Ancient Wisdom
New Spirit

Ancient Wisdom
New Spirit

*Investigations into
the Nature of "Being"*

Peter Ralston

Frog, Ltd.
Berkeley, California

Ancient Wisdom, New Spirit: Investigations into the Nature of "Being"

Published by Frog, Ltd.

Frog, Ltd. books are distributed by
North Atlantic Books
P.O. Box 12327
Berkeley, California 94712

Cover photo by Peter Ralston
Cover and book design by Paula Morrison
Typeset by Catherine Campaigne

Printed in the United States of America by Malloy Lithographing

Library of Congress Cataloging-in-Publication Data

Ralston, Peter, 1949–
    Ancient wisdom, new spirit : investigations into the nature of
    "Being" / Peter Ralston.
        p.   cm.
    ISBN 1–883319–21–8
    1. Life.   2. Ontology.   3. Agent (Philosophy)   4. Experience.
    I. Title.
    BD431.R2374   1994
    128—dc20   94–25348
                                                           CIP

1   2   3   4   5   6   7   8   9 / 98   97   96   95   94

Students today cannot grasp that names and words do not constitute understanding. They copy the words of some old fellow, long dead, into a great book and hold that therein is contained the secret and ultimate, and treasure it as their sacred possession. What a great error! Blind idiots, what juice are they looking for in those dry bones? Such as these do not know good from bad, pore over the meaning of *Sutras* and *Treatises* and speculate about them. It is like taking a clod of dung, putting it into one's month and spitting it out again, then handing it on to another.

—Rinzai (born 866), founder of Rinzai Zen

If we were to be shown right now two pictures by Paul Klee, in the original, ... we would want to stand before them for a long while—and should abandon any claim that they be immediately intelligible.

If it were possible right now to have Georg Trakl's poem "Septet of Death" recited to us, perhaps even by the poet himself, we should want to hear it often, and should abandon any claim that it be immediately intelligible.

If Werner Heisenberg right now were to present some of his thoughts on theoretical physics, moving in the direction of the cosmic formula for which he is searching, two or three people in the audience, at most, would be able to follow him, while the rest of us would, without protest, abandon any claim that he be immediately intelligible.

Not so with the thinking that is called philosophy. That thinking is supposed to offer a "worldly wisdom" and perhaps a "Way to the Blessed Life." But it might be that a kind of thinking has become necessary which must give thought to matters from which even the painting and poetry which we have mentioned and the theory of mathematical physics receive their determination. Here, too, we should then have to abandon any claim to immediate intelligibility. However, we should still have to listen, because we must think what is inevitable, but preliminary.

Therefore, we must neither be surprised and amazed if the majority of the audience objects to the lecture. Whether a few will, now or later, be prompted to think further on such matters, cannot be foreseen.

Let me give you a little hint on how to listen. The point is not to listen to a series of propositions, but rather to follow the movement of the showing.

—Martin Heidegger, in an introduction
to his lecture on "Time and Being"

Table of Contents

Acknowledgments

This book would not have come to pass if not for the contributions of several people. First acknowledgment goes to Richard Grossinger, my publisher, for coming up with the idea. Then Charles Adkins and Minnie Gok for all the loving work they put into transcription. Of course, we have all of the Cheng Hsin apprentices and students who supplied the questioning and listening necessary for these communications to take place. And I want to thank Dan Millman for his generous and kind comments.

Although there may be little direct contribution to this particular book, I still feel something is missing if I don't acknowledge the love and contribution of my wife Kim. She supplies her endless courage and support for me in all of my work.

Preface

More than two millennia ago in a fictive dialogue between Socrates and the pre-Socratic philosopher Parmenides, Plato raises such fundamental questions as the nature of reality, the essence of knowledge, and the realm of the gods.

Peter Ralston does not discuss the Platonic versions of these matters not because he doesn't think they are important. It is because they do not presently constellate our inquiry into reality. We have persuaded ourselves we are more concerned now with such items as enlightenment, love, sexuality, identity, and self-esteem. Without necessarily reifying these issues in their own terms, Ralston continues a nonideological mode of dialogue with his students quite in keeping with one of the most ancient modes of participatory teaching on this planet. That is, he initiates a discussion of real things and by a give-and-take exchange teases from his students both their own hidden categories and assumptions, and a glimmering of recognition of the realms of truth those disguise. This is quite in keeping with Plato and Socrates and the integrity of knowing they established in the fifth century b.c.e., and is revealed in Socrates' statements here:

> *Now let us go back to the beginning for the last time and ask, If there is no one, but only things other than one, what must follow?*
> *The others will not be one, but neither will they be many. For if they are to be many, there must be a one among them. . . . But there*

is no one among them; so the others are neither one nor many....
So if there is no one, none of the others can be so much as imag-
ined to be one, nor yet to be many, for you cannot imagine many
without a one.

   Therefore, if there is no one, the others neither are, nor can be
imagined to be, one or many.

   Thus, in sum, we may conclude, if there is no one, there is noth-
ing at all.

Modes of educational dialogue are not only pre-Socratic and
Socratic or even Western. Other forms were long in practice in
India by the time of Gautama Buddha and continued in Tibet,
China, and Japan in the context of Dzogchen and Zen Buddhism:

Placing a water vase on the ground, Abbot Hyakujo said: "Who can
say what this is without calling its name?"
Chief monk: "No one can call it a wooden shoe."
Isan, the cook, tipped over the vase with his foot and went out.
Hyakujo: "The chief monk loses."

And there are examples of crosscultural dialogues:

Martin Heidegger: ... indeed only the way back will lead us for-
ward.
Japanese man: Obviously you do not mean "forward" in the sense
of an advance, but ... I have difficulty in finding the right word.
Heidegger: "Fore"—into that nearest nearness which we constantly
rush ahead of, and which strikes us as strange each time anew
when we catch sight of it.
Japanese: And which we therefore quickly dismiss again from view,
to stay instead with what is familiar and profitable.
Heidegger: While the nearness which we constantly overtake would
rather bring us back.
Japanese: Back—yes, but back where?
Heidegger: Into what is beginning.
Japanese: I find it difficult to understand, if I am to think in terms
of what you have said about it in your writings up to now.

*Heidegger: Even so, you have already pointed to it, when you spoke
of the presence that springs from the mutual calling of origin and
future.*

Dialogues in search of the real also mark the evolution of the-
ological and philosophical discourse in Europe throughout Medi-
aeval Christianity, post-Darwinian idealism, empiricism, and
rationalism, and later existentialism and phenomenology, including such diverse seekers as Thomas Aquinas, David Hume, and
Maurice Merleau-Ponty. What distinguishes Ralston from his Western predecessors is his carrying out of a philosophical mode of
arriving at knowledge in the context of identity, movement, and
power. Ralston is concerned to know how each of us acts—that
is, acts to achieve goals or acts in spite of goals. He defines his
mode of dialogue by never giving confirmation nor aid and comfort to any mere philosophical discussion of abstract categories.
Nor does he merely insist upon the participants' inclusion of their
own motivations and desires in the discussion (while insisting
upon this); he insists that these be acted out in reality in the present again and again as true statements of being.

Being is not something to wrest or elucidate through brain-
power and the logician's skill. It is something to be proven on the
mat, or whatever passes moment to moment for the mat. In the
context of civilized philosophy, this is both outrageous and a ter-
ribly fair test. How outrageous it is can be imagined by picturing
Immanuel Kant or Jean-Paul Sartre having to defend their positions in exercises of simulated combat! Of course, this is not what
Ralston does with his students, but it is a reflection of the position he is putting forth—that it is not sufficient to know something by simply thinking to know it, or even to live it according
to a lofty ideal as an admirable, generous person; one must also
know how one is acting and must master acting in ways that
express his or her actual intentions. Otherwise, any form of knowing runs the risk of being aborted en route to expression.

In this regard Ralston is thoroughly modern. He embodies the
crisis of the modern world which demands committed action and

tolerates no well-meaning bystanders. Of what use is a philosopher in Sarajevo or Hebron? The answer is: only one who includes
in his repertoire appropriate responses to the precise actions occurring around him. Unless his philosophy takes into acount the
possibility of someone entering a mosque and machine-gunning
the supplicants—that is, proposes a world in which such acts
occur and must be responded to—then it is not a true inquiry
into reality. It does no good either to consign such actions to neu-
rosis, xenophobia, or other forms of patriotic or pathological madness. They must be planned on, and they must not be surprises.
To the true philosopher, like the true martial artist, there are no
surprises.

Ralston also implicitly embodies post-Reichian and Gestalt
therapeutic models of psychological discourse in which a person's
whole being is presumed to be energetically present in each new
act. Since the days of Wilhelm Reich and Fritz Perls innovating
such discourses, an extraordinary diversity of somatic techniques
have arisen, each of which in its own way challenges reality
through bodily identity and proposes a radical mode of knowing
from one's very tissues. From Frederick Alexander to Moshe
Feldenkrais, so-called physical therapists have understood they
were dealing with the ways in which models of reality are fully
somaticized and rigid body postures are maintained by repetitive
categories of thought. Ralston's radical way of training is squarely
in this tradition.

Ralston's dojo on Telegraph Avenue in Oakland, California, is
identified by a storefront sign: "School of Martial Arts and Ontology." The *Oxford English Dictionary* defines ontology as "the science or study of being; that department of metaphysics which
relates to the being or essence of things, or to being in the
abstract." One of its nineteenth-century usages contrasts ontology with psychology and cosmology, which are considered "oppo-
site distinctive forms" of tracking reality. Ralston's particular
concern with ontology places him in a sequence of philosophers
arising from Edward Husserl and including Maurice Merleau-

Ponty, who were concerned with the nature of the real as an ongoing proprioceptive experience rather than a development of and attachment to ideal categories. Merleau-Ponty criticized philosophy from the time of Plato as traveling in a direction precisely away from actual events and toward an idealized reality. Philosophers after Plato may have from time to time certainly returned to phenomena as unknown entities in themselves, but they tended then to reintegrate Platonic idealism within the rational categories they developed seemingly anew. Merleau-Ponty brought philosophy back to the notion of "an immediate perception ... a lived perception," in and of itself, not requiring fixed laws of nature or being.

Ralston is unusual for a martial artist in this regard. He refuses to accept the old forms on the basis of their press clippings or hearsay where, in the words of Merleau-Ponty, "objective reality has exhausted formal reality and transcended time." He addresses the phenomenology of the martial arts and the preconditions and effects of each technique anew.

His concern is the real. Not the real as opposed to the transcendental, the imaginary, or the metaphysical. Not even the real as opposed to the unreal. Simply the real. If opposed to anything, then to the stories people tell themselves under such unacknowledged titles as: "This is what's happening" and "This is who I am." In this sense Ralston is proposing a study of the conditions for being and for acting on the basis of actual ontological factors—matter, space, time, gravity, and the general kinesthetic and proprioceptive aspects of existence, however these are put into terminology. He does not impose these as unlived constructs. He creates situations, sets of conditions, in which they arise each time fresh, even to his own surprise. Yet he cannot be surprised by the general requirements for being and action, only by the particular novel constellations in which they continue to occur.

To a large degree what Peter Ralston does is to teach martial arts. He teaches all manner of different styles and traditions—classes on *pa kua, hsing-i, t'ai chi, tui shou, san shou,* boxing, etc.

He also teaches ontology in separate workshops and courses in which there is little or no martial practice, and he teaches ontology in all his martial arts classes too. He teaches it in the form of footwork, yielding, principles of movement, listening, interacting, and the like. That is, he teaches martial arts in a fundamental way that considers the entire range of mental and physical prerequisites for moving skillfully and generating power. He teaches these with an emphasis not so much on finished results as states of being that precede finished results. He clearly understands that when the gross move is enacted, it is already too late to teach mastery. Mastery exists in knowing precisely where a move arises prior to existing and even more precisely in knowing who one is oneself before acting. From this study comes an exact and rigorous reexamination of all postures and actions handed down traditionally, a reapplication of them, and also a separate study of the nature of being in a context in which the study of a particular martial form is not immediate to the exercises at hand.

Ralston makes it absolutely clear that he is not only discussing psychology. He does not want to prioritize wounds, traumas, victimizations, etc., as the tyrannical preconditions preventing effective action. He is also not dismissing them. He is just not giving them privilege to dominate the analysis of cause and effect. In this regard he is true to the martial tradition. After all, it little matters in a fight how one was treated in childhood. If it is a serious fight, the opponent will carry out his actions to the best of his ability, including major tricks and deceits, and the student must cultivate the same impeccability of purpose. A samurai does not "cure" all childhood abuses he may have suffered just by ontological and martial training, but he does carry out necessary deeds within their karma. Likewise, Ralston asks his students not to answer questions in terms of what emotional blocks prevent them from acting incisively on their own behalf, but what belief systems and habits of action and response confine their range of activity and lead them to counterproductive regimes of movement. This lesson then can be taken over directly into martial training.

In this sense Ralston is much like the old judo master Moshe Feldenkrais who developed an entire system of intrinsic self-knowing from examining and reenacting differentially the components of movement and thinking. Feldenkrais like Ralston believed that it is in thought structure that one is able to move or not move. He acknowledged traumatic causes for inability and inaction but asserted that this was too far-ranging an explanation and that much dysfunction came simply from doing things "wrong" on such a continual basis that one lost the very ability to distinguish effective from ineffective action—lost even the kinesthetic and neuromuscular basis for action. This could be regained only by starting from scratch with the simplest events and learning movement again anew.

Because Ralston is not involved per se in a therapeutic procedure, he does not follow Feldenkrais' course in developing treatments and healing procedures (though these may occur as an adjunct within his training). His process is much more to allow the basic lessons of ontology and the different martial arts to direct people into forms of action and self-knowing that in themselves provide the means of recovery and new activity. The self is remade through discovery of the right means. The "right means" is not a lesson in ten parts; it is a discrete set of idiosyncratic procedures whereby each individual learns to correct himself or herself. Ralston is traditionally the martial teacher in this regard. Many teachers were silent and simply did the moves. The students followed. Ralston is anything but silent, as this book attests, but his words amount to the cancelling out of a reliance on diplomacy. His highly refined linguistic techniques should not be mistaken for affective lessons or an empathic teaching style. His ontology is another form of silence, particularly appropriate in the West. His "words" are meant to frustrate, negate, and drown out the homilies, psychologisms, pieties, mythologized warrior ideals, macho propagandas, and all the other sets of meaning students bring into his school and continue to enact even while sincerely and intensely meaning to carry out simple, direct instructions. It is because of the noise of preconceptions and the malignities of parasitic motion and repetitive thinking that Ralston recreates a traditional ontological dialogue. It is to clear the space of trash and provide four walls, a floor, mirror, and succession of partners with which to train.

It is also that the world at large is caught up in the allure of false diplomacy and blustering counterproductive or irrelevant activity. Most indigenous peoples of the Americas reported, to one degree or another, that from Hernando Cortez to Theodore Roosevelt, "the white man speaks with forked tongue." They knew that treaties were mere sophistries to stall counterattacks, so they acted on their own behalf. People expressed great surprise at the seeming "deceit of the Indians" without realizing that their own culture's deceit was far greater—one of "true" words backed by false actions. The trouble is that we now mainly speak to each other with forked tongues, and such deceit is so widespread that most people don't have the slightest idea of what is happening or even what they themselves are advocating.

I should note that Ralston would not speak in this manner. The whole realm of mythopolitical and media-generated "current affairs" is for him a distraction from practice and personal responsibility. It is my choice to link his teaching to both the history of philosophical dialogue and cultural discourse. He would just smile, and he has upon reading this preface, and remind me that no one needs all this rhetoric to do the work—that in fact the rhetoric may confuse people by making them think that they have to follow all these arguments in order to understand the text. Not so; my description of Ralston is purely my own attempt to place him in contexts he himself declines.

Such large-scale events as the collapse of the Soviet Union or the spread of drugs and crime throughout the United States are clear indications that while major attention is being paid to a few chosen arenas and their events, other events are happening everywhere, events of often incalculable influence and ramifications. As the Buddhists well state, cause and effect are everywhere in *samsara,* and we go from one to another, one to another, one to another, in different degrees of trance and unalertness. Surely those who managed the Soviet Union and its departments, albeit corruptly and self-servingly, would have done a better job of extending their reign if they had known the actual criteria of effective action in that circumstance. Likewise, in the United States, we would deal more effectively with a wide range of dilemmas if we studied them ontologically and acted decisively. Instead we propose purely rhetorical or academic solutions and then carry those out. Our whole means of dealing with not only societal outcasts but with the basic members of society, from primary schools to workplaces, is based on a potpourri of unbased assumptions, nonfunctional ideological solutions, and assertions of what reality is like that have no basis in experience. The utopia we would pretend to invent, even while knowing we are not inventing it, cannot be invented precisely because there is no place for us as we are in it. Ralston makes this utterly clear:

"It wouldn't work. It would always break down. It would break down in a relatively short time. I wouldn't even give it a year.

"Because you see, we would be there. . . . And haven't you noticed? We don't have the discipline for something like that. We don't have the courage, the persistence, the overwhelming courage it takes for something like that. You don't want to go there and be courageous! You want to go there *so you don't have to be courageous.* Right? You want to go there so you can get away from this! And have a Shangri-La."

Ralston teaches us that if we are to have any way of dealing with the utterly unexpected world that is ever evolving we must return to a basis in experience. We must continually rediscover clear mind and right action. Without these, it will be difficult to deal with the problems of living in the world as it is. We will face big and little Bosnias and Rwandas, Khmer Rouges and Colombian drug cartels, without the slightest sense of who our opponents are, what they want, what they are capable of doing, and the rules, if in fact we would even consider them rules, by which they are playing. Where there are no rules, as is often the case nowadays, there always remains experience, there is still a complex range of events, and we always have the possibility of responding to things as they are. Ralston is proposing this as a principal strategy of living as well as the basis of all martial techniques. Without this examination, we remain a puppet boxer, carrying out endless forms merely because we have been taught them.

Richard Grossinger is the author of *Planet Medicine* and *The Night Sky,* among other books, and is the publisher of North Atlantic Books and Frog, Ltd.

Introduction—
Gathering the Communication

I have devoted a great deal of time and energy to communicating the work of Cheng Hsin—which is an endeavor of authentically investigating the depth and scope of the nature of "being." To the best of my ability my work has always supported a genuine look into our own "event"—uncovering the principles and dynamics that determine our experience of self, body, relationship, interaction, life, and reality. As you may well imagine, such an undertaking would assume many forms and involve a lot of experimentation. It's not an investigation or a communication that happens overnight. It takes dedicated work and serious mind-challenging considerations.

When my publisher, who was also a student, came to me and suggested that we try to capture on paper some of the quality and presence of the actual verbal communications as they occur in the workshops and courses that I do, I was interested, but skeptical. How could we go about doing that? It is true that my writing differs from a "hands-on" verbal confrontation with the material, but no writing is going to match the presence of a live encounter. So it was decided to transcribe several audiotapes of live events and see what we could capture. But which ones to transcribe? A four-day workshop is much too long, and we have literally thousands of tapes. I'm afraid the choice came down as much to chance as it did to planning. We gathered about 250 tapes that represented a good cross-section of this work and began the task of transcription. Do you know how long it takes to transcribe a ninety-minute tape, and how many pages it turns out to be?! Well, after the first eight or nine I said, "Whoa! No way are we going to sift through that much material." So what happened to be heard first is also what we ended up with.

This book is in no way an attempt to be complete or even well-rounded. However, it does include a sampling of the various aspects and domains in which I work. In this way, instead of trying to explain the principles involved, I invite you to discover them by observing (reading about) them in action. From this presentation it is hoped that the reader will be empowered to consider more thoroughly what this kind of work is all about and to apply its principles to his or her own inquiry.

Each of the considerations is a rather in-depth probe into some aspect of our experience. Often they will take careful reading and contemplation for the reader to follow the presentation. Since most of them are taken from "live" events with people actually participating in that very inquiry, it should be possible for you to join them in this (you just don't get to ask questions). You should know, however, that for the most part these talks were not given lightly or simply to lay down some information. They were interactions with people for the purpose of facilitating them in reaching into their own experience and realizing something for themselves. I advise you to read this book with the same purpose.

To this end, I would like to offer a quote from a dialogue between Martin Heidegger and a Japanese man (name unknown):

> Japanese: "We Japanese do not think it strange if a dialogue leaves undefined what is really intended, or even restores it back to the keeping of the undefinable."
>
> Heidegger: "That is part, I believe, of every dialogue that has turned out well between thinking beings. As if of its own accord, it can take care that that undefinable something not only does not slip away, but displays its gathering force ever more luminously in the course of the dialogue."[1]

I offer this exchange to help prepare you for some of the more involved dialogues to come, in which we are not working toward an easy answer but an *experience,* and so in reading them you must approach it with that in mind.

Also, the order in which the talks are presented in this book does not follow their chronological occurrence. Instead, they are presented in this order to provide information or understanding that might be useful in following talks. Or not. Of course you can read the talks in any order you like. I don't think it will matter much.

In order to assist you in orienting yourself to the communications to come, let me first provide something written a few years ago about the nature and scope of the Cheng Hsin work.

The Cheng Hsin Spirit

What is the spirit of the Cheng Hsin pursuit?

Honesty, questioning, and getting to the truth of the matter of one's own event, by pursuing transformation, effectiveness, and the direct experience of the nature of Being.

This "work" is not about proselytizing a belief system, adhering to dogma, or following a set of rituals. It is not about defending itself against differing ideas, or engaging in idle speculations. It has been created to support and encourage the work of getting to the truth of the matter—any matter. It is not intended to be an exclusive club. This endeavor is open to everyone no matter what their pursuits, as long as their interest and commitment is to directly experience for themselves what is actually so in what they are doing.

The veils that shroud a direct experience of the truth can be stripped away by committed questioning. Cheng Hsin people are those who choose to benefit from associating with others committed to questioning and understanding the very nature of our own being and reality.

I use the words *Cheng Hsin* to refer to the real and absolute nature of "BEING." To "take on" Cheng Hsin is to move in the direction of experiencing the truth of what is occurring—in this moment or in any matter.

The essence of Cheng Hsin is found in questioning our own event. We're striving to honestly investigate our actions, emotions, beliefs, relationships, and experience. It seems that in grasping the truth of any matter, the possibility arises of becoming more powerful, effective, and balanced in relation to that matter.

Cheng Hsin is non-moral, non-political, and non-religious. The intent is not to embrace a new belief system, but rather to question and challenge openly and honestly the nature of our event—any aspect of being alive. This often means challenging our existing beliefs.

I don't want to present Cheng Hsin as a "right" way of being, but simply as a commitment to uncovering the truth of being. Cheng Hsin supports direct and honest investigation, experimentation, communication, clarity of purpose, empowerment, and a commitment to authenticity and integrity in all endeavors and interactions.

The objective is not to believe or disbelieve something, not even our own beliefs; rather it is to directly and authentically experience for ourselves the truth of the matter.

The Cornerstones of the Cheng Hsin Endeavor

To empower this work there are at least four basic distinctions on which we stand. These are neither moral nor arbitrary. They seem to reflect what is simply so and embody the heart of what we are up to in the pursuit of Cheng Hsin. These four fundamental distinctions set the stage for true inquiry in Cheng Hsin. They are all actually distinctions in the very same movement or pursuit, acting as cornerstones for this endeavor. They are:

Honesty

Not-Knowing and Questioning

Direct and Authentic Experience

Grounded Openness

Honesty—Honesty is telling the truth, not only to others but to ourselves. This distinction goes beyond the conventional use of the word to a profound and real experience of a function that is as "rock bottom" honest as we can manage. In this distinction we find that our normal tendency is not one of such powerful honesty—we manipulate our own thinking and feeling, and our experience is so influenced by our beliefs, fears, and ambitions as not to be trusted as simply what is "so" without challenge. We must maintain a diligent probing into the truth of anything that arises—from our ideas on how something works to the nature of relationship and communication. It appears that direct and honest communication leads to powerful interactions and relationships. What is actually occurring is already so. We begin to participate in this when we are honest with ourselves and others.

Not-Knowing and Questioning—Paradox and Confusion are the guardians of the truth. The truth often lies in unexpected places. How can we experience the truth if we are not open to *every* possibility? How can we question or wonder without first having an experience of not-knowing? Without the power of questioning, there is only knowing. With only knowing, there is no question and so no movement, no discovery, no insight, no learning, no mystery, and no experience of the authenticity of simply "being."

Direct and Authentic Experience—We stand open to the possibility that we can directly experience something. This is the possibility that we can without belief, knowledge, conjecture, interpretation, or hearsay experience the truth of something, or the thing itself, beyond subjectivity. Prior to this we make a distinction of an authentic or genuine experience that we have for ourselves, as opposed to merely believing something or having an idea that it "may" or even "must" be some way. Since openness and questioning are always at hand in any Cheng Hsin pursuit, this distinction represents a "direction" in which to go rather than a "place" at which to stop. However, it also suggests that we are standing at the farthest point possible in our experience at this time—in other words, the most honest and authentic experience we can have in this moment.

Grounded Openness—These are two fundamental principles that we must keep in balance. To be grounded is to be real, to be committed to something, to be clear and standing on solid and authentic insights and effective distinctions. To be open is to be free, unstuck, creative, new, to make breakthroughs, to entertain radical possibilities, to embrace paradox. The dangers of groundedness without openness tend to be: an inability to learn, becoming dogmatic or closed-minded, being stuck in a belief system, never challenging one's own opinions, not being able to detect one's own lies, no breakthroughs, no transformation. The dangers of openness without groundedness tend to be: becoming "airy-fairy," abstract, merely intellectual; adopting mere fantasy or good ideas as if they are true or as if you've experienced them as real; having no real demonstration of what you are talking about; not being able to "live" your philosophy; merely believing in things rather than proving them for yourself; getting confused or flighty, having nowhere to stand, not being committed to anything. The issue of balancing groundedness with openness comes up in every form and dimension of our living and our pursuits. The purpose for maintaining such a vigil in these distinctions is to empower our investigations in being as real and as far reaching as possible.

It's important to remember that none of this is presented as truths or facts to be believed or not. The purpose here is to offer directions and possibilities for your own exploration and investigation. Remember, the pursuit is to question and discover for yourself what is actually so in the matter.

Current Forms in which Cheng Hsin is Pursued

Through a study of the body: Its design, function, movement, awareness; and the pursuit of an effortlessly effective, fully functional, and integrated body-being.

Through a study of interaction: What is interaction, relationship, ability? How is interaction constructed, how does it occur, what determines effective interaction, how is ability or skill created?

Through ontology, or the study of Being: What am I? What is Mind? What is the nature of "being"? Beyond morality, cultural conventions, limitations in our own thinking and perception, what are the dynamics and principles in which we exist, and what is the truth of our own nature and event?

Through the pursuit of demonstrative transformation: Creating a powerful and "free" human being. Addressing obstacles and ineffective patterns of thinking and emotion, and embracing a shift in the mind and body toward what is effective, free, and whole.

Note:

[1]Quoted from *On the Way to Language* by Martin Heidegger (New York: Harper and Row, 1971), p. 13.

The Art of Facilitation

Written for the Cheng Hsin Newsletter, 1990.

Martin Heidegger commented on the art of facilitation when he wrote: "Learning is more difficult than teaching; for only he who can truly learn—and only as long as he can do it—can truly teach. The genuine teacher differs from the pupil only in that he can learn better and that he more genuinely wants to learn. In all teaching, the teacher learns the most."

Facilitation is sometimes deeply appreciated, sometimes resented, yet almost never truly understood by the participant or student. It is not something guaranteed, and it is also rare. Those lucky enough to have access to insightful facilitation often just take it for granted. Very few seek it out, and fewer still can recognize skillful facilitation, or distinguish it from the art of being "pumped up and glazed over."

I make a distinction between facilitation and teaching. Many times facilitation is appropriate for teaching. Yet teaching is the passage of knowledge or technique, or some other form requiring instruction, and this is an art that can be done with greater or lesser facility.

Facilitation is an art of providing for others the opportunity and invitation to recognize for themselves something they have not yet realized. It is drawing another's consciousness to see the truth of some matter, whereas prior to this facilitation, the truth of the matter remained inaccessible, unknown, and not seen— although more than likely something was held in its place as the

9

truth. Facilitation is using whatever skillful means are appropriate to the task of assisting another's recognition or creation of a new understanding, experience, or distinction. It is providing the springboard for the participant to make a breakthrough.

The field of facilitation is immense. Its difficulty and scope are rarely known by most people. Contrary to popular belief, it requires skill and sacrifice on the part of the facilitator, just as it requires a significant amount of participation and willingness on the part of the participant. The purpose of good facilitation is rarely to have others arrive at some new conclusion. They will arrive at some new conclusion—this is almost inevitable—yet the purpose is usually to assist them in breaking free of what is held as true, or fixed, and allowing for an opening into a new possibility.

Facilitation can be likened to a boatman who ferries people across a river. It is not the boatman's job or concern where the people choose to go once across; it is to provide the opportunity to choose and to go.

Many times a student tries to second-guess the facilitator, in order to come up with the right answer and so look smart. In facilitation this almost always hampers the activity. The student is of course trying to second-guess from the framework in which he or she already views the matter, and so considers within the context of what he already knows and what "things" already mean or imply.

Often students consider the social implications of the action of the facilitator—which is most often dialogue—and often the facilitator is not working in a realm of social meaning. This is a place where people can get offended or feel indignant over what appears as something they think they understand—which is to say, they think they know what is going on.

Although some form of uncomfortable confrontation may be appropriately used as skillful means by a facilitator, it is never taken personally by the facilitator and is only done to further a breakthrough on the part of the participant. Often such offense is simply an invention on the part of the participant, clouding the purpose of the interaction, and it is not being purposefully established by the facilitator.

Another frequent and non-productive approach by the participant is thinking that he or she knows where the facilitation is going. This is usually done by holding the interaction in some historical perspective, one in which a pattern is recognized from past experience, or from reading something, or from an adopted belief schematic. This is very hard to get past for the student. It requires a genuine willingness to "not know," and this is often held as to "be wrong." Therefore the task of facilitation is almost always done in the face of opposition.

The culture as a whole, and the product of this culture—what we call an individual—are by design resistant to the ground on which facilitation must enter. Freedom always involves letting go of something clung to. This frequently appears as "dangerous" to the holding or binding force.

The function of culture and individual is one of binding, of consolidation and conclusion. This is not bad in itself. It simply doesn't provide the freeing or transformative element that is found in the death of something to allow for the birth of something else. So the breaking through of some conclusion or conviction, and the assistance in that breakthrough, is by necessity sometimes seen as "bad" or threatening.

We in this culture don't have a ready appreciation for this dynamic, and so we often fail to recognize facilitation when we are lucky enough to encounter it. As a people we must create this recognition and appreciation, and be able to see through our own reactive or resistant tendencies when facilitation is taking place—and embrace it.

Listening that Makes a Difference

From an opening talk given to students in a course on effective interaction, 1985.

Listening for a New Experience

Since you've all done some work with me in the past, I can confront you more and be straighter with you now. We're undertaking a bigger commitment—working on effective interaction—so we need to develop a more intimate relationship. Consequently I need to speak to you for a while.

I could just sit and not say anything. Hit you with a stick every once in a while, get you to sleep outside the door for weeks, or something. Perhaps I could teach you just as well that way. But that's not what I do. I talk a lot. So you'll just have to put up with me because I'm the teacher.

I guarantee and promise that if you can hear what I say it will be well worth it. What do I mean by that? Well, our work here is to set out to learn something about interaction, the principles and dynamics of interacting, and interacting effectively. What is that saying? Being skillful in relationship to another body, being, energy, mind.

I know, without a doubt, that you can experience great and transformative things through verbal communication alone. I've done it myself. Someone can say something to you and you can have an impactful experience, an experience about what they are saying such that you actually become more skillful.

I've been working at it for quite a few years—speaking to people. And I must tell you that most of you are not really listening yet. You are hearing sounds in the room, you speak English, and you've probably heard a similar rap. But merely hearing sounds in the room and speaking English is not what I'm talking about. You have to listen for what I can't say with the sounds in the room. You have to develop the ability to hear an *experience*. Even now, it's not being said, but it's here. It's available. So what am I talking about right now? I'm not talking about hearing something mysterious, and yet it is that also.

I want to tell you that if you can develop a kind of listening that one person in a thousand develops, then you could get this communication very powerfully. If you don't, then you'll get it far less powerfully. If you just come and hang out and do the exercises you'll get something, but you'd have to listen anyway. Think about it, Wart.

What's happening? You're sitting there and I'm speaking to you. So you say, "Hey, enough of this speaking business, let's get on with it." Well, what are we going to get on with? Do you see that anything that we get on with I'm going to have to say? You see, if I say "stand up" you will stand up, but if I didn't say that you would just sit there. You can understand that pretty readily. "Stand up and find a partner." See, all that is speaking and you do something as a result of what I've said. Now if I say "I want you to "listen" and "outreach," I want you to feel what your partner is thinking and how they are feeling, and I want you to move in unison with them and "join" them—if I start talking like that, now whatcha gonna do?

Well, you'll do whatever you hear, won't you? If I say "stand up" and to you that means lie down, you'll lie down, won't you? So if you learn to listen so that when I say something it's a new experience, then something has to appear in your awareness that comes about from something that is said. So a new hearing is very important, because what I'm asking you to do is to experience something new, and it's going to come in the form of my communication to you—my saying LOOK at this, or try that, or get THIS. In this work, I'm the master blacksmith and you're the apprentice blacksmith, so I'll tell you to use this or that kind of metal so you can learn ... and then you become the master blacksmith. But first you have to hear me, and it's not quite as easy as blacksmithing.

Merely because I say something and you do it, this is still not enough. It takes training. The more you train the better you get at it, and the more powerful it becomes for you. Out of this you begin to understand even better and more fully, and your listening becomes increasingly useful, accurate, and meaningful.

People sometimes say that I'm "good," and they ask "how come?" It's just that I do what I tell you to do, that's all. That's all! There's nothing else. I'm not hiding anything.

For example, I wasn't so connected when I was younger. I remember. But I understood that I needed to be and started to work on that. Over time I got more and more connected. Anything when grasped experientially becomes simpler and simpler, and more and more in alignment, when brought to life through training. I suggest it's best to understand it first, and then train it for twenty years, rather than wait twenty years trying to understand it.

If all you do is believe somebody and go through motions by rote, then you are basically waiting to understand. I recommend understanding right away. Why wait? That's the incredible process that I'm here to work with you on, and we have some great ground on which to do it. And you will have very good feedback with which to test the things I'm going to communicate.

But it's your skill that we're talking about. If you do what I say, you will become good, guaranteed. Now I don't say that just because I think so. Many people have observed this to be true. What I am communicating are the principles and dynamics about what being good IS. People who follow this become more effective without exception! The reason they get good is they DO what I say! To the degree they do is the degree to which they are effective. It has nothing to do with me. If you do what I tell you, you'll get good.

I am not talking about the symbols and ideas that I use to speak about some matter, and even less about the beliefs you develop about our chatter. As an analogy, if I were to put some words up on the chalkboard here that refer to the very event that is occurring of writing on the board, our attention should not be on the meaning of the words, it should be on the chalk and the chalkboard themselves. It just so happens that I speak in "chalkboardese." If you "do" the chalkboard and chalk, you'll get good—if you understand the analogy. But YOU have to UNDERSTAND. You have to get it. . . . YOU.

And you might as well get it now because I'm not getting any younger. This work hasn't changed really for the last twenty years. I've become a little better at teaching it, a little more sophisticated and more organized in my teaching. And I've gained a little clarity on it myself. But it's the same stuff. And you can get it by merely listening. I know listening is usually a drag. But if you can listen beyond belief—and I mean that in two ways—miracles can happen.

Examples of "Hearing"

If you wanted to learn boxing and you had the opportunity to listen to Mohammed Ali or Sugar Ray Leonard, who were two of the finest boxers ever, you'd really want to listen, wouldn't you? You'd listen very carefully, and you'd really consider what they said. But you have to do more than that. You have to *experience* what they are saying, and then "do" it. You have to "master" it.

You could get it in the moment of speaking, but most of it you won't. However, you can get it through consideration, through contemplation. You could consider it deeply and practice and train, and then consider some more, and study and contemplate, and contemplate and practice and consider.

What do I mean by contemplate? I mean turn into, turn towards, turn to face the experience, and ask, what is it? What is it? Like right now, what is listening? Really, what is listening? What else is listening? What more is listening? What greater dimension could listening be? You'll get lost, but then come back. It's work.

So I'll tell you about my Judo experience. One of the first great breakthroughs I had was when I was fifteen or so. I was studying Judo—plodding, straining, twisting, and slapping the ground a lot. I was really very average. But I liked it. I was strong and determined, but I was really very average as far as learning went. I would learn something and train very hard.

Then after nine months of study, I had a breakthrough about Judo. I don't know how or why. It seemed like a natural thing since I was thinking about Judo all the time. I was an obsessed teenager. I would go home and sit and think about it, or go out and practice on the tree in the yard. I was a white belt, quite normal. Then all of a sudden I realized what Judo WAS! What I was supposed to be doing! What throwing was. Presently what I call that realization, in broader terms, is effortless power. The goal of Judo was effortless power. But it wasn't just a thought that the goal of Judo was effortless power; I experienced something! The way I said it at the time was "Oh, it's supposed to be easy!" I suddenly got that it was supposed to be easy. It's not merely going in there, finding a technique, and levering somebody's body to the ground. There's actually a way to do that easily.

Now, what do you think? Do you think I just had the thought? NO! I didn't just have the thought, it didn't come as a thought, it was like a whole bodily experience. I could feel it, I could taste it, I knew it. Do you understand? I suddenly knew what to do, or where to look for what to do. I went back to the Judo school and started doing Judo on a completely different level. I threw people easily. I'm not saying all of a sudden I was a perfect master and every throw worked out, no. I had a lot of training to do still. But it was training from the position of knowing where I was going. Knowing what I was looking for, rather than just going through motions by rote according to what somebody showed me. I knew what I was looking for; I was looking for effortless power, that feeling. I knew the feeling, and it was easy! I looked for it and found it.

In some throws it was much more difficult to find than in others, and so they took longer to train. But let me tell you the difference this insight made. I was nine months a white belt, then I had a breakthrough in my understanding, my experience. I then went through green belt (fourth Kyu), brown belt-third degree, brown belt-second degree, brown belt-first degree, and then black belt (Shodan) all in just one year and three months—which is unheard of! So do you understand that that was a different training than the first nine months? A VERY different training, and it's the one I recommend. It saves you a lot of time.

Changing Your Experience

Know what you're going for and go for it. But in order to do that you have to experience it for yourself. Know what you are looking for, cut through the wheat and the chaff, and extract clear liquid from the dregs of my mouth. And you can, you are capable. You are a plastic event. You are a human being, and a human being is a plastic event. What I mean by that is you are not stuck. You are not stuck the way you think you are stuck. You might seem to be, but that's really not the end of the story.

There is a possibility of you becoming a master—of this, or anything else you want to become a master of—because you are a plastic event. You can mold yourself, change, or transform. I'm not just talking about your body; I'm talking about your experience—your experience of reality, how you hold reality, how you hold yourself, how you hold your own skills and abilities. But there has got to be a massive confrontation. Just because you're a plastic event I don't mean it's going to be easy.

It's not like changing yourself from a Dixie cup to a Ming vase, but more like changing from being a Dixie cup to being Infinite Space, or perhaps a cup-maker. So, when we talk about anything— say, relaxing for example—you've got to get goofy with it. You've got to relax so much it's silly, it's stupid. And there is no way you won't think that relaxing—as much as I want you to relax—is anything less than silly and stupid. If you don't think it's stupid— in other words, too much, that it's really kind of dumb to relax that much—you are not relaxing as much as I want you to relax. It has to be stupid; how could it be any other way?

I know you really don't believe me, but listen anyway and maybe something will seep through. What I'm speaking about is your body sitting here right now. Our sitting, our speaking, right now. I'm not talking about something else. I'm talking about you and me right now. You feeling your body. You thinking what you're thinking—what you know, what you don't know. Your "position" of being right now. Whatever impulses you feel in your body, whatever you think good is and bad is. If what I'm talking about is not found in the already established set of thinking and feeling, then any impulse that would get you there is going to feel stupid. See? Because this—how you feel and see things right now—is "smart." Which is to say, this is how we live, so smart-ness is seen in here. See? This is how we frame it up. Anything outside of that has got to seem stupid, or weird or strange or unbe-lievable or wrong or really mysterious or at least different. So I recommend throwing yourself into the matter until you're goofy— and not believing a thing.

Believing me is irrelevant. Watch! Believe that you are a mil-lionaire. I say you are a millionaire. So go ahead believe you are a millionaire. . . . See? You can believe it, but that doesn't put money in the bank. Notice that THAT is a different event than belief. So you needn't believe anything I say. As a matter of fact, you needn't disbelieve anything I say. Talk to me about it. I'm either right or wrong, or it doesn't make any difference. But you needn't believe me or disbelieve me.

Bob: *How should I judge my progress?*

Listen more to your experience than the results. How does your experience change, and then does the shift in your experience provide something that wasn't there before? Not whether you get an immediate result or not. You can get a great result and not have learned a thing. If you get a result and say, "Aha! I must have heard what he was saying," it's not necessarily true. If you take a look and your experience is a whole lot like it was before, if it's very familiar, then probably you didn't hear. Because the experience I'm talking about undoubtedly will be different. When you realize something that you haven't realized before—and most of this you have never done before—the experience is different. It's not the same one you have now. The same one you have now—so what? You came in with that one; why do you need to do that one again?

It's not like I'm asking you to take your experience—your body, your feelings, your thinking, the way you already know things, etcetera—and then use that to make something work out. That's not what I'm talking about. I'm talking about changing your experience. And out of changing your experience, things work out differently. Even when it doesn't make any sense, or it's not working, but boy, is it different. So if the experience feels the same as before, it probably IS.

And there are other dimensions to this. I am not always speaking about feeling, but in here I almost always am. It's like I was saying to the apprentices the other day: "When you demonstrate, always shoot for the bale of hay, never shoot for the target." Got it? Do you understand the reference? [Zen archery] If you are worried about a result, aren't you demonstrating how "good" you are? If you start shooting for the target, you're going to demonstrate how good you are, aren't you? Instead, demonstrate the art of shooting. Then "you" are not an issue, and you cannot fail, except by failing to demonstrate shooting. But all you have to do to demonstrate shooting is to shoot!

The Nature of "Experience"

Taken from an Ontological Investigation Group meeting, 1991.

Belief Is Only Hearsay

Peter Ralston: I want to work with you some more on a distinction. It's the distinction between experience and belief, or experience and concept—I am looking at a particular distinction. Once again I've become aware of how little understanding there is, how few people make that distinction. They don't really get the difference.

Now, I know you know the difference between the words: experience and belief. You already make that distinction, but that's not the one I'm talking about, and I think it would be valuable for us all if you could get the one that I'm talking about.

So I'm talking about a distinction that's not necessarily hard to get. But if you don't get it, it's impossible to get—because you don't get it.

I'm going to speak, and you're going to speak, and by the time we finish our speaking together, hopefully there will be something new. Or, at least something powerfully refreshed. Because one of the things about this business of experience versus concept, experience versus belief, is that the experience of the distinction continues to degrade into concept or belief—even the distinction between experience and belief degrades into a belief, or degrades into a concept. That continues to happen, even after having an experience of what it is I'm talking about. So, whether

21

you've made it before or not, it's time to make it again. The more times we make it, the stronger the experience becomes, and the easier it is to access.

So let's start with a story. There was a person that I knew who was very psychic. She knew things that were happening that were not commonly known … that kind of thing. Now, some of the stuff that was occurring, as far as I could tell, was incredibly legitimate, and I'm a big skeptic. We will just start there. Most of the time, it's like anything else—psychic, spiritual, scientific, you name it—we get it like a belief, right? For example, take spirituality—if I talked about the Upanishads, if I talked about Christian scripture, if I talked about the *Bhagavad Gita,* if I talked about the *Tao Te Ching,* if I talked about the *Diamond Sutra*—how much of all that do you think would be belief?

Brian: *All of it?*

PR: Sure, all of it! It would ALL be belief. It would all be concept. The Upanishads were written by people who were prolific; the material that has been translated so far makes up volumes and volumes. Now, who knows, most of it could have been crap, but we could imagine that so much effort might have been a result of some very powerful experiences. From the *Upanishads:* "When there is an other, fear arises." … Whenever there is another, fear arises.

How about Christian scriptures? We could imagine that although it's way less than a second-hand account, maybe Jesus knew what he was talking about, was coming from some experience or other. Looked like he made a pretty big impact. Looks like he had so much influence, he was impressive—if nothing else! Maybe he walked on water, maybe he raised the dead, maybe he healed people, maybe he did those things. There is certainly a lot of hearsay. But no matter whether he did any of that or not, he was at least charismatic. [laughter] He seemed to influence people. He seemed to influence people so much, that the people he influenced—who died out, by the way—changed a whole empire, stirred the Romans into becoming a Christian empire. That's pretty influential. Perhaps the Romans were impressed by the people they were crucifying and feeding to the lions. . . . In order for people to be impressed that much I would imagine there would be some experience there. And yet, when you and I start to speak about it, what are we speaking about?

When we start talking about the *Tao Te Ching,* well, it's neat and groovy, but what are we talking about? Ideas. We have an idea. I'm not putting down ideas; they are very powerful. But there's something else that's also powerful. And actually, as far I can tell, there's something else that makes ideas even more powerful. And that's *experience.*

Now when I say experience, I'm not just talking about past encounters. Like when we say a person has "experience" in something, that means they've done it many times. That's not what I'm talking about. That's fine, but it's not what I'm talking about. When I say experience, I'm not even talking about the fact that you lived through it yourself. It's a little bit in that direction, but that's not what I'm talking about either—that you've lived it yourself, like "I experienced it for myself." As opposed to hearing about something, but not experiencing it for yourself—"I 'heard' roller coasters are really scary." Or, "I 'experienced' roller coasters, I was on one myself and I lived through it—roller coasters *are* scary, I know from 'experience.'" That's not what I'm talking about, and that's what most people think I'm talking about when I talk about experience—whether you "did it" or not. Now, that's not a bad direction in which to go. It will clarify and clean up a lot if you start getting rigorous with all that you "believe" and just ask yourself, "Did I do it or not? Did I have the experience or not? Have I actually seen or experienced something for myself?"

Have I actually personally experienced a round planet? No.

A molecule? No.

A soul? No.

God? No.

Where I came from? No.

What a body is? No.

If I have a mind? No. Well, okay, I get carried away—maybe you could argue that you have experienced having mind. But if you started to get rigorous and go through all of your beliefs, everything you think about, you would probably have to eliminate a tremendous amount if you eliminated everything you yourself haven't directly experienced, perception-wise. Do you see what I'm saying? "Roller coasters are scary"—have you ever been on one? No. How do you know? You have to throw that one out. If we threw out everything we don't have personal, first-hand experience with we would throw out most of what we believe to be true. You can't speak with authority about roller coasters if you've never been on a damn roller coaster.

"The people in this country are like that"—have you ever been to that country? No. Throw it out. "This is what happened during the war"—were you there? No. Throw it out. And how about abstractions? "This is the way we should run the country." How do you know? "It's my opinion." Throw it out. I don't know where you would go to know, to experience the way you should run the country ... at least you would have to have some experience running a country. Have you? No. Throw it out. "This is what the president should do." Have you ever been the president? No. Throw it out. Do you know what it's like to be a president? No. Throw it out.

Do you see how much damage it would do to our belief systems? And all we're doing now is making a distinction between what you have personally undergone and what you have only heard about, or have an opinion about. Just those two domains. Do you know how much we talk about things of which we have no experience? Most of it. Take a look. Most of it. Now, it would certainly cramp our conversations if we only spoke of what we knew, right? So, in order to fill up the conversation at the dinner table, you have to speak about a lot of things you don't know anything about. The problem is, you forget you don't know anything about them, and so you lose a powerful distinction and an opening.

Now let's start to move toward what I'm calling experience. When you ride the roller coaster—I'll get back to the psychic in a minute—when you ride the roller coaster, isn't a lot of what's going on concept? When you're standing in line to ride the roller coaster, you're nervous. Why? Some imagination about what's going to take place: it's going to plummet your body toward the earth and you will be scared—those *ideas* make you nervous. It's all conceptual. And then when you get on the thing, I'll bet you have a concept or two. You know, like "I'm going to die!" That's a concept. Are you dying? No, you are just falling down, quickly. And you yell, "I'm going to die." Or you imagine the thing going off the tracks. Sometimes it happens. They do leave the tracks. People do die. Does that ever come up when you're on the roller coaster? Or do you just stick with, "They know what they're doing, they've got this thing riveted down, most people live." Those are all concepts too, right?

So, even when you're undergoing something, there's a lot of concept influencing the experience. Your bias in relationship to the experience is going to influence what you come up with. So when you say, "I did experience that," still . . . think about it, Wart. Aren't our biases and the concepts that we have at the time going to determine a lot of what we call the experience?

Somebody goes flying in a hot air balloon. Is that a nice experience or is that a terrifying experience? Well, I bet we could find two different people who would say two different things, right? Some of you would say, "It's a wonderful experience, so freeing and liberating, it's just like floating in the air, and you can see forever, the views are terrific." And like that, right? And do you know what you're talking about? "Yes, I did it." Okay. And then somebody else says, "No, it's horrible, you're cramped in there, and you can't even piss, there's no toilet, and it's windy, frightening, and scary! You get chapped lips and they don't serve good food, and it really sucks." Well, do you know what you're talking about, did you do it? "Yes, I did." Now those sound like two different events, for the most part. I suggest that a lot of that has to do with the bias of the person who's looking at it.

Now, if we took away whether it's enjoyable, or really neat floating in air and all that good stuff, and we took away whether we could piss, they don't serve good food, and we're scared, then there's something we might call floating in the balloon. Right? So then we might be getting a little bit closer to just the normal experience that we'd be talking about called floating in a balloon—the perception and cognition of floating in a balloon without a whole lot of bias.

Let's continue to look into the matter. And it's still not what I'm talking about yet, okay? But we are moving closer. So back to the psychic story—I said to her, "What do you *experience?*" And I was going more for the balloon thing, without bias, belief, or hearsay. She thought I was doubting her psychic ability. I didn't doubt her psychic ability. I doubted a lot of the crap that went along with it, but I didn't doubt the ability. I was too impressed. She said things she couldn't have possibly known. There was very concrete, consistent evidence that something was occurring. That doesn't happen often. And I hang out with a lot of psychics, or they hang out with me—whatever. It took a while to get her past her defenses. You know how people are—we like to defend our beliefs. But once she got past her defensiveness about whether I was attacking her or not, and she started to recognize—it took months and months—started to recognize I wasn't indeed attacking her, or doubting her, that I was actually trying to get what her "experience" was, she started to talk.

The reason I'm using this example is because it's so abstract, it's so loose, you see? It's a good one. When you start speaking about having a psychic experience, what are you doing? For example, she would "talk to Devas. . . . "

Kevin: *What's that?*

PR: Well, it doesn't matter, does it? [laughs] Devas. D-E-V-A-S. She could have been talking to goo-goo bees—don't you see that it doesn't make any difference at all? But she's talking to Devas.

Now that meant something to her. There aren't that many people around "talking to Devas." And the Devas seemed to have something to say—nothing good though [laughs].

But what is occurring? "I talk to Devas." I understand you talk to Devas, but what is actually going on? What's the experience? Took a while, you see. What's a Deva? "A deva is a blah, blah, blah. . . . " Yeah, I know, but you read that in a book. What is the "experience" that's taking place? You don't know what a fucking Deva is any more than I do. If somebody told you it was a Fred, then you'd be talking to Freds, right? If somebody said they were horses, you'd be talking to horses. So, I'm not questioning the explanation, I don't give a shit about the explanation. What is it that occurs?

In the end the whole experience boiled down to something that was far more grounded than I was actually expecting. See, when you take away this idea of psychic—the training, the book learning, people's beliefs about it, people's labels—what do you have left? That's what I wanted. What do you have left like an experience? What are you cognizant of that's actually taking place? It's hard to take out the concepts and the imagery and the way you make sense of it. Do you see? But even if you pare it down. . . . I mean, there's no Deva there. Maybe there's a sense of something. Okay, there's a sense of something. Great. There's a sense of something—and perhaps you make a distinction of entity or something. Where? You don't know. Oh, that's very different than "there's a whirling light over there that looks like Charley Brown, and speaks with a deep voice, has wings, and carries a sword."

"What" is occurring? Do you speak? Do you say, "Hi Dev," and they say, "Hi?" What *does* happen? How does the communication take place? Do you see? So, say we get to a completely different description than anything you and I would imagine, or even the psychic would imagine, when she says, "I talk to Devas." A description that's far more experientially grounded and extracted from the bullshit that makes it what it is that we believe in.

Is It Live or Memorex?

PR: In my early Zen work I had very little exposure to Zen literature, so certain notions were completely outside of my thinking.
I didn't know about them, nobody ever told me. And in a certain
way that was very beneficial. Somebody who has Zen literature
up the wazoo is going to have to go through at least ten years
before they can get past that! Their ass has gotta get sore. Their
brain's gotta rot before they're going to drop all that they know
about it—which is damning. What you and I know can serve a
purpose, but it's also damning at the same time.

In a radio interview in Nashville ... how many people listened
to that tape? Well, more than I expected. So, if you remember
one of the dialogues, he basically kept saying, "Tell me who I am."
And I kept saying, "You don't understand. It's not going to do
any good. As a matter of fact, it would be more damaging for me
to tell you who you are than for me to refuse to tell you who you
are." Of course, he had a clue because he read my book, so he
kept saying, "Well, then I'm going to find out that I am nothing,
right?" And I said, "I don't know what you're going to find out.
You could be a ball point pen for all I know." Then I tried to
explain to him, "Look, don't you get it, whatever I say or whatever you think is the truth is worthless. It's worse than worthless,
it gets in the way." ... People don't get that. Honest to God, really,
people don't get it! To me it's obvious, but people don't get it. I
know it's hard to get, but it's the truth. This is not just something
to say. As some comic said, "People kept saying, money can't buy
you happiness, but I found out the people who were saying that
were the people with all the money." [laughter] Anyway, so, it's
not like one of those. It's not like I'm trying to "fool the people"
[chuckles].

Look, what would happen—I mean really—what would happen if I said to you, you're an apple? Or you're nothing? What
are you going to do? You're going to sit down, and you're going
to try to experience yourself as an apple. Or you're going to try

to experience yourself as nothing, and that's worthless. Oh, it might have some strange value, I don't know, but that ain't the point. That's not it. Don't you get it? What you've got to do is experience your self. If it turns out you're an apple, great; then when you experience yourself, you'll find yourself to be an apple. You don't have to worry about what's there. But that's not what you're going to do as long as you have an answer.

And you know what else? There is no way on God's earth that you can understand what nothing is. Nobody gets that! Everybody thinks they know what "nothing" is. If you've been around me long enough you've probably become a little confused about it. Nothing is just kind of the best word to use—since it's a lot like nothing. But prior to experiencing what you are, it doesn't mean anything—so you *can't* experience that you're nothing. You can't do it—it can't be done. You can experience what you are, but you can't experience that you're nothing, because you're not nothing. Whatever you've got as nothing—that's not what you are. You are what you are. Whatever the truth of that is.

If I kept saying you're an apple, whatever you thought of as an apple, that's not what you are, you're not an apple. You're what you are. And if you're experiencing yourself, you might say, "Hey, I'm an apple." Or something else. You might "say" that, but the experience would be so different from the concept you had about being an apple that you would see, in retrospect, that it was completely worthless and inane and stupid—and damning because you had suffered it for so long—setting out, trying to experience yourself as a god damn apple! And that's the stupidest image I can think of, but it would be the same thing if you set out to experience yourself as nothing. It's just that nobody says they're an apple, but it makes no more sense, really. Really, it's in the same domain—it doesn't make any more sense.

So I was trying to get the interviewer to get that, but I don't think he got it. . . . Of course he didn't get it.

So, now we're kind of on the brink in our discussion. I know you haven't been saying much . . . [laughs]. So we can use this as

a springboard to see if we can make a leap. Experiencing what
you are is different from being Nothing or an apple, isn't it? Even
if afterwards you say "Nothing" about it or you say "apple" about
it. The *experience* that I'm talking about is when it's what you are.
Not whether it's Nothing or an apple. And it doesn't have to be
a grandiose experience. It doesn't have to be an enlightenment
experience. I'm not talking of a "direct experience" necessarily.
But that does push us in a direction.

For now we can just take it at a cognition level, the present
perception that you're having of reality. Experience is not what
you think about it, however. It's not what you say about it, it's
not what you feel about it, it's not the reactions, it's not the imagery and models out of which you understand it. It's what actually is occurring. What actually IS there. And since we don't know
the difference most of the time between what's occurring and the
influence our bias, understanding, images, beliefs, etcetera, have
on what's occurring, it is very difficult then to hear what I'm saying. I'm not talking about a different reality. I'm talking about
this one in a different way.

Say you're trying to remember a dream. You had certain images
and they meant something to you. It could be very abstract, like
vast space with a huge rotating amorphous plane and a crack
somehow between two domains, and you were trying to get
through the crack to understand something—but the dream is
difficult to describe or remember. That's an abstract one. There
are some concepts going on, and imagery, and you have a sense
that it means something in particular. Sometimes you wake up
from a dream, and you have a sense something happened, but
you don't know what, right? Like you were just somewhere and
you want to go back, but you can't find the door. Well, where is
it? It's on the tip of my—hmmm. Ever done that? And you think
you can just . . . get it . . . but you never do. Why? Why can't we
think it? It seems to be right there, almost palpable, you could
taste it, but you can't structure it enough to think it. It eludes
you. There may be an experience there but you can't think it, you

have no objective structure in which to think it. There's no conventional, objective, relational domain in which to conceive the
experience.

But this is not to say that it needs to occur in only one form.
For example, Katie didn't dream in pictures, or what was it? Was
it dreaming? Memory? What?

Katie: *None of my concepts appeared to me in pictures.*

PR: . . . But you can do that now?

Katie: *I can.*

PR: Okay, so say we have somebody who doesn't have memories
with pictures. There are two possibilities here. One, they have
pictures but aren't cognizant of them as pictures, out of which
they understand and then become cognizant without a "picture"
framework. Or they don't have pictures and they are cognizant
in some other way. So now, what's the experience? What's an
experience of memory? It's something you're doing, so you should
know, but generally you don't.

I'm going to keep working here, and I want you to get it, okay?
—Have you ever tried to follow some kind of scientific paradigm,
or recall a dream, or understand something somebody's saying?
See, this is it, this is exactly it. You're trying to understand—I'm
talking about something and you're going, "Huh?" Say someone
is trying to explain molecules to you and he says, "Look at it like
this: say this is the molecule and this is energy spinning. The
energy spins, bumps into the molecule, creating a vibration in
the molecule and blah, blah, blah. . . . See?" And then you go,
"Oh, I get it." But what did you get? You didn't get *it.* You grasped
the model he just created for you to understand—unless you leapt
past the model. But having created the model, perhaps you will
consider further, right?

And some people, some students, probably many, maybe even
most, never get past the models. Their understanding lies in the
model. They reproduce models and formulas, get good grades,

and leave. Brilliant ones get past the models. Those are the ones that impressed you perhaps, because they always knew what they were talking about. And you didn't understand how they did. Did you ever have that experience? "But I don't understand it, how did we get to here? We have this equation here and this problem—I can't make sense out of it." And they go—"Look, it's easy. All you do is turn this and do that and then you do this like that and boom, it all falls together, see?" And you just moan. Or maybe you get that one but you don't get the next one. And they say, "But don't you see, it's just like the other one except it's here and it's spinning like that and it's out in the street ... don't you get it?" And they can keep doing that. And you keep trying to memorize each example, so you can try to understand it. Well, the difference between you and them at that point is they understand what they're talking about, right? And maybe you understand, but you only understand the models and the formulas. You understand the "means" of communication, the vias. Hah! ... THIS, right now! Are you getting it? See, right now I'm speaking to you about something that you're valiantly trying to understand, right? Have an experience! Everything that I'm saying, everything that I'm doing is the same thing—it's models. I'm trying to make up examples, imagery, and models. Why? Because basically it's how we understand something, and if you don't have any way to grasp something it's very, very difficult—unless you do it directly, and then there's no reason and no cause, so you may just sit there for a while.

So you can see the difference between an experience of mathematics and an understanding of mathematics. Yes? No? I suspect Einstein had an experience of physics, not just an understanding of physics. Having an experience of something then understanding is like cannon fodder. I mean it just comes. Tons of it. You can make it up, think it, create it, change it, or throw it away.

Interjecting Perceptive-Mimics into Cognition

Jef: *What do you want me to get?*

PR: What I'd like you to get is the difference between experience and belief. Or experience and concept. When we look deeply enough, everything seems to be conceptual. Already we can make a distinction between frivolous beliefs or hearsay, and something that seems a little more authentic. That's in the direction of this distinction. We can make distinctions between concepts that look like they are just "of the mind"—like abstractions—and interpretations that look a lot more undeniably there—like objects.

I could try another route . . . but that might be dangerous. Well, I'll try it. Notice what's taking place in this moment, what's the experience of the moment? As opposed to the concept of the moment. When you see it as "moment after moment" it's apparent that a time thing is happening, right? You've got concept-concept-concept-concept-concept. Okay. And then there's the experience of all that happening.

So, right now you're in a room and I'm talking . . . and now I'm not, now I am [laughs]. You're in a room and I'm talking. Now, what's the experience of being in a room while I'm speaking? There's a lot of judgment going on, bias, feeling, emotions. But what's the "experience" of being in a room, with me speaking?

Jef: *Okay, to work with the distinction you're making would it be appropriate for me to notice what it's like to always be thinking ahead? Since mainly what's going on for me is wondering where this is leading, should I notice that's what I'm doing, or should I try to keep to an awareness of just being in a room?*

PR: I always want to dive into it and go as far as I can, and I don't know if that's going to serve. But if you and I say we are in a room, we might restrict ourselves. Our experience may look like we're in a room, but if we insist that we're in a room it can switch really easily into a belief. Because in this moment we might not experience ourselves being in a room, we just believe we're in a room.

Say your mind wanders, or you start reading a book or something, and you have no cognition of the room; it doesn't seem to be there. And you say, "Well, I was in a room," but it might be a carry-over that you're in a room—maybe you're not in a room. Your cognition was not about being in a room.

When people say, "Be here now," what are they saying? Usually what they're saying—and it's a legitimate say—is to be cognizant of what physically seems to be occurring right now in our perception. Right? That's what they're saying. But who said "that" is now? Or here? See, there's still an assumption there. You might be able to be now and here without being aware of what's occurring in this physical, objective perception called now. It's an assumption. But you would still say you are here, and it is now. Right? Experience is whatever way it actually is. Which is largely unknown.

Jef: *So how do I know if I'm making the distinction that we need to make?*

PR: Well, the one I started out making [laughs] is first of all noticing how much we live in belief—we think that it really *is* the way that we believe. It's pretty easy to pass up some beliefs and/or to pass up every belief for a moment, right? Some beliefs are harder to let go of—it's like you would say, "Well yeah, it's a belief, but it's true." For example, you could say about being in a room, "Oh, that may just be a belief, but it's true. It really is true. I mean, c'mon, who's fooling who? You know I am in a room." Okay, perhaps you're in a room, no problem, but be able to see when a belief is a belief.

Jef: *What do you mean, "be able"? I think I've been able to see that but I'm still here ... just sitting here talking and looking ... like in this moment I'm imagining what it looks like while I'm licking my teeth.*

PR: Yes, like that—"Imagining what it looks like licking my teeth." How much of that do we do? Make the distinction between licking your teeth and the "image" of what's happening there. The image of what's happening there is a conceptual construct; it's not occurring for you as a perceptive experience! Except that you construct the conceptual image of teeth and tongue. You conceptually construct the image and then perceive that image. And it occurs as if it is the same thing as the sensation of licking the teeth, but it's not! Most people wouldn't know what I'm talking about right now, because they can't tell the difference between the conceptualizing, creating an image, and the perception of actually feeling the teeth. It's like when you raise and lower your hand but can't see it, you still have the sense of the hand going up and down. You construct the image and see the image out of the sensations you feel, but you're not actually seeing it! So you could say I "saw" myself licking my teeth, but if we are very rigorous with it, we have to say you conceived yourself licking your teeth and saw this conceptual image. You didn't actually see yourself licking your teeth, but normally you wouldn't notice, and you live as if the sensation of licking your teeth is the same thing as the visual experience of licking your teeth, right?

Normally our cognition just goes along like that. You can see how much our facility in concept influences what we call our experience. You would say I had the experience of licking my teeth, and without knowing it, you would be including the vision of teeth, tongue, and movement, all in that statement, in that experience, without knowing that that's not *actually* what took place for you—as a perception. And we do a lot of that! So right now we're just trying to get a lever in here, to pry apart these two domains.

Jef: *So should I start noticing beliefs and then stop them, or be checking them out right now? Would that be a good exercise?*

PR: Umm.... I don't think it's useful ... or, I should say, I think it's more useful to strip things down as much as you can. If you can't strip them down any more, fine. There still remains the possibility that you can go further. It's not like we're necessarily trying to find the honest-to-God, bottom-line strip down. That's another one that we could do. But, like I said about licking your teeth; what are you actually experiencing and what else is conceptually going along with that?

When we have something physical that we can refer to—a sensation or an objective experience—then it's much easier, even though it's not normal. Do you all see this thing about licking his teeth? You wouldn't have thought of that as conceptual, would you? So, when we have something like that, I can point it out and you can see it. But it's also true in the non-objective domain. However, it's more difficult to distinguish experience in a strictly non-objective domain, because it's all non-objective; you can't see the sensation versus the imagination, the object versus an idea about it. It's not as clear . . . unless you know what I'm talking about.

John: *I missed that. . . . What's not as clear as what?*

PR: When we talk about physical perceptions in the objective domain—sensation, sight, sound, something occurring—it's simpler to see the distinction between a concept and what we perceive as an object or a perception. For example, what are you actually experiencing as your arm right now? Notice you have a visual image of your arm; well, that's not a present perceptive experience—since you can't see it, what you actually experience is a feeling, and the sensation of your arm is not a vision. It's not a vision, right? And there's room to get that you're conceptually constructing a visual image about it that's not objectively there. Or you could look at something and say you feel it, but the vision is not a feeling, it's a sight. You might have feelings "about" it— reactions, judgments—and you will draw out many relations to it, but all this is only conceptually occurring in relation to the objective perception.

Now you may say, "Well, what's the experience?" If you don't like something you would normally say "that" is your experience of it, but I'm saying that is a concept about it. "I don't like it," is not the object or the perception; it's something else, do you see?

But we are still left with the question, "What is the experience?" However, we've moved in a direction and that's the direction of the distinction I'm trying to make.

In any case, it's easier when we can find something and say, "Oh look, it's this sensation right here, this is the experience"— and/or the experience of perception. Then we say that's the experience, and we've distinguished it from a lot of other stuff—beliefs I have about it, conceptually made-up perceptions I have of it, judgments I have about it, and the reactions I have about it.

We begin to notice at this point that a remarkable phenomenon is taking place. We can actually conceptually reproduce a memory of a perception and even create a new perceptive mimic. When we mimic our past perceptive experience conceptually, in other words, when we create a reproduction of a perception, we then perceive it in our cognition. What you and I fail to do most of the time is recognize that although this "mimic" looks, feels, sounds, and tastes like an objective perception, it's not, it's a concept!

But when we start talking about what's non-objective—like an idea, or understanding something—where do you find a foothold for experience? It's all non-objective; ergo it's all in the conceptual domain, so to speak. So how do you find experience in that conceptual domain? What could we call experience?

Watch the distinction here. For example, when we talk about relaxing or following you have an idea about it, and lots of information, and then something occurs, and you say, "Ah hah, this is relaxing or this is following." So you say you had an experience of it. And this "experience" is quite different than the experience you had when you had your ideas about it. It's very different, right? That's important to notice. Now what we usually miss at the time is that the moment we have an experience—and I'm not saying it's not an experience—but the moment we have an experience of relaxing, or some such thing, immediately we conceptually frame it up so we can understand it.

We think about it, we "cognize" it. And when that occurs, it then becomes as influenced as "seeing" your teeth. And it happens like "duck off a water's back" [chuckles]—or like seeing your teeth. Thinking, conceptualizing, making sense out of it, associating, believing, feeling. But still there's an experience there. While the experience is there, and usually while it's fresh, it seems to have some real or authentic quality to it. Somehow an understanding comes or blossoms, and you can speak about it differently, you have more intelligence about it, and you "know" something else now. But quickly—because the understanding that blossoms and the intelligence that increases, and everything else that occurs, is all conceptual—we look to the only place where we can understand. We look at the concept that has framed itself up—the images, the models that we've made, the sensations, the references. "Oh, this is kind of like a sensation of swimming," and now swimming somehow always influences you licking your teeth [laughs]. Are you following this?

However we frame up an experience conceptually, it influences and then gets riveted in the place of the experience, and immediately we start to separate from the experience. And it always happens, right? This, then, stands "as" the experience, and so what is actually experienced is missed. We fail to make the distinction of experience because our conceptual understanding and the insertion of conceptually mimicked perceptive overlays overwhelms what is there.

Experiencing the Models

PR: Do you get how easy it is to think that something is real and experienced when it's not, when it's just made up? For example, you believe in the unconscious, the unconscious mind. How would you know you're unconscious if you are unconscious of it? But you believe in it, because somebody said so. It's not just because somebody said so frivolously. Somebody got a hit on something—probably a very good one, a very deep one—and invented a distinction called the unconscious mind. And then worked with this distinction and produced results—and so we believe in an "unconscious mind." But there may or may not be an unconscious mind.

For something to be effective it doesn't have to be "real." I want to use this next story to reveal such a dynamic. Mohammed had three sons, but seventeen camels. And in his will he left half to Abdul, a third to Wayameya (he was the Hawaiian one, his adopted son), and Ishmael got a ninth. Then he died. Now the sons have to divide the seventeen camels in this way—it doesn't work. But then Moses comes down from the mountain with his own camel, and he says, "No problem, I'll lend you my camel." He gives them the camel, now there are eighteen, they divide them up—a half is nine, a third is six, and a ninth is two. When we add up nine, six, and two the total is seventeen right? Okay, so now the camels are all divided up. So Moses takes his camel back and rides off into the sunset.

Got it? What the metaphor is being used to reveal is that something fictitious can be introduced to create results, but that doesn't mean it takes on reality. In other words, it doesn't mean that it is actually that way. We *can* create something for the purpose of making a result. And it will produce a result. That doesn't validate what we created as something other than fictitious, or a place to stand. We do it all the time. You can introduce something, and then pull it out again. In science there are many examples in which you can introduce something, things happen, and then you pull it out again—things still happened.

If we use that story as a metaphor, you can see that the whole notion is a metaphor for other things we do.

Brian: *What we tend to do metaphorically is create the camel that....*

PR: We create that we're looking at our teeth! That we experience looking at our teeth. We forget it is a concept.

What we want is the distinction of experience. It's not a concept. So we are starting to get closer to this distinction. What people tend to do with it is get a sense of what I'm talking about as experience and then turn it into something else, because the moment you have an experience of something, you understand it. You "formulate" it so you can cognize it. Understanding and cognition are like this [grabs a pad of paper and holds a pencil touching the middle of the pad]: okay, this pencil touches the middle of the pad. See, and it's perpendicular to the pad; this is like a model of understanding. Now, you can understand it, by drawing out relations. You see—actually you compose or determine—relationships between the shapes, and this means something to you. [He begins re-positioning the pencil and pad, changing their spatial relationship.] Now understand this. Go ahead. Okay, understand this. Now, keep watching right there, right there in space, okay? Now, understand *that* [pulls the objects away and points to empty space]. It's harder to understand, huh? You don't know what to understand because there is nothing there. Without the form there are no relationships that can be seen; no associations, no meaning, no references. Understanding demands that something be there. The moment we understand something there's a relationship, however it's constructed. . . . See, when the teacher was trying to teach you two plus two equals four, she probably got two oranges and two oranges, and then said two plus two is four! And at some point you understood what she were trying to say, right?

Bob: *You want us to go in the other direction?*

PR: Something like that.

Kim: *So . . . when you get that two oranges plus two oranges is four, and at some point it shifts to an understanding—which would be along the lines that you can add anything, or grasping the concept of numbers—what is the experience in this?*

PR: The experience is of an abstraction.

Kim: *I'm confused between the experience and the understanding at this point. What are you pointing to?*

PR: [Peter goes to the board and draws a smiling face] Different, huh? [laughter] See, this is cognition. Your cognition, your understanding, comes out of making sense of the pattern that's there. The patterns mean something to you and you recognize them.

This [holds up a pad] even means something to you. What if our thinking is like that—I mean all cognition, all thinking is like that—then nothing is just perceived, nothing is only experienced. It's patterned, it's created out of relationships made in patterns of feelings, shapes, and ideas.

Kim: *So is there experience in feeling?*

PR: Feeling is like thinking, only different. So why wouldn't there be a pattern? This is what we understand. And why wouldn't there be experience in feeling? If you have experience in thought, if you have experience in perception, why not experience in feeling?

Kim: *When you were talking with Jef, it seemed to me that in the speaking of experience you were subtracting emotion or feeling as things that aren't the experience.*

PR: No. We were talking about sensation. And I was extracting what's not the sensation itself. Neither an emotional reaction or an abstract thought are the sensation itself.

Kim: *So if he's running his tongue over his teeth, I get he's not seeing it, but making a picture of his tongue going over his teeth. And that's not "seeing" that happen. But you'd be feeling your teeth and feeling something.*

PR: Yes. You're even cognizing the teeth, but the cognition is built out of feeling the sensations that you have. The "look" of the teeth is added to the cognition conceptually. Which is quite amazing. However, what is the experience in all this?

An Insight (Breakthrough) Is an Experience, But It's Only Known as a Concept

PR: Let's try another doorway. What is an insight?

Bob: *I think insights are another kind of concept. When I notice something that I haven't noticed before—like when I look at an oil painting and I notice that all it is is paint on a surface, and there really isn't*

*any image there. It doesn't have to be an image. The first time that
happened I called that an insight, but to me that's still all conceptualizing, and it's just either a different concept or another kind of concept than I've ever had before.*

PR: The concept that was occurring before the insight was concept
also. Right? If you're talking about recognizing paint on the canvas rather than a picture as an insight, then the concept or concepts have changed. What happened that the concept changed?
How come you suddenly saw paint on the canvas?

Bob: *Well, I don't know . . . I can't remember. All I can say is that I
was ready, something was ready for that to happen.*

PR: Okay, and that's an explanation.

Bob: *Yeah, you're right.*

PR: An explanation and a guess.

Bob: *Yes, okay.*

PR: Well, what's an insight? It doesn't have to be just that one,
right? You have other insights, don't you? What's *insight?*
   Let me propose that insights or breakthroughs are experiences.
Let's think for a moment that is what they are. The moment you
have an insight or a breakthrough a concept arises out of which
to understand the insight and breakthrough. Before he got paint
on a canvas, something was there, and immediately thereafter he
conceived, "That's paint on a canvas, not a picture." But I'm suggesting the recognition followed the insight or the experience.
The moment you get something like that—a breakthrough of
some sort—you go "Ah." When you go "Ah," you think something or feel something, and then say something. This is the way
you understand it. What preceded the conceptual formation was
an experience. Which will always be followed by a concept, or
you won't understand it. You might have experiences that you
don't have concepts about, but you don't understand them. You
could also understand them wrongly.

Eric: *I've been having experiences.*

PR: Having experiences? Well, what's occurring?

Eric: *. . . It's nothing that I can handle in any way or have anything to say about in any way, shape, or form. And that's not very useful, so immediately I come up with something that I can do with it. I can't deal with it until I have something that's useful and something I can play with. Although I notice that even though it's weird and different, I'm not any smarter necessarily. I'm not any more anything, except that I'm experiencing that that's what's going on. What does happen is that I notice I'm only experiencing what I'm experiencing. Like when we were talking about being in a room: until we say we're in a room, I don't have being in a room as an experience or as a concept. When I conceive of being in a room it reminds me to look around and see what I'm in—I'm in a room.*

PR: When it's "weird," immediately that's a relationship to what's occurring: it's weird. That's also conceptual, right?

Eric: *It's not weird at the moment that it happens; it's only weird as I sit here, and the concepts that arise out of it are weird because it's not normal for me to be doing this. I can actually sit here and experience myself conceptualizing.*

Experiencing a Concept

PR: Sometimes I ask people, "Have you ever experienced a concept?" Because it sounds like I badmouth concept. It would be silly to badmouth concept. Have you ever experienced what a concept "is?" It's an "anal clenching" experience. Concepts aren't what you think. When you experience what concept is, then it's an experience, not a concept.

Katie: *Were you speaking of experiencing concept generically or experiencing a concept that I'm having now? A particular one?*

PR: You can experience a particular concept, but if you get what a concept "is" it doesn't matter which concept it is. If you think,

"What is a generic concept?", all you do is conceptualize. It wouldn't be an experience, right? Because you would just be thinking about what a concept possibly is. See, you'd have to actually experience conceptualizing in order to experience what a concept *is*.

So to balance out the speaking—a lot of times people think I'm badmouthing concept, or I'm badmouthing feelings. If you want to know my opinion, both concept and feelings are actually the same. Can you imagine no concept? Of course not. Imagination *is* conceptual. Take a look at the power that conceptualization is. It's our whole life. All that we *are* is pretty much concept. The whole social structure, reality, the whole universe, none of it is possible without concept, is it? It's not possible, it couldn't occur in our experience.

Consider the abstractions that we're able to entertain. I mean, it's far beyond what you "know"—far beyond what you think. It determines what you can do. Think about a frog catching a fly with its tongue. Can you catch a fly with your tongue? That's pretty good, right? Zap that little sucker out there, whapp. Catch that fly and zap it back in here. And it's quick. That's a very basic occurrence. Yet, can you imaging the genius it takes to create that?

How about thinking? Incredible! I mean incredible. Thinking! What if we took your thinking away? You would have next to nothing left over. But regardless of quantity, think of the quality. Are you a quality thinker? Just think about thinking—what it provides, the power that it is. So maybe we're stupid with it, but still consider the magnificence that thinking is. Incredible!

Feeling! Consider the genius that feeling is! We don't know what feeling "is," we don't know what thinking "is." So, I'm not putting them down. It's just that there's another distinction besides thinking and feeling, and that's the one I keep working on. That's the one I keep trying to draw out. And the distinction other than thinking and feeling is experience—which is what allows us to get what thinking "is" and to get what feeling "is." Rather than just being "in" thinking and being "in" feeling, experience allows us to see the activity that they are—the magnificent activity that they are. . . . Incredible.

Eric: *It's just too there, it's like inherent, and I can't experience it as a concept. It's just that way. It's really different than what I thought you were originally talking about. I can sit here and experience. Wow, experience, wow. Wow!*

PR: Unless it's actually an "objective" concept. Remember what I said . . . about a danger in what I said I shouldn't go into, but then I said I would? If we chip away at this distinction, we just set up a dynamic. You say "this is a wall" because you say it's a wall. It's not really a wall. And yet you and I see a wall. Well, over there we see a wall. This is a blackboard, a shoji screen, space, distance, light, sight. [Makes a non-linear leap.] You see it's all gone now [laughs].

Jef: *What's gone?*

PR: If I'm drawing your attention to sight, then you have got to see, right? You do see, right? Sight, living color? Sight, distance, wall, feeling, thinking!

Well, let's try this: that's not a wall [points to the wall]. THAT is not a wall. Are you feeling your body? You're not feeling your body, there's no body there! Without the concept "body" there is no body there. Without the concept "wall" there is no wall there. Without the distinction "distance" there is no distance between us. Sight? Feeling? These are simply phenomena. So, take those away. If you take that away what do you have left? Not much.

But, you still have that there's something pushing itself forward that you don't have much to say about, right? Okay, good. Who said *you're* the one who says? That's one of our confusions. You don't seem to have any power in relationship to the wall being there or not being there. Without the concept "you" and "power" it doesn't make any difference. There's no wall, there's no you, and there's no influence of the wall. Strip it down—take out all that you can see is conceptual or assumed, until your experience is really fundamental—then press yourself toward what's still there. But without what you conceive you don't know what it is. Still, you have this sense that there's something there. You may be right. But do you see how much of it is concept? And when you get down to objective concepts like sight, distance, wall, space, it seems to stop there—it's difficult for you to get those as concepts. That's okay.

Eric: *The wall seems to stop wherever I stop challenging it. If I look at that wall and challenge it enough, it stops being a wall.*

PR: It'll stop being a wall, for sure.

Eric: *But I've got to challenge it.*

PR: But it doesn't stop "being." Since when it stops being, we're not talking about anything anymore. See? ... I didn't make this up. Don't look at me.

Okay, I thought that experience would be a useful distinction for you to make. So, with this kind of challenge, you can still get a really good and useful hit on a distinction between merely believing in something and having some kind of authentic relationship with it, right?

When my teachers would show me something, teach something, and ask me, "Do you understand?", if I couldn't do it—if I couldn't experience it for myself, then I would say, "No, I don't." It's clear that the only useful place, the only useful part of the understanding in that case, was what I could do. So obviously my understanding was lacking, because I couldn't do it. I was missing something. But I understood him from day one, intellectually. I spoke English [laughs]. That's not it.

The Relation between Belief and Suffering

PR: So you had homework about getting some freedom from the source or foundation of suffering—whatever we called it. What are we calling it? What's the jargon for the day? Or yesterday, or whatever?

Jef: *The Big Banana.*

PR: Okay. So we have some limiting beliefs. When we eliminate these beliefs our immediate suffering goes away. Right? Yes. But then it comes back. What's so that it comes back all the time? That's what we're calling the big banana; and we are investigating the possibility that eliminating beliefs is like freedom. So, what happened with your homework?

Eric: *It seemed that there were beliefs coming up that were responsible for generating my suffering, my pain, but it always seemed like there was a deeper belief out of which they were coming. These first beliefs could be anything, and they were expendable. But what they came out of was not. Like ... people are dangerous. There's something real about that, and I mean* really. *I can came up with all kinds of different beliefs about it, and I can change those like that [snaps fingers] to suit. If they're working, fine. If they're not, well, I'll come up with something else that works better. But something doesn't change.*

PR: Those deeper beliefs?

Eric: *Yeah, the deeper beliefs. Those beliefs will just hang out, unless something hits me hard enough to show that those beliefs aren't working. And it's always something traumatic, like some work here at the school, or something horrible in my emotional life. And then I'll have to really examine those beliefs. But, unless I'm forced to do it by some kind of horrible trauma, I will not challenge those beliefs.*

PR: Of course, there's always the horrible trauma of living with those beliefs. Sometimes that can be horrible enough.

Eric: *I can just juggle that one with various little beliefs. I've got this sea of swirling beliefs ... it's all horribly painful, I mean it's just horribly painful, but it works ... or it kind of works.*

PR: [laughs] Yeah. Kinda reminds me of the story that I'm going to make up right now on the spot, of a guy in "The Twilight Zone," working very, very hard to save himself by climbing everything because he thought he was going to drown. And clinging to things because he thought he was going to fall. In regard to all of the activity and effort that he was exerting, he would say, "Well it works, I'm still here." What he didn't know was that he'd still be here anyway, no matter what he did. He wasn't going anywhere. At some point he found out it didn't make any difference what he did. He's still in the same event. Then he got he was in hell and couldn't get out. So all those things he did didn't really work anyway. Oh well. It's just a story.

So, these beliefs . . . people are inherently evil, or they're out to get me, or whatever—we could challenge them and still what happens? What's underneath that?

Eric: *That I'm incomplete, and that I need something added at all times.*

PR: That's pretty fundamental. Again, what if being incomplete and needing something at all times is right there at the heart of the matter? Yet, what's the experience that we're talking about? When we say we're incomplete, and we need something else, that's the activity we're talking about, that's the concept we're talking about, the framework—what's the experience that we're talking about? What is this "incomplete" . . . as an experience?

Bob: *I noticed that beliefs would come and go—beliefs about self-image, a belief that it's important for me to keep up appearances for other people. At work I noticed this, and dropped it, but it would always return. I could just drop it. Yet I don't even know if I ever really dropped it. I just kind of put my attention on something else. But I couldn't get what was under it. I just percolated some thoughts about what it might be . . . like the beliefs that give rise to pain. The only other sense that came up was that maybe there's something that I don't want to go away. That felt true, there's something that I don't want to go away. There's something that I don't want to disappear. I came up with answers like "I don't want me to disappear, I must survive, yack, yack, yack." I tend to throw away the yack, yack, yack because I've been doing that for about eight years now. But, nothing else came up, nothing beyond what I just said.*

PR: You all know what I mean when I say cosmology, yes? I'm not talking about beauty school [laughter]. Cosmology—what I'm saying is how we see the universe. The conceptual structure or framework in which we see "life" or how existence is occurring—like the hierarchy of being alive. Contextual belief systems we live within. If we can "see" ourselves "licking our teeth," although there is no such perception taking place except as a conceptual interject, imagine how our cosmological beliefs influence our experience. And everybody has a cosmology. We more than likely have a combination of cosmologies, several, even if they're inconsistent.

For example, you have a scientific paradigm out of which you think of things. You also have a spiritual one, a religious one, or something like that. You may have a cosmology of what the universe is like, in which there is a god, a heaven and earth, and that's a cosmology. Or, one in which there is none of that; everything is chemicals and it all arose from the Big Bang, and that's a cosmology. They are all belief systems out of which to hold things. And you have more than one. You have your favorite— maybe it's the one that provides a groovy spiritual domain, you certainly have a psychological framework, and probably you have a pragmatic one, and then you've got one you live in for your daily routines, right? In any case, you've got a cosmology out of which you view your place in the scheme of things.

So, I'm looking for the source of these beliefs here. When you eliminate particular beliefs the pain goes away, the suffering goes away. Suffering and pain come out of beliefs—something you believe in. And when you stop believing in that, the suffering goes away, along with the belief—*if* you stop believing in the right one, the one that's causing the pain, so to speak. And yet the beliefs and the pain continue to arise and come back; even once you've been free of them, they keep coming back.

So we are asking what is this driving force? What is suffering? Why suffer? We seem attached to it. That's an avenue I'd like to pursue at some point. Because if we really are attached to it, then it might be a good thing to know. Then we could go ahead and enjoy our suffering. [chuckles] Okay, so that's not so popular.

When you're thinking about your cosmology, what's underneath it? What is "this" right now? See if you can experience it without a cosmology. Without a hierarchy, without a structure, without a paradigm, or at least clean it up as much as you can. So maybe just a basic "you" sense and "other" sense, with very few variables. See if you can eliminate your hierarchies, the way you see reality, the way you see the world. Religious, spiritual, scientific, any other way—eliminate it all. And then take a look at the question. Because all you get then is experience.

Kim: *Eliminating the cosmological belief systems—if I'm hearing that correctly—as well as the many layers of active beliefs, the pain does disappear, . . . but then I'm lost as to what it is I'm looking for.*

PR: Well, right now what we're focusing on is watching it come back. . . . Why does it come back? If it's gone there should be no need for it to come back.

Kim: *Well, in my experience, I take a belief back on—and I can manipulate the belief so it may not even be the exact same belief anymore; it has a little different twist. I have a lot of different frameworks and patterns of belief. When they disappear though, the pain disappears. And as I go through eliminating beliefs, then there doesn't seem like there's any pain there anymore. So, what I'm asking is, what am I supposed to look into?*

PR: That it comes back.

Kim: *That it comes back appears to me to be that I take on the belief again.*

PR: Why do you take on the belief again? From where does it come, from where does the demand and the motivation come to take on a belief again? Especially one that you've already noticed causes pain?

Kim: *You're speaking about it like, why would you take on something that causes you pain, like it was a bad thing. I don't know that I get my pain as a bad thing.*

PR: You liked it when it was gone.

Kim: *Umm, yeah, but then there's something in me that places some value on the beliefs I held, and now . . . .*

PR: So what's that about? That's what were after. If having the pain isn't a bad thing—and you *do* say that it is—then you have to get where it isn't a bad thing. Like where it really isn't a bad thing. Where you really do want to have those beliefs, right? So that's pointing at what we're calling—since we don't have a name for it—the big banana.

Kim: *Okay. Well, I was looking in that direction—now I'm trying to work something out—I was looking in that direction and. . . . Well, I want to be a certain kind of person. This is important, you know?*

PR: What kind of person is that?

Kim: *In the specific case I'm thinking about, I have pain because someone doesn't like me—I want to be liked but it's more important for me to be able to speak my mind truthfully. So, if that puts me in a position that I'm not liked. . . .*

PR: So you're saying it gets down to basic values, and wanting to feel like you can be "yourself" with another and still be accepted?

Kim: *Or something.*

PR: And there's a pecking order; some things will go before others which are more important.

Kim: *Right, when you were talking about a hierarchy in our cosmology, it made sense, that's what occurred.*

PR: Well, when I was talking about cosmology, I was actually speaking about the context, the framework or structure that it is—and you could have very different ones. A hierarchy is just one framework that you can have. That's a very simple one. But it could be quite different than that and so you'd think about things very differently. If you look at the universe, life, and your position in it, from a general scientific perspective, then you think of it one way. If you look at it from a Christian religious perspective, you look at it very differently, right? And how you feel and think is very different. And so, that's the cosmology. That's what I'm talking about.

Kim: *Well, something that I have gotten a hit on a couple of times is responsibility, and the sense that somewhere I feel I made a choice, or I'm making choices. In particular, religion is a great description of that....*

PR: So that reveals a cosmology, see? That you make a choice, that you've been making a choice about things, comes out of a cosmology in which you make choices, create your life, etcetera, etcetera. It's a certain framework in which you hold things, such that choosing would be a possibility, and a thought. So when I spoke about looking toward this underlying dynamic and, as best you can, eliminating your cosmology, then you don't know whether you make a choice or not. See, you have a sense of making a choice, but you don't know if you make a choice or not without your cosmology. So keep trying to look at it from a very innocent or fresh point of view.

Kim: *Now, even in looking at it from a fresh point of view, I still interpret there's something there that I interpret as choice, or responsibility. And that's what I'm talking about.*

PR: Okay, and unfortunately in this work and our endeavor, it doesn't seem like it makes much difference to. . . . Well, let's say choice and responsibility in the matter seem to be more of a point of view. They might come out of some sense of experience, but what we need to do then is to dive into that experience. What is the *experience* that you're calling choice or responsibility? It might not even look like choice or responsibility. And from where does that come?

Why do we suffer? Why do we create suffering, over and over again? Even when there are possibilities of freedom, or lightening up at least, we don't pursue them for long. We continue to suffer. How come? What's the story? That question is so general and so abstract that we needed to do work to ground the question. And we still need to do work to continue to ground the question and to drive into it. Otherwise, we just sit around asking, "Why do I keep suffering?" Too abstract.

We've made some distinctions, seen some dynamics that we can work with. We might be wrong, but as long as we keep a vigil, it gives us a springboard from which to jump. All of the time, all that we are ever working with are the models, so to speak. All we're working with are the things that we construct to speak about it. Everything you and I have offered up so far in the course of our meetings has been that, hasn't it? You see, it's all models, it's all made-up, it's all ways of thinking it, even the big banana. Obviously the big banana, because it's not a banana, probably. I would really be surprised if it turns out to be a banana.

That's why I'm using the term big banana, because nobody's going to take that seriously, right? But still you have to be careful. See, even that there is an underlying motivation that drives us back into suffering is an assumption, but it's a good one—for now. We still have to keep a vigil on it however. We don't know that there is such a thing. Obviously, we don't know what is going on, so we can't say for sure that it is this way or that way. But we move in a direction. And the direction right now is to uncover, to experience what moves us to believe in things. What moves us to have pain?

This is our eleventh meeting. So in the first ten meetings we were basically trying to find our question, and move into it. I think we're pretty close to our question now, we're starting to concretely move into something.

Katie: *I have made a lot of progress into an experience of beliefs that are fundamental. I've gotten to one that I keep saying, "Well, I would get rid of this one if I knew how." And I hold very firmly that that's true. I also have this belief that of course I could get rid of this. I definitely hold the idea, "I would if I could." There's too much pain here.*

It's very painful. So if you would just tell me how to do it, I would do it in an instant. And at the same time, there's also that sort of nagging sense that says, "No, that's not true, I wouldn't give this up," or at least I don't give it up. Even now that I have an experience of it, I don't give it up.

PR: You have an experience that it is a belief?

Katie: *I have some sort of experience around a belief that causes me pain—something about being "hidden," and a lot of things that come out of that. I have this idea that if I knew how not to be hidden, I would do that.*

PR: Hidden? Sounds pretty vague.

Katie: *There are a lot of specifics, like I must be mediocre, but when I look into that the motivation to be mediocre goes into an issue of being hidden, or an issue of not surrendering—and there were other things that came up around that. When I trace it back they go to the same place, even though it doesn't sound like they would.*

PR: You trace them back to where?

Katie: *I trace them back to this place that I now call "being," I have a need to "be" hidden. The very source of various pains seems to go back to this.*

PR: Are you hidden? Hidden is something like protected, right?

Katie: *Yeah, the closest that I felt tonight about what is behind the hiding is that fundamentally I am alone. And then out of that I need to not be seen. . . . There's some "I"ness that can't come out, the real me can't come out.*

PR: I would guess three things in the matter. The primary one is that you don't drop the belief because you don't actually get that it is a belief, even if you say you do. In other words, for you it is real, it is the truth. So you don't get it as a belief. If you get it as a belief it will unhook the reality of it, and then you can indeed drop it. So I suspect it's still anchored "as" the truth. That's one thing.

What also plays itself out is that it serves something, and it might be useful for you to get what it serves, because if you're unwilling to give up what it serves, you're probably also unwilling to drop the reality of it. It does serve something, and what it serves might be something more fundamental than the belief. I don't know.

The third possibility that came up for me, which actually got more wind as you spoke toward the end, was that you don't know what you're talking about. And what I mean by that is that what you're identifying as the belief isn't really what it is you need to be talking about. Or what you're identifying, how you're saying it, how you're thinking and looking at it, isn't really what it is you need to be talking about, it's not what you need to be addressing—that's not what needs to go. It's perhaps a camouflage to what needs to go, a distraction, a snow job, or something, and probably a really good one. But it sounds like it's still a little vague and amorphous, somehow. It sounds like it's not quite the heart of what you need to be speaking about.

I would imagine a way to go about it is to look at the beliefs that you think are most concrete. Take the reality out of them, really get them as beliefs, and have them disappear. If they come back, find out what they're serving, and have that disappear. At least for the time being. Sometimes you have to trick yourself. So ... either they keep coming back, or something else will arise, and that will probably help you get more in touch with the real point. Because probably, when you get rid of those beliefs, something else will persist. Something will persist. And so you can ask, what is persisting? Then see if you can get clearer on what that is and go for *it*. And then do the same thing with its reality. As long as it is given the status of "true," it will stay. That's one of the reasons why I asked you, "Are you hidden?" And you connected it with what I would call being existentially alone. Alone just because you exist—the experience that we have of being existentially alone—that you are absolutely, totally alone. So, in there is a possibility of being hidden. There's something pretty fundamental in that. Now if you just hold that it's true that you are alone, then that's not a belief. You are alone.

Katie: *And it's a problem.*

PR: It's a problem being alone?

Katie: *Or it used to be a problem.*

PR: Okay. Now see, there might be a belief that it's a problem. It also might be a belief that you are alone. But still, that might not be the problem. There might be a belief that it's a problem that you are alone, or that it's painful to be alone, or that it means certain things to be alone. Or that you have to be secreted so that we can't find you, so we can't hurt you, or whatever. All that could definitely be a belief. Try to see what belief or beliefs seem to generate this pain.

Okay, why don't we continue with basically the same question. I think we have gotten deeper into it, so we will keep storming the castle, until the walls come tumbling down—that's a metaphor. Keep plunging into the banana until we've gobbled it all up—that's another one. So, it's basically: "Where is this suffering coming from?" I think it would actually be useful to get that. Where does this belief and pain come from?

Thank you, and good night.

Thank you.

Listening for Being

The following communication was taken from talks given to apprentice-instructors in 1983. James Kapp: "Those of us who have been associated with Peter Ralston for some time have found that profound listening and contemplation are required to approach the experience of which he speaks."

The Skill of Hearing: Merging with the Experience

PR: Hearing is a skill. It's like being attentive and sensitive to what's occurring when we are fighting—what we call "listening" in the context of internal martial arts. It's a skill, and if you've ever been attentive to your consciousness while you were engaged in a demanding endeavor such as fighting, you know that your listening ability fades in and out, that it can be better or worse. Sometimes you drop it, and then notice that when you dropped it, you didn't get what was going on.

However, when I'm talking to you and you don't get it, you don't notice that there was anything not heard. But when you're fighting you notice you don't get it because the person hits you, or surprises you; and then you notice that you weren't paying attention—if you were conscious enough to notice that you weren't paying attention.

There's only one way for you to be here. It's very difficult for you to sit there and hear me. Very difficult, I know. You want to go to sleep, you want to think about something else. Your mind is constantly working and you get distracted, or maybe you'll hear

57

something and go off on that, and half an hour later you come back. It's like when you're listening so well to an opponent and they throw a punch, and you dodge. Then you think: "Oh boy, I dodged, I dodged, wasn't that good," and POW, they hit you.

See, it's the same kind of listening. It's knowing the experience that is happening. When you listen to somebody verbally, the same thing has to happen—knowing the experience that is happening. When you're fighting or playing games, the function is the same; you have to know the experience that is happening. Now, when it's done verbally, obviously the experience that's happening that you're to notice isn't necessarily how the energy is flowing through my body, or what my body is doing, since they aren't the issue.

There is only one way for you to listen that is not painful. Otherwise it is painful, it's a struggle. It's a struggle to stay awake, it's a struggle to be here, it's a struggle to listen to the words, and it's a struggle to figure out what I'm talking about. The only way to listen is to *experience* what it is I'm talking about. It's the only way. Other than that it's a struggle—and other than that it's not listening! So you're not even getting it. It's a struggle and you're not listening. Beyond that is discipline.

The discipline is: when you fade out you come back, you fade out, you come back, fade out, come back, fadeoutcomeback [faster]. It's a discipline.

Doug: *I'm sorry, I missed what you just said.*

[laughter]

PR: I don't mind questions. . . . [laughs]

You have to live the experience we're talking about, what's being addressed. If there's one experience happening, then you're doing the same thing I'm doing. It's not difficult for me because all I have to do is experience it, and then get it across. What's difficult is getting it across.

The level of hearing shouldn't be this low. The level of hearing in this room is appallingly low—for who you are. For what you've gone through. If you were just people off the street I would say you're doing really well, but I won't bullshit you. You are much more capable of hearing at a much deeper level.

There is nothing outside of this. There is nothing outside of the communication that we're talking about. What's outside of it? You have two choice—you either listen or you don't. What's outside of that?

You think there is something else, or somewhere to go. You go outside into your "life" and think this doesn't apply. How can this not apply? You either listen or you don't listen in your life. But listening is not as simple as mastering your attention, since it is determined completely by the way you "hold" the world. At any moment, the world or reality is the way you "hold" it, the way you interpret it. You hold the world "is" some way, period. What's outside of holding the world? What's outside of the way you hold the world? NOTHING! Right?

You think, "Oh, there's this talk about the way I hold the world in Cheng Hsin, but that's just some philosophy; when I'm out in my life, forget it." That's the way you are holding the world! There's nothing outside of that. That's it! Every moment! When you encounter somebody you can listen or not. All the time—at a checkstand at the grocery store, walking down the street, being with your girlfriend or boyfriend, or when you're fighting.

And yet you hold it as if there is something outside of this, something outside of this communication, that this is just some philosophy—[gestures waving his hands] like here's your whole life and here's Cheng Hsin over in this corner, and here's some philosophy that we talk about every once in a while, kind of stuck in this part of Cheng Hsin. You hold it that way; and that's absolute nonsense. It's not true. It's not the truth.

Marcel: *You talked last time about having to get outside of our experience, so that we can get past our limits. And then you talk about it not being something outside of ourselves—and I'm confused. If it has to be outside of the way we hold it or how we experience it, and yet it's not something "out there," then where is it?*

PR: [laughs] Where is it? [laughs] . . . Michigan.

[laughter]

Marcel: *This is real confusing.*

PR: When you get to the point of increasing your ability to hear, we'll put more attention on that again and again, so you can hear it. Figure it out? Maybe never. Don't worry about it. We haven't even really talked about the way you hold things.

You have to put in your time. How come? What would happen if you didn't put in your time? Nothing. Is the time it? No. Is the time necessary? ABSOLUTELY!

Insight: Get It, Lose It, and Get It Back

Judy: *I've noticed that when I have an insight, or something becomes clear, that then my mind will take over and I lose the experience. But I notice too that if I just keep asking a question, rather than taking time to fix it into place conceptually, if I continue the inquiry, the tendency to want to put that insight into place doesn't stop the process of living out of the experience.*

PR: Right, good. Well said. Insight is in the realm of that which generates, and not that which is generated. If we take a look at something that has been generated from some insight or other, we are not actually looking at the insight but at something that arose from it. We generate through insight. Which is to say, some construct comes up: "Oh. look at this principle" or "Look at this thing about me," or whatever. The moment it's generated it is no longer the insight, it is a concept. Ordinarily we recognize things through generation; in other words, we generate it, we "conceive" it, and then we look at it.

So the moment it's generated we have a new concept. What you noticed quite well is that the moment we experience something, we start having thoughts and feelings about it, and that's not the insight. The insight is what generated what you conceptualized and found to be so interesting.

The moment you've done that, however, you start identifying what is cognized "as" the insight, rather than as what has been generated by the insight. The insight is what generated that. Then you start having thoughts and feelings about what is cognized—and these are all coming from a mechanism that's already fixed in set patterns.

As we continue doing that, it becomes useless and dead, and even counterproductive. But if we notice this dynamic, and instead stay with what's generating the concept, then we keep the openness and generating power alive, rather than getting stuck in some fixed conclusion. One of the ways to do that, as you actually brought up, is to continue to inquire. Because when we continue to inquire we keep cutting into the generating process rather than the generated process. That's very important to see. "Being" comes from the generating not from what's generated, not from what's already formed. And so following that method you are aligning yourself with "being," rather than "been." [laughs]

Judy: *What would also happen was I would think, "Oh good, if I inquire then something will happen," so I even put the idea of inquiry into a box.*

PR: Yes, that goes on, right? There's a tendency to identify—just notice it, and question again right now . . . and now . . . and now. . . .

Such a vigil is absolutely necessary, because even such matters as the source of being, which isn't a thing, we attempt to bring into thinghood. Thinghood on a radically different level, like the absolute NO THING THING. "The absolute . . . ah yes, I know . . . the source is no time, no space, so this sense that I experience as no time, no space, that's the source, I see." And you've heard that the source is creative, so you'll add: "I see, there's a little paradox, so this experience here that I have of paradox and no time and no space, that's the source, I understand that." Uh huh.

And it's not! It's a magnificent, and I mean magnificent, representation of a something that it's not. It's like creating a new realm in which to represent something that's not representable.

And when I say "thing" I'm not saying thing, but our language has no word for something that's nothing, you see? If you can do that with the source of being, you can certainly do that with anything that arises in consciousness—by representing it with something more objective.

Jef: *Any experience of the source then would have to include that that's not it.*

PR: Any experience of it, yes. That's why I point to "direct experience" and say it is not conventionally an experience—it's not a sensory, perceptual, mental, psychic, emotional, or any other type of experience—it's not the way we commonly hold experience. It's not really an "experience."

Scott: *It seems like the natural thing for our mind to do is to try to make insight or breakthroughs into usable "things." There's nothing else for my mind to do, except make it into a thing, or shut up.*

PR: Shut up the mind?

Scott: *Yeah, shutting up the mind, not the source. I mean, the mind is always going to be trying to make everything into a thing because that's all it can do, really.*

PR: That's true. So just notice that, and now? ... "Oh look, there's something, and?" ... Don't get stuck with it. It gets very, very complex. It's like trying not to have any thoughts. You sit there not having thoughts. "Boy, I'm not having a thought now." [laughter] "Boy, I haven't had a thought for several minutes now. I'm really cool without these thoughts. Look at all this no space. Great, no thoughts.... Wait, what am I doing, am I thinking? Is this ... what's this? ... Shut up! Shut up? Who? Where?"

You sit there and it looks like you haven't had a thought and then all of a sudden you recognize that the thought that you didn't have for this period of time was nothing but a thought. In other words, it was a concept. Totally. Concepts—like space and distance, and not having thought, and how cool you are now.

[laughter] Once you notice that, you just start screaming. And then it's all over. The mind is really very clever.

No-thought is actually a completely different matter than the thought of no-thought, than the concept of no-thought. It's outside the realm of the mind. It's like the difference between dark and light. Like somebody turned on the light, and only then do you realize that anything you would do within the dark is always going to be within the dark no matter how much light it looks like you're doing, you know? That's not a good analogy but no analogy is good. Then all of a sudden the light is turned on and boom, it's radically different!

Doug: *So is it like, "You'll know it when it happens"?*

PR: Kind of like you'll know it when it happens. But more like you'll not-know it when it happens. [laughs]

Remember when you first fell in love? If you have. [laughs] Remember before you fell in love—or had that experience that everybody calls love—when you were a kid and you didn't know what they we talking about. Is that true for everybody? Maybe you've never fallen in love or you were born in love, I don't know. But when I was a kid people would say, "You're going to fall in love, you're going to love 'girls'." [laughs] You'll fall in love, get married, and have kids. That's the concept. And I remember asking, "What is that?" and my Mom said, "Well, you'll know it when it happens." "How will I know?" So there's this concept communicated about falling in love, and you'll know what it is when it happens. And then you feel something that feels very different than what you've felt before and you say, "Aha! that's love." Right? Did everybody do that, or am I the only one? You say, "Aha! That's what love is. That's what falling in love is, that's what they meant."

How do you know that? Why on earth do you accuse those sensations and that experience of being what was represented to you years earlier? It's pretty interesting what's communicated beyond the words. Probably it is actually communicated inde-

pendent of the process of telling you. And the fact that you were
told about love, you recognized it and labeled it. That's all.

Unformed Mind

Let's take a look at a veil that mankind has already created. This
is one that's already so, and it's a product of humankind. I think
in this case our problem is the same thing as our ability. It is the
power that we've developed as "beings" called the ability to *represent*. Something about consciousness turning in on itself. I've
said that before and meant it completely differently than I do
now. It's the power to create "mind"—to create a way of understanding or interpreting things and non-things by creating a
"model" or paradigm in which to "cognize" the matter. This is
what most people call "knowing," or awareness, or perception.
Where we've gone with it, or where we've stopped with it, is no
longer viable—it won't ultimately work.

I think we are an obsolete species. The current design of humanity is kind of like a dinosaur, and we'll of necessity die out. We're
non-functional in a sense, or rapidly reaching a place where we'll
be non-functional, and we'll have to be replaced by something
else . . . god knows what. [chuckles]

It seems to me the possibility that exists is one of being replaced
by something that has the power to represent but at the same
time has the power to know or distinguish the difference between
a representation and the presence of something. Perhaps we will
be replaced by consciousness knowing consciousness-as-such, not
consciousness knowing its symbols. To our mind this is not even
something we can think or know, but it has been done. And it's
done periodically, by one of us. It just has never been done as a
species.

Let me see if I can clarify this for you. For example, there's not
a car in the room, but you can know of CAR, you see? That's a
power that an amoeba doesn't have, it's like it "don't know from
car." It's a leap to not have the presence of something and be able
to create the notion or the symbol of it. In this we can create a

conceptual picture of it. This picture is an indirect perception of what was already an indirect encounter with the thing in the first place. We can create the thought of it, we can create the label of it, and we can consider all sorts of qualities that are associated with it.

So we say "the thing IS." We don't say "it is here," but we say it "is." Yet we don't notice that the qualities of it, and the picture of it, and the label of it, aren't it, and never were. They're not even it when it's here, but we don't make that distinction.

Now for objects it's not that big a deal. That's why we've become so technologically successful. Because when dealing with objective reality it's really no big deal. For us the presence of an object and the notion of an object work really well hand-in-hand. We do mess it up, we run into that constantly—like when we're wrong! "I thought it was blue." "No it's green. See?" "Oh well, I really thought it was blue."

So it does have its problems, its drawbacks—sometimes deadly ones: "Oh I didn't know it was loaded!" [laughter] But we've generally been able to handle that one for the most part. We've learned to live with it.

But you see there are endeavors where it really breaks down. For example, you can see how much it breaks down in practices such as Huan Sheng [an "esoteric" form of fighting skill practiced at Cheng Hsin]. That's why we have to understand what it is that we do, such that these breakdowns occur.

There is something I'm steering us toward. Another example of the direction of this communication might be seen in an historical account. We hear tell, in the early days the word "God" was not spoken out loud. People weren't allowed to say it. The purpose for that I'm sure got really weird after a while if they re-created the purpose to be "because it's sacred." But the purpose of such a disposition isn't because it's sacred, and it's not because it's bad to say it. You're intelligent people, you all see right through that one. But perhaps there's a greater purpose. There is a possible purpose behind doing that, and that's the central issue of what

I'm talking about today. You see, the purpose for not doing that is because you can't.

The concept isn't it. The word isn't it. Whatever that word was referring to is not knowable in any conceptual sense. Probably in the very beginning, whoever did that, whoever set it up that way, did so to keep drawing attention to the fact that you can't think it. You can't THINK God. You can't symbolize God. I mean, we do, but it ain't it! You can't represent God in any way that makes a difference. And the spoken word "God" has nothing to do with God as a presence, an experience, you see? So this probably was a neat thing to begin with and then it got weird. [chuckles] Like all things do.

So, I could say there's an experience here that I can't tell you about. I could, but all it would be is an empty symbol and a misleading representation, and so it wouldn't be it—so there is absolutely no purpose in putting a word on it. The minute I say there is no purpose in putting a word on it, your minds rebel against that—don't they? "How am I supposed to know it then? I'm lost, I'm stuck." And we rebel against that.

You think I'm holding something back. "Tell me, come on, I'll understand it. You just tell me and I'll get it." That's all fine, but I can't speak about it not because I'm holding something back, but because something is being pointed to—and the value lies in the presence of it, not the symbol, not the word.

I know, just like you do, that most of the work we've done here at Cheng Hsin has basically "slipped by." When you look at the work we've done, you look back at some notions, some words, some symbols—concepts that you've collected in our talks. And from time to time when you're taking action you're able to create the presence of something that looks similar to what I've talked about. You're able to get into the presence of something that when you symbolize it, when you conceptualize it, you say something about it that looks similar to or identical to the things that were said when I was teaching, and so you say, "Ah ha! This is it." And from time to time I'm sure you're not able to do that. You go out there and it just doesn't work, or it seems strange, or stupid. That's just because what your actions are based on are the concepts, not the presence of an experience.

Our task is to uncover the presence of something, not to develop the symbols for it. That's why when we start to go over point A and point B, and there are all sorts of other points, I say, "Well, let's not waste our time with the other points." We're not trying to develop a rationale to believe in. We have plenty by now. We're continuously trying to bring in the presence of something, the experience of something . . . referred to as Cheng Hsin.

So what we're doing is immensely difficult. Why is it immensely difficult? Not because we have to learn how to do a thousand push-ups. That's pretty simple. It's hard, but simple. I mean, you know what to do. You get down and you do push-ups every day until you can do a thousand of them. This stuff is not difficult because it's highly complex, demanding our mind to keep many complicated relations in place. It is both hard and complex. Those are issues that come about. But why it's really difficult is because of this issue I've been talking about—directly experiencing it. Getting into and then staying in the presence of it is immensely difficult. Not because being in the presence of it is difficult—being in the presence of it is easy. Not having the presence of it is difficult. Bringing it about is the first obstacle. Staying with it is the second.

"Doorways"

There's something that I've referred to—in *The Principles of Effortless Power* it's referred to often. There are several places at crucial points I'd say something like, "Look, it all boils down to this . . ." or "this is fundamentally important . . ." or something like that. The issues are apparently different, where I'd say, "Forget everything else; if you don't get this you've got nothing"—that kind of thing.

Now here is the very important part: distinguishing the difference between the presence of this, what this is, and the concepts that come to it, is one of the most fundamental things we can do at Cheng Hsin.

As an analogy—there are certain principles that are like doorways into something not immediately accessible. When we experience a principle like "listening," we are getting to a door— "following" is getting to a door. Those are two of the things I mentioned in the book that are of the most fundamental importance. Then there are other things which if we do them demand these doorways—like "leading." You can't do leading without what's prior to leading. You just can't do it. It doesn't come around. So leading is at once a doorway. Do you understand that? Following accompanies leading, because if you don't do following or if you don't do listening, you can't do leading.

So you can do leading and not even worry about following and listening. You don't have to worry about them because you can't do leading without them. So it's a doorway by itself. But it's the presence of what's inside the doorway that we're looking for.

Sometimes we get in the presence of it—you get in the presence of it or I get in the presence of it. Sometimes in a big way, and sometimes in a little way. Then we say something like, "Ah, following! That's it!" or "Listening! That's the answer to being effective!" But see, the concept that arises from this experience is not what we think it is; it is not the "thing itself." Now that is what you really have to get. The concepts that we use to represent it are fine, the symbol is fine. Take following, for example. If I'm in the presence of it and I say, "Ah, following!", what I'm doing is using a word and a notion to point to this experience that I'm in the presence of. Then I say that it is following. It's all right because I'm more concerned with the presence of it than I am the symbol of it. It ain't following. The functionally active principle is not the notion or the symbol or the qualities that go along with following.

Although the notion does seem to fit. When you have an apple, you get RED, and RED seems to fit. So you say, "RED, it's kind of RED." And ROUND and APPLE. It's RED-ROUND. But it ain't red and it ain't round, it's an apple. But red and round are close. They seem to fit. Something seems to fit there. But if what you're looking for is an experience of FRUIT then apple is only a doorway, and the qualities and notions of an apple aren't really of service at all.

When you're in the presence of it the concept is not a problem. It's when you're not in the presence of it that the concept is a problem because then you get into the presence of the concept. That ain't it. It never was. It never really was.

Scott: *There is a difference between the concept following and this state or presence of something that really works very well. What I'm curious about is it seems like there is something that we're doing that is following—you're moving and I'm following along. Now that's not the concept of following, but is doing that just another doorway? It seems like following is different from listening, or it's different from these other things, but are these all really the same thing? I don't really know how to ask the question, actually.*

PR: Your concern is to be able to function effectively with somebody. You wouldn't learn listening unless it increased your ability to interact. If you are listening and yet you are ineffective interacting with someone, then listening would be seen as useless. Or if you were following them but unable to function more effectively, or if you were using your Cheng Hsin Body-Being, or leading, or anything else, and you weren't functional, you weren't accomplishing something in the area of mastery, you really wouldn't care much for those things, would you?

Scott: *No.*

PR: Yet we have to start learning to live with the flip side of things, the paradox of things, or the double-edgeness of things. For example, listening is basically useless all by itself. Yet if we don't leave listening alone it's not functional. If we don't do listening beyond, or despite, or separate, or distinct from anything it does for us, it won't do for us. It won't be true listening. It won't be functional.

There's a paradox here. The only reason we care about listening is for the application of it, its functionality. Yet we have to leave it alone, otherwise it becomes impure. Our mind gets in the way, we will start pushing things in front of it. Then it's not pure listening; it becomes projection. So you see, it's a paradox that the greatest functionality that we get is, in the same moment, completely useless; and the only value is in its uselessness. This doesn't make sense. So be it.

We have to start coming to terms with things that don't make sense. This is why human being is on the way out—because of our difficulty coming to terms with things that don't make sense, and yet are still true.

An Open Question

Do you remember a long time ago I asked, "What is the perfect state—a state that in itself is mastery?" We started to analyze that, and question it. What would the qualities be? What would have to BE, to get the state that could handle everything? That was kind of a play into the presence of what we are talking about now. You notice we never—I never, so we never—tried to say it, to define it. And I would definitely never try to say it. Because then people would go away with the symbol. By leaving it open, at least we're left with the continued possibility of discovery. We developed a feeling for it, we moved towards it like a question. And as a result of that we were left with a question, and so it becomes more of a presence, you see?

It looks like on the one hand there are questions and on the other hand answers. It looks like there is question-answer, question-answer. The question only serves the answer, and the answer settles the question. Yet it's not like that. A question isn't the same thing as an answer. The question is an openness to the presence of something, and the answer is a closure, the symbol, or the concept of something. Because of the way our mind works we try to move to answers, since we want the symbol or concept of things in order to understand them.

Scott: *When we have the answer that absolutely forces the question to close, it sort of squeezes something out and then the question disappears.*

PR: So break down this notion that question is something to serve answer. It's not. There is so much power in truly questioning. Much more than having a question so that we can get an answer. It's creating an openness so that we can have an experience—of the BEING of something. Not to have a closure to that. So Cheng Hsin is like that, a question. The perfect state is like a question. The presence of something is like a question. It always will be because the PRESENCE ONLY SHOWS UP NOW, and now only shows up in process. By process I mean it shows up now, now, now, now. It never shows up as an answer. When it does it's historical and a symbol.

See . . . there is a tape recorder. Bingo, an answer. You notice how the tape recorder suddenly appeared? The only reason the tape recorder is really showing up now is because we're talking about it, and that's a process, you see? But the pole back there disappeared because we're not talking about it and we're not looking at it. Even objects only show up as a presence through process, not through "objectification." I mean really! [chuckles]

Scott: *It really wasn't there and it was easily within my field of vision.*

PR: And it has colors and lights and everything.

Scott: *Yeah, yeah.*

PR: [chuckling] . . . So hang open for a while—like in the practice I call "Waiting." These things have to be cultivated. Waiting is very difficult because of our wanting. It is like what the Zen Buddhists used to talk about—"taming the mind," getting the mind to stop running amok answering everything. Waiting is allowing the mind not to answer. Which is crazy for the mind because that's its job. So we call that no-mind—when it's not answering constantly. We call that no-mind simply because the purpose for the mind is to answer, in order to survive.

Trapped in an Ability

Say, as beings, we developed a great ability. And this ability was to answer. Another way to say that is the ability to represent, to picture, to record in that way, to model, to symbolize. Answering is conceptualizing. When we get in the presence of what truly is, it shakes our bones more than the symbols do. Right? Like being in the presence of the function of you-as-a-being. We call us-as-a-being our mind, or say that the function of us lies in being our mind.

Joe: *Why can't we be in the presence of something when we stop at the symbol of it?*

PR: Like I was saying about following, we can use the word while in the presence of following and there's no problem. The symbol fits the presence, but the presence doesn't fit the symbol. I mean not at all. When you bring the symbol up, the presence doesn't fit into it, but the symbol fits the presence fine because it is a symbol of the presence. It lends itself to the presence, it lends itself to whatever that process is, or that principle is, that we call following. That's what it's for. Like if I were to say I'll symbolize following with a square, that this square represents following. Then when I put a square up on the board here that means following. So we say that this square refers to the presence of following. But vice versa? Not at all.

I've talked about how come this occurs. The presence of something is only in the present. In the next moment it's not, and so whatever was experienced a moment ago does not now exist. What does is the concept of it. Right-about-now isn't now, it isn't this moment. The moment doesn't look like anything, since in order for it to look like something it has to be interpreted. And for it to be interpreted it must be held in some conceptual context or "model" in which it makes sense. Right-about-now is the concept of what was. "About now" isn't "it." It might be an identical replication of the perception of what was, because it's so fresh. But as you've noticed, it's only a replication of where your awareness falls, and what you can interpret depending on the paradigm for interpretation that you are using. But that's mind-boggling.

Like you noticed a while ago that things disappear when you have no reason to cognize them. You couldn't allow things to disappear and have it that they really do disappear just because they disappear for you. So we say THEY ARE, right?

Joe: *And that they're just not seen.*

PR: Right, and they are waiting for you over there, for you to see them or use them or something. This is how we hold reality, and there doesn't seem to be any problem with that to us.

"But wait, you're not saying it isn't real. It's really real, isn't it? This is not a child's game or a philosophy, it's really real! I mean honest-to-god real." You think that. And that's fine. But that we don't know "what that is" isn't so fine ... and that we don't know "that it is" is even less fine [laughs]. But we don't have to challenge that right now. There is no reason to challenge that until we notice something else. Such as "now" isn't. "This" is a concept. Of what? Of "this?" Well, no, I mean really-this, and this cognition of now is a kind of trailing-off concept of the moment.

Now consider what I'm pointing to when I talk about following. Obviously following, in this case, isn't just trailing along after someone. Just as listening by itself isn't enough, but there's something wonderful that comes about when you listen and when you leave listening as useless. But there—do you see? The only way you can get in the presence of listening is when it's useless. Because if it is useful it gets to be what? It is like that thing over there [points to a cup] ... See, it became useful. Something comes into our awareness because it's useful to us, and then it trails into a concept, and it's not truly functional as a concept—it's only functional as a presence. Yet everything will fall back into concept because it isn't present. Because the last moment isn't present. But we have to relate to the last moment in order to make sense and continuity, and we will do that. So this moment of experience is primarily a concept.

That's mind-boggling—that this is a concept and not the presence of something. We don't know what it is because we are seeing this indirectly, and we're falling back into concept. The mind can't use direct experience, it's not useful.

Well, do you see the point I'm making? It is the presence that we're looking for when we talk about listening, when we talk about following, when we talk about leading, when we talk about the Cheng Hsin body-being, when we talk about anything. But now we are looking for the "presence behind the presences" ... that's what we're really looking for. We'll leave it nameless because we want it to show up as a presence, not as a concept. So that's why the most I'll usually speak about are the doorways, like following, and leading, and listening. And those are incredible doorways, but you must understand that by themselves they aren't it.

Scott: *When you're saying following is a doorway, you're not referring to the concept following, you're referring to the presence of doing following and then that's still only a doorway to the presence of the thing which following is a doorway to....*

PR: Yes, and the concept of following can be used as a doorway to the presence of following.

Scott: *Right. Right.*

PR: But only if you make it that way. Only if you go past the concept to the presence of it. That's why when you're out there having trouble, and you remember to follow—which is a conceptual act—then you can start getting into the presence of it. In this case, the concept could be a doorway, and in that sense it's useful, but other than that it's not useful.

Scott: *It seems to me an ability we want to develop is to become clear on "presencing," or getting into the presence of anything, so that we can get the presence of presencing? I don't know ... well, we don't want to presence things.... [laughs]*

PR: Why not? It's not a bad practice to put a cup in front of you and try to get in the presence of it. Try to stay in the presence of a cup. It's not a bad practice.

Scott: *I can dig that. Whenever I drive home, since I've driven that way hundreds of times, I have all these memories—like when I almost hit that thing, and when I saw a beautiful girl here. As I drive along I can see something and a memory will come up. For instance, I notice that seeing a certain sign is pretty much the same thing as seeing all my memories of the things that happened around the sign.*

PR: Yes, it acts like a "place holder" for your concepts. But don't even try to map out a way to study what it is I'm pointing at. Perhaps it is better to notice that there is a presence of something that we cannot conceptualize. It doesn't fit in a notion or a concept. We cannot "answer" it, we cannot do anything with it. It doesn't fit into the concept following, it doesn't fit in the concept leading, it doesn't fit in the concept listening . . . or even in the presence of those. And those are great!

Do you see what I'm saying? Not like we're bad because of it. It just doesn't fit—it's not in the same realm. It looks too much like nothing to go into concept. There ain't no concept for it.

Yet it doesn't mean there is not a presence that can be grasped as an experience. It's just that we cannot "think" it. We get to have a concept of a quality of it, or a concept about a doorway to it . . . but we don't get to have a concept of it-itself.

Through the study and the mastery of these doorways we open up to IT. And must keep opening up to it—keep experiencing it, or presencing it, until it becomes profoundly it! I am certain that that's what the founders of the great human movements did; they kept getting more and more into the presence of whatever it was that "sourced" their communication. It's even dangerous to call it whatever "sourced." Then we start thinking there is something there. As if it's kind of floating around and we've got to dive into it. It's not there . . . it's HERE.

Scott: *Like I've got to bring its presence in here—I mean, I've got to presence something and . . . hmm.*

PR: Just keep openness. That's why "waiting" is such an important practice. Because waiting is just openness. That's all. It's learning how to tolerate nothing, and uselessness.

Like in the Principles Course the other night I said what I do is so useless. And people valiantly tried to console me and tell me that it wasn't [laughter]. That's very nice, but still, it is useless. It really is useless [more laughter]. It's very difficult to be in the presence of such uselessness, but necessary.

In the *Principles* book I suggested a study of the non-items. The presences of these things I've been discussing turn out not to be items AT ALL, and are fundamentally non-graspable. I've said that most of what Cheng Hsin is about are the non-items. There's no object, there's no event, there's nothing there—there is no "item" in which it could be. So it's a lot like a non-item. And it looks a lot like something intrinsic, in other words, inherent; something that is not an object, and nothing that has to be produced. All of these non-items may be the only way to talk about what we're talking about, or the only way to look into what we're looking into, but still they have to be recognized as useless.

For example, the times when you really get into following, when you decide to practice your following and that's all you are doing—you're not doing it to beat this guy, you are just training following—and you notice things start to turn out. But all you are doing is following, right? And things start to turn out anyway—it's almost a secondary matter. Of course you need a test to make sure you're really listening and following. Because you might not be. If you don't have a test you won't know. With a testing ground you get to notice when you get distracted or try to "use" it, and so lose it. Because following as itself is useless for your own survival, for having things turn out, yet it's one of the most valuable things for having things turn out.

So we must get into the presence of that uselessness—the presence of that useless stuff that has things turn out. But see, even having things turn out is useless. I mean, isn't it? Totally useless. It really is [laughs].

We won't work on that right now, but I can see you want to go with that one [laughs].... Get into the presence of that. You want a method to train? Well, here's a thought: train to get into the presence of that useless stuff where things turn out just because—like a side effect—kind of intrinsically turn out. Then from there look into and open up to what *is*. What is "this"? ...

Something magnificent and yet so paradoxical arises when you're doing something useless, absolutely and purely useless. Something that has nothing to do with your survival really—like pure following or unadulterated listening—something that doesn't have anything to do with your winning; that's when you are the most masterful you can get.

Outside the Stream of Humanity

Don't even try to conceptualize this, don't try to framework it. I'm talking now about a step beyond the stuff that we already have trouble with. When a doorway like following or leading is present, don't stop there—open up even further. That's a killer. When it starts to work, don't stop there. Don't stop with it working.

Scott: *That's going to be such a temptation. That's going to be the irresistible temptation of all temptations....*

PR: Yes. Still, open up to what is beyond your cognition. On the one hand, it has to work, and on the other hand it has to be totally useless. What is this presence? What is so that allows such a paradox to be? What's that?

Scott: *This is funky because we're talking about getting something to be present, and when we get it present it ain't there.*

PR: We must learn to live in paradox. Absolutely, because Consciousness lives in paradox. It spits upon convention. [laughter] You have certainly conceptualized a lot about it. Now what to do is remember it will remain nameless.... Don't call it the nameless, though.

[laughter]

PR: This is why the Ontological Workshops that I do are so important, not the workshops *per se*, as, say, a four-day event, but the thing it lends itself to. The four days aren't that important, they're just four days, right? It's not the hours, it's not the exercises—it wasn't sitting in a chair that did it. It's what it lends itself to, and what it lends itself to doesn't show up in a way that you can hold onto—as you've probably noticed.

However, NOTHING is all that we need to take from it. When you want to directly reach into something, what you need to do is look into nothing. But look into nothing like it's a presence, and then whatever shows up you will receive very directly. When you look into something, you don't see what's not the something that you're looking into. I'll say that again. When you're looking into something, you're looking into your own meaning, your own interpretation, and the "objectification" of whatever your perception is about—your own concepts. So you've got to keep feeding it back into nothing, or get stuck in a vicious circle created by your framework of assumptions and conclusions.

For example, let's say in this moment you have no experience of me, okay? So then you look at me, and you want to pick up what's going on. What you see mostly, right now, is your concept and meaning of the object you say you perceive. Now be honest … it's just whatever you see. I'm not trying to destroy that—or you shouldn't try to destroy that right now, because we have to look through it. People try to not look at what they see, when they're trying to see its essence, so they create a concept of something not there.

You want to see something about me in the moment arising NOW. Because, if you're going to interact effectively, for example, no matter what you're going to do you want to know what's coming NOW—RIGHT NOW. What is really going on, before it goes on!

As you attempt to see me, or what I really am, you look into my appearance. You don't find it in my cheek. . . . See? You don't find it in my eyeballs. . . . You don't find it in my fingers. When some of you sense me you look at my cheek and my eyeball, I think. Do you notice I don't spend a lot of time looking at people's cheeks, eyeballs, and fingers?

Yes, I'm looking at them now [chuckles]. But this is where "nothing" comes in. If you pay attention, if you just grasp it right now, you can get it; and I guarantee in the next moment you'll lose it. I just want you to know that. The reason you'll lose it is the same dynamic I'm talking about. The dynamic we LIVE in— turning into history—we don't live in an experience of turning into NOW. We turn into history. We turn our attention to history, and we also turn into history—like turning into a pumpkin, we turn into history. Do you see what I'm saying? We keep turning into history. We are historical.

We have to notice that we're constantly turning into history, to even have a ghost of a chance of turning into now. All of your thinking about it, is just prep it isn't really looking into it. Everything you do to think about it, everything you do to look into it, may be necessary, but it's prep. It's preparatory for what you need to do, which is to directly experience it, and that looks [snaps fingers] ... like nothing. Still, it takes a lot of discipline because it goes totally against the grain of our conceptualizations.

It's like there's a stream that's pushing you. This is why you lose the breakthroughs so fast, and it's why you always will. Because it's like a stream, it's a stream called "REALITY"—a stream made up of the way people hold life. I'm not even talking about the stream of nature, I'm talking about the stream of humanity. You are part of the stream of humanity. Actually it's more like a torrential river [laughs], or like a torrential flood. Any time you try to move into what's true, or into the presence of something, you have to look past the stream, or outside of the stream. The moment you take your attention off looking into the truth of the matter, you go phfff! right down the stream.

One of the components of the stream is a negation of anything that's not in the stream. Do you see what I'm saying? One of the functions of the stream is to negate anything that's not part of the flood of the stream. So, anything you do that's outside of the stream, although it's a presence when you're there, the moment you hit the stream again, when you slip into the stream, the stream pushes you again and there's a negation of what you just experienced. It becomes "NO GOOD," or "this is stupid"—even fitting the experience into your belief systems or fantasies is a function of the stream and negates the experience completely. And that's the stream of humanity. It is ON PURPOSE. Changing that stream is an immense undertaking.

So now, when you look into me and you want to know what is coming up for me, you have to look into nothing, because what you keep seeing is your concept of me, your objectification of me. You hold me as an object, right? Well, in the "object-known process" you noticed that you really don't know what any object is. You "say" object, you conceptualize object, you get object, you suspect object very, very strongly, you demand object, but you don't directly "know" or experience object. All that other stuff we call knowledge or perception. So the moment you objectify me and say, "He is that way," what is that way? You say I "am." Then you say I am that way. And the moment you say "I am" you're going to say "I am that way." For you, there IS a way that I am, otherwise you wouldn't say I am. Right? If I was no way, you'd say nothing. I know this is hard to follow. . . .

Joe: *I is that?*

PR: Yes, I is that. In the same moment both are there, in the same moment of being! See? . . .

Joe: *No.*

PR: Don't worry . . . but stay with me now, because you know that although it looks fantastic and it looks heady, I'm not talking heady here. One of the values, one of the ways we get to see that I'm not just talking about heady abstractions is to really study Cheng Hsin in demonstrable forms such as Huan Sheng. Because Huan Sheng is founded on this, and if it's just a philosophy, there's nothing called Huan Sheng. In other words, philosophy doesn't show up in Huan Sheng, it doesn't show up as skill. It shows up in a book [laughs], not in your fighting, and in your fighting you've already noticed that we have just scratched the surface. You've been introduced to quite a bit, but it is just what you've managed to actually presence that changes your skill. And it does, doesn't it!

This is just trying to get at some of what I'm talking about. I say what I'm talking about "IS" it. I'm not just talking "about" it. I'm not talking about this abstraction, and then there is something else called Cheng Hsin, and that I'm pretending they are the same. I'm saying it is the same. And you may not be able to see it right now. It might keep looking heady to you, and the reason that is so is because what I'm trying to communicate is outside of the stream.

If it were just some heady philosophy I would have to be very, very committed to keeping all this up. I don't mean just with you but with everything that I'm doing. I'd have to be very committed to bullshit. And as you've noticed, I seem to be very accurate about the things I say. I seem to be consistent in a very unusual way. In other words, I'm not keeping you in the dark. You might think so sometimes, but I'm not. It's just that you can't understand it sometimes, so it looks like philosophy or it looks like some conventional belief system.

The resistance coming from the stream of humanity is the only thing that wants me to stop. It's very difficult. I've committed myself to speaking outside the stream, but I don't get any support for speaking outside of the stream. Where do I get support from you to speak outside the stream? Maybe I get support from your being, but not from you. The way I get support from you, speaking about all this, is when it looks like a fantasy, or it looks like you are going to get some power, or something good. Right? That's where I get support from people, but that's part of the stream. That's just a nice twist to the stream. I know this; you should know it, too. It's all right. Somehow in the stream we've got to get into a position where we want to look outside of it, and so in that respect at least there is some value.

If outside the stream were a totally inviolate world, if it were totally impossible to access, then communications like the onto-logical workshops would not be possible events. See? In four days I can take somebody outside the stream. And what they do is immediately put it into some concept or other, because that's just the way it goes, that's what we do. We have to fess up to that. That's the beauty of it, since there's nothing else you can do. The only way you can have it BE, is to BE it. So when you aren't being it the only thing you can do is represent it. See? Like the cars—they're not actually in the room; the way you bring CAR in the room is to represent it. You have a thought CAR, maybe you pic-ture CAR, or whatever. Right? Isn't this true? Am I lying?

Joe: *No.*

PR: All right [laughs]. You have to represent it to bring it into the room; to get CAR, there must be a representation here. So when something "isn't," the only way you have access to it is in repre-sentation. That's a power, but it's a power of humanity that has lost its true functionality, because there's no presence experienced in relation to the representation.

John: *Oh god, to really have the power under our control we have to have something else in addition to the concept.*

PR: Yes, you have to be able to distinguish between concept and experience.

John: *So the thing is to really conceptualize in a way that is most appropriate.*

PR: We are swept away by conceptualization, we are swept away by the representations and the symbols. We are swept away in the stream. But it is worse than that because we are not only swept away with conceptualization, we're swept away by directions of conceptualization—things we say are TRUE about reality and about each other and about the way things work. It's a very forceful direction in conceptualization, it's not just random, like "just conceptualization." We're swept away by conceptualization that is forcefully directed for a purpose.

The direction changes a bit over time. There's something that stays pretty much the same in humanity, but if you take a look at humanity one hundred years ago, there were different assumptions. One thousand years ago even different assumptions. Right? What hasn't changed throughout is that whatever the assumptions are they are always assumed and believed. But it wasn't the same kind of assumptions. And I don't mean just whether the world is round or not. That's a pretty big deal really, but I don't mean that kind of thing. I mean what it is to be human. I mean a scope that we are not going to go into right now [laughs], just guess at it.

So I'm telling you how to do this. When you look into me you get that everything you hold as me is not me; what you see is concept and object. When you take your concept and turn it back into experience then you become sensitive to what's actually present. By "turn it back" I mean you just keep letting it go as fast as it comes up, and then you look into it newly, it's the only place to look, in this way you are looking into nothing, like an openness—see? In contrast to nothing, what do you pick up? For example, if you look at someone as if he has no intention and you look into his intention as if it's no intention, what shows? Do you see what I'm saying? As an analogy, if you put a white background behind some black specks, black specks show up. See? But if you have a black background, or a lot of concept and projections in the way, it's very hard to see what's there. The nothing is like the white background behind the black specks.

Look into nothing, because every time you draw a conclusion, you're gone, it's history. If you constantly keep pushing this "nothing" to the foreground, you will be sensitive to what's arising in every instant. You will get a feeling for his intention and act on it before you can conceptualize about it.

Okay, let's see if you get what I'm saying. Find a partner.

The Power of Being in Your Body

The following are excerpts from talks given by Peter Ralston to Cheng Hsin apprentice-instructors in 1983. He addresses subjects ranging from responsibility to our own growth and the nature of being in the body.

Responsibility

PR: Have you ever had a vision of going to some place like . . . Shangri-La? "Wow, wouldn't it be nice to just go to someplace where people are good and life is wonderful, and the sun is shining and. . . ." Yes?

[sounds of assent from the crowd]

PR: See, the reason it's not possible is because you would be there.

[laughter]

Judy: *I was afraid of that.*

PR: Notice what you need in order for a Shangri-La type place, a beautiful place, or even a place away from here. . . . Say we get a place up in the mountains and we start a community that's based on truth and love and peace, getting conscious and breaking through everything,—to go beyond the mediocrity that we live in, and the suffering that we live in, and the pain that we live in that we just put up with from moment to moment—to go someplace to create an environment where our purpose for living is to experience beyond our present level of experience. . . .

It wouldn't work. It would always break down. It would break down in a relatively short time. I wouldn't even give it a year.

Because you see, we would be there.... And haven't you noticed? We don't have the discipline for something like that. We don't have the nuts, the courage, the persistence ... the overwhelming courage it takes for something like that. You don't want to go there and be courageous! You want to go there so you *don't* have to be courageous. Right? You want to go there so you can get away from this! And have a Shangri-La.

Why do you want to go to Shangri-La? Well, what's a requirement for Shangri-La? The requirement is that everybody else is cool! Everybody else is doing it! Right? You see? *You're* the barbarian! And you'll be good if everybody else is good. Right? And if you run amok, they'll be so cool that they'll just mellow you right out [laughter]. Or they'll teach you the ways of peace and love. See, but it's all their responsibility!

... They'd ask you to leave!

It takes a lot of discipline. That's why we need Shangri-La. Right? Because then it's their responsibility, hmm?

Being Present

Last time and the time before last I talked to you about staying in your own body. Perhaps there is some misunderstanding about that. When I ask you to stay in your own body, you have to understand I'm not asking you to stay in your own mind. I'm asking you to be present, and the only place you can be present is in your body.

Don't listen to me like you are an audience, because if you are an audience you listen to me as if detached, and everything is happening over here. I want an experience to occur for you. I want you to be inside the experience of the room, the experience of what's going on. And I want you to do that from a position of being responsible for your experience right now, because that's the only way you can do it. If you are not responsible for your experience right now—in your body, your mind, being alive right now—"this"—who will be? Not just thinking about things, not this internal stuff going on with you, jockeying for this, strategizing that, and figuring everything out—that's not what I'm talking about. I'm talking about being responsible for that—that goes on, fine—but I'm talking about more than that.

By more than that, I mean less [chuckles].... Less stuff, more presence! More simplicity. More simply here. Here, see? Less away. Less "stuff" going on, less figuring out, less personal orientation, less wasting time with all your bullshit! Wasting time with all you hold as you—figuring it out, believing, disbelieving, right, wrong, judging, placing, siphoning, censoring—you know, all the activity that you spend ninety percent of the time doing with any communication. Then there is no communication. Ninety percent no experience, except what you already have. You already have that! Why waste your time with that? I know it's the most precious thing to you, that's why you waste your time.

Isn't it getting old? It's like a butterfly you catch. It's a very pretty butterfly. It's so precious that you hold onto it real tight ... and it gets old [laughter]. But you've stopped noticing that it's not only dead, it's all crumpled up, it's moldy, it's rotting. It's not really that precious anymore, because you held onto it so tight. I mean, take a look! Take a look! I'm not talking about anything that's outside of your ability to perceive right now in this moment.

You have resistance. You say, "Aw, it sounds like he's making me wrong."

YEAH!

[laughter]

PR: Yes, if you want to put it into right and wrong—actually, I'm saying YOU are held so tight it's not worth anything anymore, too much is dead, too much is rotting, it's killed. It's not a butterfly anymore when you do this. It starts to rot, you just haven't noticed that. It's not that much fun anymore, hmm? It's just mechanical ! It's old hat! Don't you notice? It's old! It's old! It's again, and again, and again, and again. It's not thrilling. You're not even excited about it. I mean what excites you is outside of that. Isn't it?

You sit there jockeying for some ego-position—judging, figuring out, being you—and it isn't even thrilling to you! There is not a person in this room that it's thrilling to, because that's not thrilling stuff! From time to time when you get thrilled, it's because of an experience outside of that! Something new! Something alive! Something that was like the original butterfly. But ninety percent of what you do isn't that . . . and I think I'm being generous.

So you have to be responsible for that. Because unless you are responsible for that, there is no hearing beyond it. You think "that" is hearing, you see? It's common, almost everybody on the planet agrees that's what hearing is. Something gets thrown out, you decipher it, judge it, censor everything, put it in its place, box it and squeeze it, so it becomes just like you, and you've "heard" it.

But if it becomes just like you, you didn't hear it! How can you hear something if it becomes just like you? If it becomes just like you, it's already like you! You already got that, so there's nothing really coming in, right?

Now, if you waste time feeling like, "Oh I'm so bad, I can't hear," that's just wasting time too. Or you can waste time saying, "Well, fuck him, I don't really get this hearing stuff." That's wasting time also. See? All that is you. It's not hearing. Neither of those is hearing. If you waste time going, "Well, I'm going to be real attentive and listen this time; I'm really going to hear this thing, I'm going to hear if I have to . . . is he talking?" That's wasting time too, you see?

Being in Your Body

PR: Okay, everybody put your attention in your bodies right now. Just sit there. Close your eyes for a second. . . . Just get a sense of your own body here. Get a sense of your own experience. What you feel. . . . I want you to allow the communication to come to you. I want you to be open and let it come to you. I don't want you to have to strain and struggle for it. I don't want you to go through all these gymnastics. I don't want you to beat yourself up. I don't want you to make yourself wrong. I don't want you to make yourself right. I don't want you to do any of that. I just want you to let it come to "you"—which is what you are being responsible for right now.

That means when you look out from your eyes—so go ahead and look out from your eyes—when you look out from your eyes it's not like you are back there looking out. That's not called being in your body. If you are "back there looking out" that's called being in your "mind." When you're in your body, all there is is a sense of "being," and the experience of whatever it is you are looking at. Not being behind there looking out. Do you understand?

I want you to be centered in your body. When you're centered in your body there's no thought about being centered. Being centered isn't the thought about being centered. It's being in your body, it's just being your body. It's truly being in your body so that everything simply becomes a function of itself. It's not exclusive to you, you don't feel like it's exclusive. It's not like you're an isolated thing; you as a thing is really not the consideration when you are in your body, when you are centered. You're not self-possessed when you are centered. You're not saying, "It's me against the world." You "are" . . . being. That's all.

Judy: *I noticed that once I get an experience it's not something that I'm going to forget. Whenever I really grasp a communication it's not like I have to strain to remember it. If I want to write about it or speak about it, I don't really have to have the words; if I'm going to write about it, all I have to do is put my attention on the experience and the words come from there.*

PR: Yes, because you have an experience. Like I was saying to John the other day . . . you have to look for that which wrote the book. Do you understand? *The Principles of Effortless Power* has more information in it, more experience held within its form, than you'll probably assimilate in quite a few years. And there's more than that. I could write another book. I could write many more. That's not the point. What you have to do, rather than memorize the information in the book—which could be a handy thing to do—is know that which wrote the book. You have to experience that which wrote the book.

When I do a class or a course, you have to understand where it comes from. Experience the experience. If you experience the experience, and half of chapter three is written down, you could write the other half, with absolutely no error, without even a thought of right or wrong, you'd just know. You'd fill in the blanks, no problem. You could write chapter four.

Consistently, again and again, year after year, in this form, in that form, on this subject, on that subject, I present this communication, and none of it gets lost and none of it is inconsistent. It all concurs, all of it fits and works and repeatedly proves itself to be valid. I sure couldn't memorize all of that!

So you all want to do that, you all want to have the experience that is where the book came from. Do! This is all done to save you time, and energy, and errors. That's why it has all been created. The Cheng Hsin endeavor was created so that you could save a whole lot of time. I said that many, many years ago. People don't seem to be saving a whole lot of time, though. You seem to be dilly-dallying.

Changing Your Mind

PR: We look inside what it is we have frozen in our own "mind" for some solution and the solution doesn't necessarily lie there. It doesn't necessarily lie somewhere else, either.

The first thing we have to do is notice that we don't know what anything is. Take healing, for example—we must notice that we don't know what healing is. Acupuncturists, psychics, herbalists, Western doctors, us ... the first thing we have to do is to admit that we don't know what healing is. So why limit it to something? Or exclude something? We don't even know what it is! We don't even know how to keep our own bodies alive, and so we're going to say how to heal us? We have a lot of information about things, but we don't know what they are.

Okay, let's do a practice. Everybody notice that you are looking at the world in a certain way. Now what I want you to do is pretend that you "are" your body. Perhaps you feel a lot of mind chatter today, you have a lot of conceptual activity in your head, a lot of "looking out," and so when you put your attention onto your body you also have a lot of attention on the mental activity in your head. Well, how about the bones in your head? Feel the bones in your head. Feel your ears and face, and all of the bones—in your head, and the skin. And now feel the rest of your body. Just be there. Pretend that there is no mind. That all you have is just this body, just this flesh and bone. This experience of flesh and bone. Keep surrendering to that, keep flowing into that, like letting your mind, your self, flow into that. Pretend that that's what you are, that your body is your self.

Now, I want you to notice if what you are doing is getting self-conscious. In other words, conscious of your self, like how you look, or if you are mentally "looking" at your body, things like that. Notice that if you "are" your body, you are not self-conscious. See, you feel the bones in your face but the bones aren't self-conscious, are they? Your eyeballs aren't self-conscious. Your flesh isn't self-conscious. It's just flesh, bones, the experience of being. The flesh doesn't see itself and the bone doesn't see itself. It's just an experience.

If you have a sense of existence, like self-consciousness—which is all right—then you are not being your body; you are being your mind. Self-consciousness lies in mind activity, not the body. If you are mentally looking at your body while you are trying to be your body, like conceptually imagining or viewing the shape of your body, that's not being your body, that's being your mind. Because you're looking, you are imagining your body conceptually. See? So when you are being your body, you are just being. There's no other stuff going on. Also, it is always present, and it's easy; it's not a struggle since there's no turmoil going on. [Peter goes to the board]

Let's say this is your body. Okay? [draws circle on board]. . . . Although you don't really define yourself this well, try it. Frequently you're just kind of a sense behind your eyeballs looking out, right? Or the experience of your awareness floating around, or maybe you moved into self-consciousness . . . and you have identified with certain thinking, feeling, beliefs, and sensations. Well, instead of becoming your body, you became self-conscious. [He draws several lines with arrows pointing toward the circle of "self."] This is what's going on. All the world is seen in relation to what's coming to you as a point of reference. So even when you include your body in that, it's self-conscious because it's in reference to your "self." The consciousness is going to what you call self, as body, you see? It is the body judged by this self mechanism. In other words, if I look at you, or we look at you, you notice us looking at "you." You are conscious of your body. That wall there is in reference to your body; it's like the wall is looking at you, too, see? "What does that wall mean to me? What does that person mean to me? What does that picture mean to me?" This referencing occurs without notice.

For most people this is just the way it is, so it is difficult to understand. It's the experience you are having right now. You have a sense of being inside looking out, but at the same time this looking out is in reference to all things "coming in" or being related to you. In other words, everything revolves around this point of view. This body-self. So when you are being your body, self-consciousness dissolves into the body, but it's not like you are "behind" or "inside" looking out. And since it dissolves into the body and you experience from the body, these lines of attention aren't coming in, referring to the body-self; these lines are going out. It's like awareness radiates "from" the body, not back into it.

In other words, that wall is a wall. It's not the wall in relationship to you. It's the wall. People looking at you is not people looking at you, it's *people*. "Oh, 'this experience'—this dog, this danger, this pleasure, that wall." Awareness is going out from the body, and so there's no self-consciousness. You don't see your self, really—it's as if you don't exist. This hand is this hand. Usually you are looking at yourself, looking at your mind, your exclusive sense of you. When you are your body, you're not "looking" at your body; it's simply the experience of all that is going on, including your body, but not a self-consciousness of your body.

Another way of saying this is the world is seen as how it affects itself, not how it affects you. Everything is let go of, and so is seen as how it affects itself. You don't see it as how it affects you— "What's that for me? What did he mean by that? Oh, he's looking at me" ... and all that. It's just, "Oh, he's looking, that's his experience." You experience "that" experience. It's not like you couldn't add anything, but then that would be just your experience of that experience. See?

It's the experience of that person "looking," or this wall "being." Times when people get closer to that are when they are absorbed in something—like gardening or some hobby. Like when you're gardening and you forget about everything else. You're really involved with it and nothing else is going on. At those times you don't think about yourself, right? Everything is just dirt and plants, and you're simply doing whatever you are doing. Perhaps for moments or perhaps hours, depending on how much you are involved with it, what needs to be done is done. You don't question if you are going to do it or if somebody else is going to do it. What needs to get done is done; if it's being done it's being done. See? You're not thinking about other things, you're not thinking about your body. You're just totally lost in that work. That's the closest most people come to the kind of experience I'm talking about. Yet usually it's limited to just one activity.

Also, it's not like you are "pushing" out; the experience comes to you. You don't have to push your awareness and attention outward, the experience comes to you. With "lines in" the world is seen as affecting you—every color, every shape, every noise, every person, every thought, are all seen as how they affect you. It's all about this self-conscious body-mind. Whereas with "lines out" you disappear, since you're radiating from here. It's natural, it's not like you're reaching out to penetrate things . . . that's the mind trying to handle things. Do you see what I'm saying? It's just "things being things."

I first called it that when I was in New York . . . hmmm, when was that? Sometime in the mid-seventies. . . . Anyway, I was walking down a street in New York and I noticed that there was something radically different than the last time I was there, which was a couple of years before, and I asked myself, "What is this difference?"

I started noticing as I walked that there were people and trees and buildings. And I noticed I wasn't holding anything like I normally would. Instead of everything being focused on me, instead of the whole world being "me"—how I fit in and what I'm doing— it was itself. Do you have any idea how much the whole world is usually you? It's your reactions, your concerns, your interpretations, your thinking. I mean even when you are thinking about cars, it's in reference to you. I like that car—I don't like that car, it's an ugly car. It's in reference to you, you see?

So I was walking down the street and . . . "Whoa . . . it's 'THE WORLD'. . . . " [chuckles]

I noticed it was the other way around, like a sense of radiating, a sense of "lines out." There wasn't anything impinging or pressing upon me. I hardly noticed me. I noticed me in a very full sense because it was, umm . . . just "being." But not in a self-conscious sense, not an isolated sense, just an experience of what is, that's all. I was part of the experience that was going on. And the dog was, too. I experienced a dog. The dog was growling or something, and I wasn't afraid of the dog because it didn't mean anything about me. It was, "look, that's an interesting experience." There's an experience [growls], and there's a fence, and there's a tree, and that's a road, and people . . . people, wow, what an experience! And it's a natural occurrence.

This can occur through a shift into being the body. That's another way of saying it. I think it's an interesting way of saying it because it is an experience that occurs in relation to how we hold the body and sense perceptions.

But you have to understand the difference—that's why I'm telling you this—between being your body, and a concept or feeling of being your body. The mind's idea of being your body is not being your body. The body is simply body. It's not some thing in relationship to this body. There's no concern about this body. There's an experience here, it's a bodily experience. But you don't mentally image or feel a body, it's just experience. You still have a sense of over there, so if there's an over there, there's going to have to be an over here. So you still have reference, but it's a tacit reference, it's a not-thought reference. It's not a self-conscious reference. It's not something you think about, and it's not an orientation; you're not orienting yourself to everything. There is simply an experience of something—perhaps through the function of your eyes, or sounds through your ears, but without a thought of those functions. There are no personal concerns, it's absolutely simple, there's nothing you have to do about it.

Practice it. See what it is. It is what it is. Ways of playing with it—because the mind needs methods—are: get centered, don't think, be your body. Don't feel your body from a subjective point of view, "be" your body. Don't think, just experience, be present and centered.

As an analogy: in some dreams it's like you are not really there. You have a sense of being there, but you are not a person, you are not one of the characters in the dream. You are just watching the activity of the dream. Have you ever had a dream like that? You didn't identify you. You are not thinking YOU—this body over here, that person over there—you are just conscious of the experience of whatever is taking place.

David: *Not like an audience.*

PR: No, not like an audience. Because you are not the issue. You are not self-conscious. If you thought about it, you wouldn't know if you had a body, or if you were "placed" anywhere, really. Just that somehow you are cognizant of all this stuff arising. It's a little bit like that, but that should be taken as an analogy.... It's very important to get that it's not like an observer, or detached, or anything like that. Absolutely not detached. Absolutely not an observer, not an audience. But there are some similarities.

Scott, are you having a hard time being here?

Scott: *Yeah, I am.*

PR: You're waiting to go, you have something to do?

Scott: *Yeah.*

PR: Well, try being your body.

Scott: *Well, it's my body that wants to leave.... [laughter]*

PR: I'll bet it's your mind that wants to go. When you are simply being, you have no desire to be anywhere else. That is the experience, and you don't want to be anywhere else. You don't want to be at the end, or in the beginning, you see? If you are through with a technique, for example, and you are standing there, you are not motivated—it's not like you are restricted—but you are not motivated to be anywhere else or do anything else other than what you are doing. So notice that when you are motivated to be elsewhere, you are not in being, you are not aware of what I'm calling being, or you are not in "this."

When this is uncomfortable, it has to be conceptual. You see? There's motivation ... that force we were talking about to do other things, to be other places, to go eat, or something. All these forces that are both pushing and pulling ... pleasure, pain, comfort, and discomfort. So being in this experience is complete and you don't have to be anywhere else. You don't feel like you have to be anywhere else. It's a very good clue. You don't feel moved to be somewhere else. Or have your mind screaming, "GOD, shut up, let's end this!" That is something else, it's not part of simply being.

Clint: *If you are just being, why do anything?*

PR: You asked that before.

Clint: *I know! [laughs] I'm afraid I wouldn't do anything.*

PR: Maybe you wouldn't. But you wouldn't be bored [laughter].

Clint: *I guess it doesn't really matter.*

PR: But look at the way you hold it. You hold it that you'd be bored. "Oh my god, I couldn't go into being, I'd be so bored."

Clint: *I'd have to do something, you know?*

PR: You probably would. When you were hungry you would eat. When you were tired you'd sleep. If you wanted to build something you'd build something.

Clint: *But why would I want to build something?*

PR: Because it was there to be built. It's like being a "function" ... or like answering the door—if somebody walks up to the door and knocks, you answer the door. If somebody else answers the door, the door is answered. See? A plant is a plant.

Clint: *But why would I do anything?*

PR: Because you're alive.

Clint: *That's what you said last time.*

[laughter]

John: *... Must have memorized it.*

Marcel: *It seems similar to the issue of responsibility—it's not a burden it's just something that's occurring.*

PR: Mmhmm. The statement before was, you don't feel moved to do anything else besides what you are doing. Whatever you are doing, you are doing. If your blending with your partner, you're not moved to do anything else, you blend with that movement. If you're sitting you're sitting. If you are talking you are talking. What needs to be done will be done. That's all.

Clint: *As I'm looking at it, I just realized I was looking at it from the point of view of what I'm going to be doing next. . . . I'm not seeing how it's just what I am doing.*

PR: Talk to Scott—he has been dwelling on what he's going to do next. Probably has lots of good ideas. [laughter]

Scott: *It's like a raindrop not falling up.*

PR: Yes. Right, right. Notice that when you are truly listening to somebody you are not thinking about what they are saying. If you are thinking about what they are saying, what are you doing? [laughter] You're not listening to what they are saying, you are not experiencing their experience in this moment.

Feeling-Awareness
and the Force of Life

*Talks given during a "Function Course" class in 1984
on the nature of the life force.*

PR: Often where people get hung up in relation to "energy work" is in looking for the effects—the tingling, the sense of flow, the heat, the shift in awareness. They think the effect "is" the energy—or how I prefer to say it, the feeling-awareness—and so they try to produce the effect. As a result, they are not in touch with what creates the effects. Their attention is more on the effects than what creates the effects, and what creates the effects isn't the effect itself. It's not even a sensation, or the awareness of what happens after things are affected. So I think it's best to look at energy or life force as what we feel "with"—what we experience as feeling and awareness.

This grounds us in something present and occurring as well as opens us to something plastic and unshaped. The issue I am talking about spans the field of what we call our body-being and our awareness—every aspect of being alive. It is a multi-dimensional phenomenon. We find this feeling-awareness in mental, emotional, and physical domains.

So we are working on getting into the source and nature of this feeling-awareness. This is obviously something YOU have to go ahead and DO. I want to make it very simple. I like to play around as much as the next guy, but my job is to make things more accessible and simple, and not just another game. We are already playing a lot of games—we call it life—and we play all sorts of games which really aren't very effective. But we can create more empowering games, like consciously using and getting in touch with the source and nature of our feeling-attention. It's pretty simple. It's simply what it is. It's not mysterious, and not beyond your comprehension.

It's not something that you don't know of or you're not capable of—obviously. For two reasons. One, you are alive. That shows you embrace an absolute capacity, because you're alive—the life force, the force of your life, is an occurring event and you are somehow connected with it. The other reason is because you're questioning and investigating your own event of being alive. You wouldn't be here if you weren't ready to be learning. In any case, when you turn your attention more directly onto the matter, there are new experiences to be had.

Feeling Is a Form of Intelligence

You pick up a lot more information than you allow yourself to know. In other words, you are working with a tremendous amount of information—and you will work in relation to it in one way or another, but you don't notice that.

Often many associations will come up. I was watching people play some game the other day and I could see some of their associations like: "No I shouldn't do that. I'm not allowed to play like that, it's not fair." Perhaps we took on a lot of assumptions and do's and don'ts when we were children, but don't remember most of them. We hesitate to feel deeply into our own life force. Perhaps we're afraid that getting to the source of being alive may require too much responsibility on our part, and that if we get into it too deeply we may lose control. But sanity hasn't helped a great deal so far, right?

Regardless of origin, or validity, inherent in every feeling is a great deal of information and the drawing out of many relationships. In these feelings a sophisticated and complex form of intelligence is made simply and immediately available, yet most people have little sensitivity to this fact.

Concept Isn't Experience

There's nothing wrong with using visualization or imagery to direct the feeling-attention. It's just that most people don't understand that what they are imaging is only a conceptualization and not the life force itself. Very few people make that distinction. When you are using a conceptualization or a visualization to move feeling-awareness in a certain way, you are just creating something for the energy to do. You've already created a concept and so you are having the feeling-awareness move in that way, and you think it's the same as the concept. It's not, it's just moving feeling-attention in that way. You gave it something to do, so to speak. Given that you want what you are conceptualizing to be actualized, it must take its place in distance, space, process, substance, or interaction.

Even Mind Is Life Force

The source of this feeling-awareness runs your mind also. The force of your life is not any less responsible for what you think and cognize than it is for your breathing and walking and living. The force of your life wouldn't stop there! It does it all. Your thinking is only feeling-awareness doing that. Whatever the force or source that provides or "gives" this feeling-awareness is the same force that provides being alive, and your life functions—walking, breathing, metabolism, healing, etcetera. We can see that it must be prior to intellect or cognition since we cannot perform these functions with our intellect, nor do we cognize most of them and certainly not the source of them. We can also see, or must infer, that this source, this life force—whatever it is that provides the feeling-awareness—must also have the attribute of "intelligence" or consciousness, since it provides or "gives" intelligence, awareness, and cognition. This connection, this source, is often overlooked.

When you obsessively think, however, then you are pouring your energy into THAT. Which is fine, but it doesn't get you anything but that—the thought, the abstraction. It has no real actualizing power in itself. What goes on with your intellect are too many filters, so you get in the way of using energy directly. You think about it, you don't do it. So you see, when we create a picture of something, often the picture, the thought, stands in the way of just doing the thing, or just feeling it the way it is. Like in relation to your body, the thought of your body stands in the way of feeling your body because the thought of your body is not your body. Even the feeling of your body is not your body. And very few of you realize that.

The thought or image of your body is the thought or image of your body, it's not your body. I know it's the only thing you can know or think about relative to your body, but it's still not your body. When you are pouring energy into the thought of your body, that's where your energy is going. It's going into the thought of your body, and since the thought of your body is not your body in fact, actualizing any skill, or shift, or state, or action in your body is hampered.

You pour your energy into abstractions. What I'm calling abstraction is the use of intellect, or the domain that has no basis in just "being" right now—such as thoughts, images, fantasies, fears, or feelings that have nothing to do with "being" right now. There's nothing wrong with that—it must have significant value, you all do it so much, so habitually, it must be worth something. But in any case, pouring energy into beliefs, opinions, judgments, abstractions, emotional reactions, or all sorts of mental-emotional positions is pouring energy into beliefs, opinions, judgments, abstractions, emotional reactions, and all sorts of mental-emotional positions, and that's why most people are so ineffectual and dead. Make a distinction between simply being alive rather than being a surviving "mind," and in this you'll have more power and freedom. That distinction will be very valuable to you.

If you want to actualize something in the world, it has to be aligned with the way that it is; you must actualize it or make it real outside of merely thinking about it. In other words, you can't actualize something in time and space that doesn't meet the requirements of time and space. Make the distinction between pouring your energy into your intellect, and consciously using feeling-attention more directly, in your body, your psycho-physical existence, your being alive, your interactions. If you understand that distinction, your abilities will accelerate rapidly.

One component of that is simply letting things be. I'm a fan of radical experimentation, and you can be too if you want. Maybe you'll find some small way to work with things more effectively, a trickle, but if you don't want to give up the trickle to go for more juice, it will stop there. That's just an analogy—try not to take it too seriously. In any case, don't be afraid to throw it all out and see where it lands. Constantly begin again. Rip off your own beliefs, your own attainments, create new possibilities and make them real.

Developing Functional Interactive Skill

The following lecture/dialogues were taken from a one-day workshop on the nature of developing skill at freeplay in the art of effortless power in 1984. The principles, obstacles, and dynamics that are addressed are relevant in any relationship that demands skillful interaction. The dialogues go in and out of training periods, so often what is said is a result of issues or obstacles that have arisen during that period of training.

Laying Some Groundwork

[A training period just ends. . . .]

PR: So that's really the crux of the matter, right? When you are training a technique it's not against your partner's will; they allow you to do it. However, in freeplay what you are doing is against their will. Even when your partner is not acting against your will you can still have a hard time finding a technique—the precise time, the precise place, right? Doing it easily, keeping your balance, and keeping your structure are hard enough when it's a choreographed routine; during freeplay many more dimensions enter into play and the difficulty level rises dramatically.

I know, I watch you. When you do freeplay there's more pressure than you need, or you call in the old standby—Umph! Well, you may get them to go down, but you're still using too much strength.

Sometimes in freeplay you do a technique which is good—but what do I mean by good? I mean that it's balanced, it happens easily and smoothly, and creates a result to your surprise.

Now let's just say for the moment that a quality of "good" is that it happens to your surprise. In other words, the ease of getting that result is to your surprise, not necessarily that it takes place, that it occurs, but that it occurs that easily, that well, and that cleanly is to your surprise.

If it's not to your surprise it's because you made sure it was going to happen. If you made sure that it was going to happen then, one, you're probably too involved in getting that result to begin with and, two, you probably used too much strength. Because how else are you going to ensure that it's going to happen? You're going to do the things you know how to do, right? You're going to "force" it enough so that you know it's got to go, and then it's not to your surprise. It might even work out, it might even work out well, but there's too much effort and it's not the best technique, because it's not to your surprise. Do you understand what I'm saying?

In your own experience you should have times when techniques appear to your surprise. Those of you who've never had a technique appear to your surprise, you have something new and exciting to look forward to—but if you've been working on the Cheng Hsin principles, if you've been working on following and leading and compressing, or the principles of the Cheng Hsin body-being—if you have been faithfully working on those things, rather than just winning or merely winning, if you have put attention into those things—then, from time to time you will have had techniques come up to your surprise.

Because it's a mechanical event—albeit a psycho-physical mechanical event, maybe a metaphysical mechanical event—but it is a mechanical event. It's nothing mysterious. It's nothing you can't discover. But it's like being in a closet and trying to see the vastness of space. That's a mechanical event also. And although there may be an equivalent relationship between the space in the closet and the space of outer space, the experience is rather different. And even though we might say outer space is there while you are in the closet, your relationship to it is conceptual. So your relationship to it is non-existent, really—as an experience—so it's not very useful. What I'm trying to say is that although the mechanical events of winning freeplay, or anything else, are simple mechanical events, you shouldn't draw the conclusion that you know what they are.

You shouldn't draw the conclusion that what you consider to be a mechanical event is what I'm talking about. Because what you consider a mechanical event may leave out something that I'm considering, or that neither of us are considering. So don't jump to conclusions too quickly.

If you don't take it personally, and start allowing what's there to be what's there, with the devastating quality that it has nothing to do with you, then we can start talking about mechanical events.

James: *I see the distinction of the physics of it, . . . and that doesn't mean you're a machine. I can imagine one idea of what you're saying as being like a machine, a mechanistic way of behaving, and that's not really what you're talking about. . . .*

PR: Right, those are all conclusions you draw about machines. So you hear correctly—that I'm not saying that. When I say mechanical, it's dangerous to draw conclusions like you just pointed out. That it means being insensitive, that it means working like a mindless mechanism. No, in part I'm talking about mechanics, but highly sensitive mechanics. If we could construct a robot that had the perceptive qualities, timing, movement, all of the mechanics for using intrinsic strength, sophisticated programs for interaction, everything needed to win at freeplay, it would off your ass. Do you see what I'm saying?

It would beat you. You know it's true. I mean, if we could design it to have all the sensory sensitivity that it needs, the perceptive abilities, a sense of timing, and an absolute knowledge of physics, movement, compressive ability, it would never make any mistakes—given that it didn't go into error. It wouldn't have impulses it wasn't designed to have. And we would of course design it perfectly to shift its weight properly, to always use intrinsic strength and compressive power (we'd build it with springs) [laughter], and to know when to attack, how to attack, at what angle you're losing your balance, how to change appropriately, we'd design it so that it can see and feel everything, and with all sorts of highly sophisticated feedback loops.

You could see that designing such a mechanism would be a challenge, and playing with this robot would take tremendous skill. You would be slammed into the wall across the room, wham! Like that. And all with a relatively low degree of pressure ... we could design that into it. So that's mechanical, right? It's completely impersonal. You can turn it off [laughs].

We could throw in some soul, but it has nothing to do with being effective, it just goes along for the ride [laughs]. Maybe you could add some artistic flavor, have some emotions. If they get in the way of what's supposed to be happening, or if they serve what's supposed to be happening, only then do they make a difference. In any case, I don't care if you are emotional or not.

Alisia: *So are you saying that this is all just a mechanical affair and we just add stuff to it?*

PR: Yes. Do you still see no mechanics to it?

Alisia: *I don't see all of the mechanics to it.*

PR: Trying to see all of the mechanics to it puts you in a big ball-park, but you still don't even see THE mechanics to it, just THE mechanics. The mechanics that you see, *you* for example, are that there is something over there, but it's pretty much objectified; you don't really see a "person," you don't see their weight, you don't see their balance. You see an object over there—conceptually held most of the time. Once your eyes have alighted on the object, you don't even really look at it anymore. It's as if your eyes alight on an object— a "target"—click, click, click, click, and you go for it over there! As long as you can distinguish the color pattern of the thing—this isn't it, this is it—then you know basically where to charge, but that's pretty much where most of you leave it.

There's a general distinction of distance and the mechanics of distance. There is identifying the object by distinguishing color variations in your field of vision, and then there's direction, moving in some direction—exactly how much? You really have no idea exactly how much . . . it's just kind of "go that way." So there's identifying the object, distance, direction, and then moving in that direction, and in gross that's about it. That's about as much as you've got.

Some of you others are trying to design your structure a bit, make more subtle distinctions in distance, direction and process, and you try to use compression. So the mechanics become more distinguished. And then some of you have gained a bit more sensitivity and consider outreaching. You don't outreach most of the time, but sometimes you do. You think, "Maybe I should outreach and feel what's there so that I can design my actions more accurately—structure my body, shift my weight underground, compress, maintain proper ongoing processes like timing, etcetera."

But none of you really, some of you almost, but none of you have really gotten—even though I've said it a few thousand times—that a technique is a PROCESS that begins somewhere before it starts, and ends somewhere after it ends. And that everything that takes place inside of that is a mutable event. It's not the fixed event that you are conceptually stuck with and think that you must drive through. You don't need to do it that way, and yet most of you do it that way.

In other words, forcing it, struggling with it, fighting what's there. See, that's a result of making it a fixed conceptual event. You're going to uproot them and it doesn't make any difference what changes occur between now and then, you just do your technique. Boom! Did it work? No? Try again. That kind of thing.

But there is another way of doing it which is constant and yet fluid. The whole process is mutable all the way, changeable; the whole process is arising and taking form as it unfolds.

That it arises more or less in relationship to your concept is a tribute to your conceptual ability. And if it doesn't, and you change to meet the circumstances—which are changing like that [snaps fingers]—then that's a tribute to your ability to be present with what's there.

The only way it's going to coincide with your conceptualization, really, is if you ignore what doesn't match how you think. This is easily done since everything else is pretty conceptual also, so it seems to work out, more or less. And when it doesn't, you figure that it just didn't work out. You don't notice the great gap between what you conceptualize and what occurs from moment to moment.

The only reason it will seem to turn out the way that you think it will, is if it is what you suspect it is, since pretty much when you attack you are involved in trying to do something in particular, and have separated yourself from the changing relationship and the unfolding process. And so you have to force it in order to have it turn out like you planned.

Let's look at this simply. You see something, either a body standing there or moving. If you know they are moving "this" way, you attack THAT. You see a body. If they are standing there, you attack there. In other words, you attack them standing there. But by the time you get over there, he may not be standing "there" any more. He may have been standing there when you started, but now he's standing here, you see? Or he may turn his body so it's not as advantageous for you. Or he begins moving somewhere, you can see him moving and so you extrapolate to attack him moving—like shooting at a duck. Do see what I'm saying?

James: *I lost you when you said "seeing moving"—are you saying that that's the same as neutralizing?*

PR: Well, I really didn't say that exactly. But it's about all kinds of things. See, if I see him standing there, and I have the concept of pushing him and then try to push him and it happens, I think I'm pretty good! But the only reason it happened like that is because when I designed what I thought would work to uproot him he was standing there, and as I moved through that process in every moment of the process he was standing there. So as I begin the process of uprooting him he's standing there, and now he's standing there, and now he's standing there, and now he's standing there, and now he's standing there—all while I take action . . . see?

He's pretty much standing there like he was when I first conceptualized the event. Do you see what I'm saying? So the event turns out as I planned. But if he moves back, and I do my push like I planned in the first place, it's not going to work because he's no longer standing there. He moved!

Now, when you are in competition, or when you are in freeplay, then they are going to do this! They are going to act against your will! That's their JOB! But you don't take that into account. So let's handle some things really quickly—where do you go when they mess up your plans? You try *harder.*

Now of course if you have no ability with your techniques, if your techniques aren't very good and you have no stability and no training, well then, your "content" is lacking. . . . If you try to make a fruit salad and all you've got is potatoes, it's hard! You can make french fries maybe, but fruit salad is out of the question. You've got to have techniques, things to work with, Okay? We are not working on techniques today, but I wanted to mention that. Also train techniques, it's a good thing to do.

So, they are going to mess you up, right? That's their job! Now the sooner you get it through your head that that's their job, that they are doing what they are supposed to do, the better off you'll be in competition. Most of the time that's not the way it's held. The way you hold it is they are supposed to do it wrong so you can do it right! But that's not their job!

Now, if they make mistakes, that's good for you—you can take advantage. But you should change that attitude—that you want them to mess up so you can do it right, and if they don't, then they are fighting you—because it really gets in the way. They ARE messing you up, it's true. But see, they are doing their job. They are doing what you are doing. You are messing them up too, remember? They are doing what they are supposed to do.

So I'll say it this way: we have to find out how we can play with somebody who is messing us up. When somebody's trying to thwart you, how do you uproot them thwarting you? How do you play "that?" How do you handle "that?" Do you understand? Not how do you handle it when they are just standing there. Not how do you handle it when they are simply doing a technique, because that's not the case anymore. If you have a violin and try to blow it like a trumpet it won't work well. You must play the instrument that you have. How do you do it when it's against their will?

Kapala: *Well, the thing you do is change your state of being, to transcend the mechanics, and I hear you saying that that would be less if you can't do mechanics. So the goal is to "be" the mechanics, isn't it? To experience the beingness of the mechanics?*

PR: First of all, you're kind of moving ahead; and you are jumping to conclusions.

Now for those of you who are training as apprentices, I just want to use this to point something out, so you can see where or how he is thinking. How is he thinking? Did you hear what he said? Do you see how he is thinking? Do you see that he has drawn conclusions and made assumptions relative to what he has heard? He's inaccurate, having drawn the conclusions and made the assumptions, and you can also see he has some other beliefs that are influencing the conclusions and assumptions he has made, and this is what is directing him in his question. You see? Because he's trying to move somewhere. He's trying to move into where he wants to go relative to his beliefs. Do you understand? You would have to go in and find the conclusions and assumptions, which in this case are pretty obvious, and the beliefs, destroy them all, get down to the nitty gritty and get him to really get that the conclusions, assumptions, and beliefs are not it, and that they won't serve. Because that's your job. You have to learn how to hear these things and in this way, that's why I bring it up.

Now, this is a freeplay workshop so we won't do that [laughter]. When I work in different places I'm not always doing that. Sometimes I'm very easy . . . so the apprentices are saying, "Well, how come he didn't jump on his case?" Because it's not always my job to jump on people's cases. Sometimes it's better to do something else—whatever's appropriate. Understand? That doesn't mean that if he were an apprentice I wouldn't jump on his case.

Okay, back to you. You're moving into it and questioning, that's good, but it is mechanical. So the consideration and the issue are both still mechanical. We need to find out what the mechanics of it are. Okay? "Being" those mechanics is another matter. We'll get to that. We've got to do first things first.

Where to Look

[Another training period ends . . .]

PR: When you get in trouble, you get in trouble because of what has happened before. In other words, because of what has happened before you realize that you are in trouble. If you get in trouble, you're in trouble because of what happened before you got in trouble, not what happens when you get in trouble. So pay attention to what's happening before you get into trouble.

James: *Peter, when you were talking about "being in touch," I don't feel like I have a concept or even a minimal alertness to be able to say that the touching I'm doing is what you are asking for. I usually have a different kind of a touch than real outreaching—or feeling my opponent's whole body. I very rarely—unless I'm really trying to make a certain technique work out—have any kind of thoughts about the location of her feet, and being alert like that. In other words, being that much "in touch." I guess I'm curious about what we are implying, or what we are shooting for with this "outreaching" kind of touch.*

PR: We are noticing some of what the psycho-physical ingredients are—for example, our attention wanders, or our attention goes to what's "important," our attention shifts from thing to thing, it's not all-inclusive—and in order to be effective it has to be inclusive. So if interaction is designed in relation to our attention, our cognition, then our cognition has to be inclusive of the entire event, since that's what our actions must relate to. We have to be directed by the whole interaction in order to be directed by the whole interaction. And I want to suggest here that in order to be effective our actions have to be effective in relation to the whole interaction.

However that's going to be. If you grab an elephant's leg and start yanking the leg to the left, the elephant just says, "Hey! What are you doing down there?" You've got to move the WHOLE elephant. Either you have to grab the whole elephant and move it physically, or you have to get the elephant's attention and bring it around that way, or get the elephant to react to the left, but the *whole* thing needs to be moved—you've got to include the whole thing.

Scott: *I noticed that frequently when I started playing I was too far away. I needed to take a step to do my technique, and the timing of that was too slow. I'd take the step rather than having it come together at once.*

PR: So you noticed that a lot of times as events were taking place, you'd see an opportunity for action but too late, you were too far behind the unfolding event. By the time you got there he did something about it, right? By the time you could adjust your body or take a step to do something, he'd change?

Scott: *Yeah, or he certainly could have.*

PR: Okay. Now I want to suggest ... because of how you said that, it might draw us to the conclusion that we need to speed up. That we have to move faster, we're too slow, we have to do the same thing faster. Maybe that will work, maybe you could squeeze out some workability by doing the same thing faster.... but I want to suggest that you should concern yourself not so much in terms of doing the same thing faster, but doing something else. Like a shift in the way you are approaching it, such that the whole timing frame shifts from one of cognizing something and then trying to catch up with what has already happened, to one in which action is arising at the same time as the cognition. Making a new distinction of immediacy and effectiveness, so that things can happen all at once, like whoompf. And if you don't get the "whoompf" timing frame, well, I just don't know what I can do [chuckles].

Shift your timing frame, how things appear, so that when they appear you are already taking action in relation to them. But that's a little unusual, like patting your head and rubbing your stomach. It feels weird. The mind says, "Wait a minute, I can't do timing like this; I have to do it kachunk, kachunk, kachunk, this is the way the world really is! Kachunk, kachunk, kachunk, kachunk. If I go whoompf—wait a minute, I can't have something appear at the same time I have something else appear—my perception and my action be at the same time. No can do."

Anyway, this is something we'll talk about later. By perception I don't just mean vision. I used to do judo blindfolded—it made no difference whatsoever, not one iota of difference. Not one . . . except, you know, I couldn't find the water fountain. [laughter]

What else did you notice about the mechanics? Didn't anybody notice that they would get in trouble because of what came before?

Jef: *I noticed a bunch of times that I was going to get in trouble . . . just like you said. I'd think, this is it, this is what he was talking about right now.*

PR: You should put more attention on that. You don't ever get in trouble out of what happens at the time. When we're talking about the body, all things appear in process. So you will always get in trouble at some point before you get in trouble [laughs]. When you say you are in trouble—like you have been trapped or outreached, you are losing your balance, you're getting thrown off, you feel at a disadvantage, or something—it's what has happened before in the process such that it came to be that way.

If you can't recognize what happens before it's going to come to that, then you can't adjust in the place or time where it's most effective—the "before" place. Because by the time you are in trouble it's harder to adjust; you are already in a less capable position. So you are trying to handle something when you are already off balance, when you are already in trouble, you are already a problem. See what I'm saying? You are already pressed out of shape, they already have the advantage. So you are at a disadvantage, they are already winning in some fashion—you are already losing, you are already a little out of control. That is already so, and from that position you are trying to handle it. It can be done, but you are already disabled. And from a disabled position trying to be capable. Whereas if you handle the process before you're disabled, you are in a very able position to handle it, and from that able position you can handle it more easily, you can handle it very easily. And take the advantage. So these things you should consider. That's why I pointed it out.

James: *I noticed appropriate body posture just allowed for changes to be handled without me having to be concerned about it.*

PR: Okay, good, good. These things should be paid attention to, and now to open it up even more, consider that what you are paying attention to is nine parts conceptual and one part presence—as what's actually there for yourself. That what you're paying attention to isn't really the presence of what we are speaking about when we talk about freely balanced, relaxing, or whatever. It's nine parts conceptual and one part there. So it's only one part ability, see? And that one part ability shows up for you as an increase in capacity. Imagine what nine more parts would do. But if there are nine more parts, that might require a very different feeling—so just keep opening up. You got something, now get it more, or more deeply. Not just this is the way it is. You understand something now, and it may be even bigger than that. When

I say relax, you relax. All right, now relax even more than that. Don't stop there.

There are times ... like for example, I had some dreams that communicated or presented certain principles or insights that I had no way of knowing about at the time. I could feel them, I could sense something. I loved it, I enjoyed it, I was immediately exhilarated by the experience, but I didn't understand it. Like in one dream an old man taught me the staff; it had nothing to do with staff, it wasn't a "staff" dream. I thought it was at the time but ... what it was was an incredible simplicity of movement—an accuracy in the physics of things, in the timing of things—and it all came about with incredible simplicity, so that it looked almost casual and certainly easy. At the time I had that dream I was Mister Complex himself! [laughs] I was beat 'em up, spit 'em out, do every little thing I could do. And so when I had this dream my heart went WHAT IS THAT!? Wow, that's something! It thrilled me.

I had other dreams about body experiences which came to be the Cheng Hsin body-being. I had another dream that in one beep, in one sound out of a person's mouth, the dynamic of mind became clear.

Things would arise that, at the time, I didn't grasp. It was only when, years later, I would experience something and would recall the dream that I understood what it was really about. I didn't know what it was at the time, I didn't have a place for it, but I had a sense of it.

Who knows how these things arise? Did a dream arise and so suggest movement in a particular direction? Or was I moving in that direction so I had the dream? Or maybe because I had the dream I then had a new possibility for investigation so that eventually I moved in that direction. Or maybe it was just totally a coincidence. In any case, once you get a sense of something, keep trying to move in that direction, without having to know where the end is.

James: *I'm wondering—whenever I'm trying to do something that you have talked about, all that talking becomes abstract. But it's the only*

access I have to what it is you're trying to communicate. For example,
when I'm playing with someone I notice being in trouble before I've
really monitored myself about it, and yet still I'm not quite able to see
it coming. I want to see it, and I don't see it. Never really getting to see
it becomes awful for me. But I'm curious and I'm wondering . . . what
is that? . . . It just keeps squirreling around.

PR: Don't try to see it with your thinking, your cognition. . . .
Watch, I'll show you. Find a partner.

All right, now I want you to look into their eyes. Now, notice
you are looking in their eyes, and probably what's happening is
you're thinking about it—you're wondering, "Why am I doing
this? What am I supposed to see looking in their eyes? Oh, they're
looking at me!" Okay . . . so you have reactions about looking in
their eyes. Now what I want you to practice is shifting from having reactions about looking in their eyes—thinking about it, having feelings about it, reacting to it, wondering, all that—to just
looking in their eyes. When you lose the simplicity, the rawness
and realness of it, then shift back again.

I want you to feel it. It's a very big shift, although you're not
going to go anywhere. Just shift. Just look—"Oh my god, someone's there." Or, "Oh, right now I'm reacting!" Okay. Now just
look in their eyes. Feel as if you move into their eyes and you're
conscious of them—you see them actually in that moment looking at you when you look in their eyes. Practice that. Practice
shifting to actually looking in another's eyes, and see them looking at you in that moment. When you see them seeing you, there
are no words to that moment. Keep doing this until you get it,
until you get that there are no words to that moment. There's
nothing you can say at the time, when you actually do it. But
notice that the moment you do it you'll probably think about it,
and then you'll react to it, or you may react to it instantly. But
make a distinction between moving toward looking at them right
now, and the other stuff—thinking about it, reacting to it.

The chances are very high that if for the last couple of minutes you think you've done nothing but look in their eyes, you're

really out to lunch. That's called conceptually looking in their eyes. That's called holding the thought, "I'm looking in somebody's eyes. Yes, here I am, see, there they are. I'm looking in their eyes." That's not looking in their eyes. That's conceptually looking in their eyes. I want you to move out and actually look into their eyes. Feel vulnerable. There they are. But it doesn't mean anything. Just bingo. And then notice you quickly make it mean something, or you shut it down or get exhilarated, or you get confused, whatever you do . . . I want you to make the distinction. Do that. Make the distinction between really looking at somebody, when you do, and what's not really looking at them. All you are doing is standing there looking at them. You see? Notice there's a distinction between when you actually look at them and when you talk about it and think about it, and feel about it, or "Well, let's see, should I look at them this way, should I look at them that way? Am I doing good?" [chuckles] "Uh oh, I'm fucking up, I'm thinking about it." All those other things are a different domain, when you actually do it there are no words attached. You just talk about it afterwards, maybe a split second afterwards, but you talk about it afterwards.

Okay, good. Thank your partner.

All right, so did you get it? Do you see the difference? That when you actually look in somebody's eyes it's a different event than talking about it, thinking about it, thinking about what it's going to be like, or even thinking about what it is like? And there are no words when it occurs. There are no words, there's just the experience. Just whatever's there when it occurs. The words are a separate activity. So when you are playing with someone, allow the words to be a separate activity so that you keep aligned with the present or arising event. Hold it in a context such that the words are going to put you back into the present, to help you keep being here. So as you go to the words, the words push you back. Keep telling yourself to go back. Go back. Can we dig it? The place where freeplay has to occur is in the wordless place, the event itself.

It's All About Relationship

[Another training period ends. . . .]

PR: I know how to win because I know what the game is. See, winning is always a relationship. It's always a relationship. You don't have any winning without relationship. What determines winning? You have to know what the game is. You can't play the game and you can't win the game if you don't know what it is. So then we have to realize what is winning the game? You've got to know what winning the game *is!* What is losing the game? You need to know these things.

So now, about this matter of doing something against an opponent's will, we are going to do some exercises to show that against their will is not as big a deal as you think.

[More training exercises. . . .]

Listening for what the other person knows has everything to do with the relationship! And you don't really get that. It's one of the most obvious things in the world and nobody gets it! That what they know, what they perceive, what's going on with them determines the relationship with you! So it's important to experience what they know, or don't know.

Marcel: *I didn't pay attention to him, or what he was doing, after I started doing something. It's just like you were talking about. I assumed that they would be staying the same, and didn't notice enough what they were perceiving and responding to; I wasn't feeling what they were going to do. The moment I started my actions I would end up in a struggle.*

PR: Okay. So now what could we create that would handle that?

Marcel: *Well, maybe that now, now, now, now . . . thing.*

PR: Okay, now, now, now, relative to them. What is that?

Marcel: *We're following their activity?*

PR: Following! Yes, following! You see? I don't overemphasize it. How you can take advantage of them when they are moving and have it be exactly the same as when they're still is to keep following! Do you understand what I just told you? Say you've got two cars driving along. They are both going along at one hundred miles per hour; if they are both going along at one hundred miles per hour then, relative to each other, they are still. Do you understand? If one's going 100 mph and the other one's not, it's going the other way, then it is very difficult to do something with the other car; you can't handle it. Because you are not following them.

You must follow your opponent so that you are already with whatever is occurring. They have a stance. You look at their stance and you think, "Well, I could push him off this way. I could throw him down that way. I could uproot him like this." Whatever is true relative to his stance, or what's true about stances NOW, is NOW true NOW, and NOW, and NOW, and NOW, no matter what changes he makes. Right? Do you understand?

You must stay with your opponent in every moment. It is essential. In any given moment they will be in some posture or other. When they adopt any stance it can be destroyed. You can position yourself in relation to them such that their posture, their action, is no longer to their advantage. For example, no matter what stance they take they will lose their balance if you apply a force in a particular direction relative to that stance. Every posture or stance has its weaknesses and strengths. So in every moment if you simply recognize what is so in that very moment, what position they are taking, then you can relate to that and destroy that position. It's true, see? If I take this stance, can it be destroyed? Yes, of course. Well, how about this one? Okay, how 'bout now, can this be destroyed? Yes. How about now? Yes. How 'bout now? Yes. How about now? Yea? Well, how about now?

Do I have to go on? [laughter] I mean, no kidding? Do you understand why I went through that? I'll do this until you get it! Now, now, now, now, they are always in some stance or other, some activity, some intent, some posture. They are always at any particular instant in a particular stance, shape, action, perception, strategy, motion. If you can destroy their posture now, then you can destroy it now, now, now, now, now, now, now, now, now, now, now, now, now. Do you understand? Even now you can destroy their stance, or their action. Got it?

However, you can't do it unless you're with them now, now, now, now, now, now, now. Do you see? If you could be with them as they are moving and freeze-frame it, then you can see here's a stance, here's a stance, here's a stance, here's a stance, here's a stance.

The only thing that keeps you from handling their intent, their action, their stance at any moment is that you're not with them, you're not following them, you're not attached to them, you're not on top of them. If you can handle their positioning in this moment, and they change it, then you are the one that must change in order to be able to handle their activity now.

Got it? Do you see what I'm saying? Following! You are not following. Understand? Following is better than any technique, or trying to force the situation. What you need in order to follow is perception or "listening." Listening, outreaching, joining—following? See? [laughter]

Joe: *I don't think I'm really getting what is implied in that....*

PR: Well, do you understand that what the opponent knows is a big factor? See, I'll use a very simple example, so that we can understand. If I have a gun and I'm going to shoot you, how can I shoot you? What is necessary? I'm looking at you. I can feel my arm here, I know what a gun is and how to use it. I can point the gun, I can pull the trigger. And then a bullet will fire, boom, and hit you. Okay? I'm looking, I see you and I do this action, and it goes kaboom! You're dead. Do you see what I'm saying? Now, say it's pitch black, I've got a gun but I can't see you.... How can I shoot you?

Joe: *If I make a sound.*

PR: Very good. Boom! Thank you. I heard that. You see? This is one of the things I'm telling you. They are not dumb! The minute you speak then I know where to shoot. What do they know? What do I know? If it's dark, what do I know?

Scott: *So is that the same rationale as when I throw a rock over at Jef and you hear that and shoot, that kind of thing?*

PR: Everything, everything. See, dig it, what are you doing when you throw something?

Scott: *I'm faking you out.*

PR: You're faking me out because what you are doing is creating a sound. I'm listening for a sound because I can't see you. And so my attention goes over there! How come? Because of something I hear. What I *perceive*. What I "know." You see? How many ways can you do that in freeplay? You have to be intelligent, that's all.

Marcel: *So in part at least it's a very simple matter, it's knowing what you need to know.*

PR: That's right, and you guys are trying to be clever. Lame! Do you understand? I'm in the dark here with a gun. I can't see you. That's a fact! Do you know what I mean? If I can't find you, I can't shoot you. Maybe I can start shooting randomly, boom! boom! boom! boom! boom! If it's a Western I'll shoot twenty-six times! boom! boom! boom! [laughter] Maybe I won't hit you, maybe I will. It's all random, a shot in the dark, so to speak [chuckles].

So, now you can handle this. It's not trickery. You want the interaction to work out. That lies in handling what is, not in being clever. When we are being clever we are trying tricks. We're trying to fool them and trick them. That's different than handling them.

You shouldn't think in terms of tricks because that's always going to end up being lame. So, I hear a sound and I shoot into the sound. I see something, I shoot into the seeing. This is all it is. What do they know? If I've never seen a gun before, and there's a gun right here, even if I see you and I want to kill you, I won't reach for the gun.

Liz: I recall something in your book about "seeing what they see." But I also interpret that as "to guess what they know."

PR: It's every way. You should consider it from every point of view. What is their capacity? What do they know? What is their knowledge? What is their skill? In other words, what is their skill level? What are they good at? What can they pick up? So, in short, what do they "know"—what is their experience? In this moment what are they seeing? What are they perceiving? What are they thinking? What are they being clever about? You can handle somebody that's being clever, just like you can handle somebody being stupid. It's the same domain. Stupid and clever are in the same place, really.

Now that is an interesting assertion. You can handle somebody being stupid. Somebody being clever is just like somebody being stupid; they are just being stupid in a clever way. In other words, they are just being stupid with all sorts of complications or variations. But it's the same thing, they are no more intelligent, they are not really more intelligent. They are no more present, they are no more astutely with what is, they are no more skillful than somebody who is being stupid. Somebody being stupid is not dead! They're alive, they are having some perception, they have some distinctions they can make, we are calling them stupid relative to—once again, it's always relative—we call them stupid relative to you, or stupid relative to what you think is smart. Clever is the same thing, it's just sideways. Stupid is simplistic, clever is complicated. But it's the same thing as simplistic. Simplistic is stupid grossly. Clever is complicated simplistic-ness. Just breaking it up into all sorts of clever pieces, but you haven't really gained in any kind of real skill, understanding, or depth—do you see what I'm saying?

So in any case I don't recommend it. It's not mastery. It never will be. It cannot be mastery. You can verify this for yourself. The experience is not really even worth having. It's not worth it! You notice when you are clever and you trick somebody, you fool somebody, what do you get? At the most you get a little glee at having fooled them or tricked them. Do you have a sense of mastery? No, you never have and you never will. Do you have a sense of real capacity? Understanding? Skill? No. Unless you have an experience of real skill or capacity—sometimes you know you can handle somebody and it looks like you are tricking them, but really you are just being skillful and that's a different experience than tricking or being clever.

So understand that what the opponent knows is very important for designing what you do, and to know how they will react to what you do. You must experience what's going on with them. Also, notice that following is a critical element. When I speak about principles like following and listening I'm not just full of hot air. You should get it. And then you should get it more, and more. You should really understand what I'm trying to tell you about listening. Which is about knowing what they know, knowing the experience that's there, knowing what's going on. Listen to your own body, listen to them listening, and follow it all.

So we talked about competition and you thought I was going to teach you something else, right? [laughter] I will. [laughter] So are we getting clear on this? Perception? Following? Relationship?

Relationship (thus effectiveness) Is Found in an Experience of THEM

[Training period ends. . . .]

James: *When I'm interacting with someone, it seems I'll always be unconscious of something. I stay open to a certain point and then I commit myself to do something, and if I'm lucky or I'm a little more skilled at that particular maneuver than they are, then I catch their actions in what I'm trying to do, and if I'm not then my commitment to what I wanted to do will be foiled by them, or used against me. I guess, I have to stay open. . . .*

PR: So you can see that sometimes you do something and it's foiled. It's foiled by what they do. You have to see in this then that you are not in fact following them, in the sense that you are not doing your action relative to their foiling. You're doing your actions relative to something that's not there. Which is to say, they are foiling your actions. You're doing the action in relation to something that's not the case. You could be mistaken conceptually; in other words, it never was the case, you just made a mistake about what was occurring. Or perhaps they change—in any of the myriad ways they could change relative to you—so that they are foiling you. Then what you need to do is get that what you have to handle is their foiling, not your actions. Now I'll say this probably a thousand times today, and maybe one or two of you will get it—you'll know if one or two of you really get it, you'll win a lot—you have to handle their foiling, not your actions!

Your action is not what counts [banging the counter with his fist]. . . . You're not interacting with your action! You're interacting with their action! If you just charge in blindly with some action of your own, what the hell does that have to do with anything?

What they do is what's important! What they do! What they do is what's important! You're uprooting THEM!! You're throwing them, remember? GET IT! THEM! THEM! THEM! THEM! Everybody is so concerned about their own action, it's so BLIND! You never see THEM! It's IMMENSE!!! [laughs]

Okay? What they know, what they do, what they see—you have to create the relationship relative to what's there! You can't do that if you don't follow them. Do you understand? You must follow them, and you can't do that if you don't get what they know, what they are doing, what they see, what they are reacting to! They are going to foil you, they are going to thwart you. That's their job. You have to interact with them thwarting you! You have to turn their thwarting you into your advantage! Their foiling into your uproot. Their mistake into your throw. Whatever they are doing, their loss of balance, whatever is going on with them, you have to turn it into your uproot, your throw. You can't do that if you are not following, if you are not always with their positioning. We'll just stay with that for now.

[More training. . . .]

PR: You're still not actively engaged enough. I want you to feel their movement and follow them with your feeling. Have your ⑨ whole body feel their whole body moving. If you lose them or are disconnected for a moment I want you to pick it up like catching a train, like running along beside a train before grabbing it. In other words, when you move you should be in sync with their movement. So whenever you touch them you are already in sync, you are already following them, and then you can concentrate on their changing actions. Remember what we went through with this issue of "now," or change, change, change? When they have a stagnant stance, that you can handle. Now they have changing stances. You have advantage and disadvantage with a changing stance. The disadvantage is that it keeps changing and you've got to follow it, stick with it. But if you follow the changing, the advantage is in its very motion; they are already giving you some ⑨ energy, some power. You can use that. They are already committed to something.

Because you are trying to do what I ask you to do, it turns into an obsession about what YOU know. And then that's still what ⑨ YOU know, and you lose them even though we are talking about what you know about THEM. You see? And then you get crazy with "you" again. What do "I" know? What can "I" do? That's more like the domain of cleverness, because that's what YOU know. The domain of skill lies first in what THEY know, and how you can relate to it. But if you go into a thought process about it, thinking: "How can I handle what they know?", they already know something different, so immediately you are no longer relating to what they know.

You have to feed these thoughts of how you can handle what they perceive back into feeling them, just as you must turn your vision back onto them. Do you remember what I'm talking about? You may think that you moved back into looking at them, being with them, experiencing them, but really haven't; you are conceptualizing them rather than experiencing them now—what ⑨ they know, what they don't know, whatever's there. So as you turn back into them, and you have thoughts arising from this turning, or you have some feeling of them and you have thoughts arising from that—"What can I do about it, how can I handle it?"—you have got to turn these thoughts and reactions back into them, them, them, them, them, how can I handle it? Oops, them, them, them, them, them, them, how can I handle it, them, them, them . . . Okay?

So be silent. Relax. Feel them.

The "Before" Place

[A training period ends. . . .]

PR: Actually, you are already good enough. Sure, you've got to earn your chops, you've got to go around the block, and you have to try things out and experiment. You have to think about things, and work them out. But I tell you that you actually know more about what's going on than you think, and you can handle it without thinking about how to handle it. For the most part, you know how to handle people simply by listening to them. You don't need to think about it as much as you think you need to think about it. You see, it's already there, happening at a speed must faster than you can recognize in your thoughts. Do you know what I mean?

You don't have to get it up to think the thought of how to handle them. Just feel them. You know what you're doing; you're not stupid either. You know what you are up to; you're not going to forget because you don't think the thought, "What shall I do, how can I throw him down, should I go against his balance, should I uproot him, is this easy?" If you don't think those thoughts, do you think you'll forget what you are doing? Are you that stupid?

[laughter]

Well, okay. All you have to do is stay on purpose. Staying on purpose, you don't have to have any thoughts—not one thought. You do not have to think in order to stay on purpose. All you have to do is stay on purpose. It's not a thinking matter. You don't have to have any thoughts. Be with them, and do what you are there to do. Okay? Go ahead and do this thing.

[Training. . . .]

PR: When you get in trouble, you get in trouble because of what came before you got in trouble. What comes before you get in trouble? What they know and what they don't know are critical for determining what they will do.

What do people know? What don't they know? What can't they handle just by the very fact they are standing? What will they react to? What they will react to will be in large measure relative to what they know! And won't be related to what they don't know.

People react to what they cognize. And what they cognize is oftentimes full of conclusions that aren't true, assumptions that aren't there. But they will react to these conclusions and assumptions relative to whatever their perception is about. If you can see the conclusions and assumptions they are making, you'll know how they are going to react. If you want to do something and you don't want them to react, you have to do something they don't perceive, or assume, or conclude. Do something that they don't know.

A lot of you aren't indeed handling what's coming before; you're handling what's coming after. Silly people. Why are you handling what comes after? It means your attention is on what you think they are doing, which is actually what they have already done, and on what actions you plan to take. Instead of handling what is actually occurring, and so what comes before you get into trouble, you're waiting until it's a problem. And then you're trying to be clever, so you're being stupid [laughs].

In other words, you're not simply seeing what's happening. Someone approaches you, his mass is moving towards you. Handle it before it touches you. Somebody attacks you, move before he gets pressure on you, before you lose your balance, before you are trapped, before he moves into a position that is hard to handle. Don't try to be clever and second-guess them, because you're often wrong.

Try to handle . . . [claps] you, you, you, attack me. [Peter points at three students who rush at him. He handles their rush before they are able to formulate an attack.]

Okay? Do you see? Try to make it simple, handle it before it becomes a problem [laughing]. They have to come over here, they don't have any choice about that, do you know what I mean? Handle what comes before. Don't wait until the last minute.

It's Only ONE Relationship

[Another training period ends. . . .]

PR: Other people have an intentions of their own, so they're doing various things on their own, right? They are not just handling this event. So now what should this tell you about yourself? . . . Are you learning? Are you learning from others? What should this tell you about yourself? When I said, "Notice that about your partner" and everybody noticed that about their partner—guess what, you're their partner! . . . Get it?

You're not really being in relationship to them. You're not neutralizing them and staying in balance. You want to reach the point where you can be as successful at staying in balance and neutralizing them as if it's all you have to do, even when you're also handling them or joining them. So you're doing it as well as you can, and your own agenda doesn't get in the way.

How does *your* activity of handling them get in the way of your handling *them?* You make it two things. You have two separate things, two activities—you and them. So the only way you can turn that around is to make it one activity, one thing. How are those two activities going to be one thing? It's very simple. It's THE relationship. ONE relationship. If you have your attention on what their experience is, and what they know, and you're in relationship to that, it doesn't make any difference whether it's coming or going. If you're in relationship to their experience, and you're handling them, and what you see arise in them is an attack, then you have an experience of their experience of attacking you.

While you neutralize that attack, in the same moment you can also join them. Both at the same time, it's one experience, one thing, not two things. You don't have to go back and forth. It's just one thing. When you get the "Sublime One-Thing" then you're starting to master interaction, and this is what freeplay is all about, not these airy fairy notions that are dogmatically believed. . . . [laughs]. I have to entertain myself, you know? [laughs]

So let's get this sublime one-thing. Which includes what they know, what they don't know, handling them, their stance, following them, outreaching them, listening to them, neutralizing them, joining them—so, in brief, all we've discussed today is the sublime one relationship—or more simply put, THE relationship.

Now I'd like to do a guided meditation with you:

> I want you to feel what all of that was like—what all of that is is everything we've done so far today. Feel it. Feel it. Include the frustrations that you've felt, include the feelings of imbalance that you had, include the feelings of inappropriateness, include the feelings of balance, include the feelings of when you did it right, when it was smooth, when it was easy, include it all.
>
> Just feel all that activity, as if it's happening to you now. Feel it, as if all of that activity is occurring right now. As if it's right now in your body. Like you're soaking in it.
>
> Soak in the experiences of the day, the sensations of today. Not so much the thoughts, you can let the thoughts and images and pictures be there, but mostly the sensations of today. Balance, frustration, pressure, smooth as silk, moving freely, and every other feeling.
>
> Include the experience of them. When you were wrong, when you were right. When things happened easily or to your surprise. When things happened that were surprisingly difficult. Feel the sensations in your body. Soak in it. Soak in it.

Soak in it. Feel it. Feel it. Don't think about it. Don't investigate it. Just feel it. I want you to get it here. HERE. Feel it until it drives you crazy. Until you're almost ready to scream because it feels like there's too much sensation, too much feeling you don't know what to do with it. So much wrong, so much off balance, there's so much ignorance, there's so much crybaby, there's so much determination, there's so much fear, there's so much sensation, there's so much ...

Feel the sensations. Soak in them. And while you're soaking in it, listen to it. Listen to it. What is it telling you? Listen to it experientially. By listen to it I mean turn into it, move into it, embrace it, turn to face it. Don't think about it, listen to it.

You're listening to the experience, the sensation, the feelings in your body, the whole of today, all the sensations, all this experience as one thing. Listen to it.

What is it telling you? Everything you need to know is being told to you, right now, right there. Everything necessary for you to be a perfect master. Inherent in what you are feeling right now, in all the sensations you felt today. In all the off balances, and all the slamming together, and all the doing it right, in all the feeling, in listening to your partner, and all the ignorance and all the concepts—in all of that field, what is it telling you? It's telling you what's not correct and it's telling you what is correct. Because there is no other way. Do you see? What is correct is what is correct. Obviously. That you engage in all these feelings that were not correct means that you don't necessarily acknowledge what is correct. So right now, I want you to listen to it.

You have to listen to the experience of the incorrect sensations—the ones that banged, the ones that strained, the ones in which you lost your balance, the one's that were inappropriate, when you were out to lunch, all of those. You have to listen to the frustrations, you have to listen to them with great intensity—until you can hear what they are telling you. But you have to hear it experientially.

So sit with it, sit with it. Listen to it. Feel it. Don't try to change it or you won't hear, you won't hear. Don't change it, feel it. It's already that way. You are not in fact moving now, so it's already that way for you. If you got up right now you'd make the same mistakes that you did then. Do you see? So don't change it now sitting in your seat. Feel it, listen to it. What's it telling you?

Sometimes it's screaming at you, "Look at this! Come on, see!" It's telling you something very simple sometimes. Sometimes it's telling you something very subtle . . . feel it all. Sometimes it's something really obvious that you're not listening to, you're not admitting. Sometimes it's a very subtle thing you're not hearing.

Listen to the experience. Don't judge yourself, it's a waste of time, listen to the experience. Don't make it okay. Don't make it bad. You make errors—it's true, you make errors. You fuck up. It's true. Don't try to put a bandaid on that. You fuck up! Be responsible for it. When it happened, more than likely, you were hardly there [chuckles]. Don't make it anything other than it is. When it happens well, it happens well. Beating yourself up isn't going to do any good at all. Feel it. Get responsible for it. Feel it.

What is it? What is it? What is it? What's it trying to tell you? Listen to it. . . .

Okay, now in a little while I'm going to ask you to interact again with your partner, I'm going to ask you to do this again. So now with that in mind I want you to turn into this experience. In other words, I want you to see what you can learn from it truly. So that it shows up in the next interaction, not just conceptually sitting on the ground.

Feel the sensations. Feel what it is you have to make corrections in. What are you going to have to change? What feelings in your body? What sensations do you have to listen to? What attitudes do you have to give up? What do you have to awaken to? What vulnerability do you have to feel? What do you have to let be true? . . . Whatever is so. What feelings do you have to have so that you can clean up all of that? So you can have a sublime relationship with your partner?

Don't think about it. Feel as if it's happening right now. I want you to imagine being with your partner and having everything work beautifully. Feel it in relationship to what you were feeling before—the fuckups, the pressure, the loss of balance. Keep that close to your heart; otherwise you'll just fantasize. I'm not asking you to fantasize. I'm asking you to create a real possibility for experience. I want you to create this experience. Feel what it would be like.

What do you have to do to keep in balance? What do you have to do so that you don't bang into them? What needs to be so so that you effortlessly neutralize and join them? Feel that happening right now, as if it were happening right now.

How wonderful. Feel what it's like being with them totally, feeling every movement in their body, always touching their balance, always being appropriate, neutralizing everything they are doing, always being in balance, flowing smoothly like silk, allowing results to take place easily. Feel that happening.

Contrast it with the experience of what you were doing. Do this right now, I'm serious. Do it until you can have the experience of what you were doing move into the experience that I'm asking you to create now. Until it's really that way for you, right now. So that when you stand up and play with your partner it is that way.

[More training. . . .]

Jef: *Could you clarify what the experience is like that you are pointing to?*

PR: Feeling perfect, playing smoothly, easily, with effortless results, always in balance, always feeling the person there . . . always feeling them, always being in touch with whatever is occurring in each moment, being inclusive. Inclusive is a word I use to indicate feeling everything. Don't deny anything, don't ignore anything. I use the word include or inclusive. But you have to seek out what I mean when I say inclusion. Inclusion is ability.

Can you imagine a perfect relationship? Feeling your body in perfect relationship? Or at least being close to it, moving strongly in that direction? Good.

Given it's not perfect already, consider: what are you ignoring? There is something you're ignoring. There is something you're not including—there has to be. Because given the relationship is just a psycho-physical, metaphysical event, there must be something that you're leaving out, or there is something that you are incorrect about, or you would already have handled it. Think about that. I know you may think that you can never be incorrect, but consider it for a moment. There's something you're misjudging—in your impulse, in your feeling, in what it means, the way it is.... There's something you're ignoring, and maybe more than one. If you handle that—if you know how to handle it, how to neutralize it, how to be with it, or how to balance it, or move with it, or how to borrow it, or follow it, or join it, or whatever ... how to think it or feel it—then you would have a perfect relationship. So what are you ignoring?

Okay, now back to interaction, and I want you to continue to hold the question, "What am I ignoring?"

[PR speaking during training]: Do you ignore their thinking? Do you ignore that they are just doing their job as best they can? Do you ignore that you space out? Do you ignore that your attention wanders? Do you ignore them? Do you ignore the physical realities of the world—distance, space, physics, timing, alignment, movement—do you ignore the simple physical realities?

Do you ignore what does not work? Do you ignore what works? Just what are you ignoring from moment, to moment, to moment, to moment. Consider this! Okay, stop.

Now calm your mind. Don't get frustrated. Empty your mind.... Think about ... a tropical island with white sand and swaying palm trees and a warm breeze. Fish jumping out of the shining sparkling water. Soft grass with luscious strawberries growing in it and mangoes hanging from the trees....

Okay, I wanted to shake you out of your patterns of thinking. Now, find a new partner. See, there's an instant relationship ... like instant coffee [laughs]. The moment you add yourself [laughs], there's instant relationship. Okay, be appropriate, do some freeplay.

[Training ends....]

PR: Now, those of you who will get better than the others are the ones who hear me best. And by hear me best I mean experience what the truth of the matter is ... best. Your level of skill will increase to the degree you've heard me during the workshop. So if I told you everything you needed to know about mastering this art—say I could do that—and you heard ten percent, then you'll only be able to do ten percent better than when you came in here. If the actual matter of effortlessly effective interaction was addressed fully in my communication and you experienced what that is, then you can't help but be profoundly better, can you?

The Power of Questioning

The following are selected portions of three separate lectures given by Peter Ralston to Cheng Hsin students or apprentices in 1983.

What Is the Center of the Truth?

PR: If you had an infinite line, and then you established the center of the line—impossible, right? Of course. But what if you could find the center of the line?

All right. Say you did. The center, then, of the line would be the same as the center of a plane. How come? What's the difference? And then there's the center of three dimensions. What's the difference between the center of a line, the center of a plane, and the center of three dimensions, given that the center is the same for all three?

Harold: *How do we know that it's the same point?*

PR: I said given that this is true.

Harold: *So what's the point, you've got a given, it gives you something.*

PR: [laughter]

Harold: *... But you'll want to take it back later on. ...*

PR: [laughter] Of course I will!

So the center—let's call it a point—the point in each case is absolutely not different in any way, shape, or form. The context is different. The form, the point, is not different at all.

What's the center of somebody's mind?
What is the center of space?
What is the center of time?
So what's the center of everything?
Where is the center of you?

John: *I don't know how to answer these questions. I don't even know how to think them.*

PR: The experience, not the answer, is what's important. We are asking questions now. So I'm broadening our relationship to center. You notice that we don't live our lives in the questions that I just asked? In other words, our life has no relationship to the questions I was just asking. One way you can notice that is how we break down. If I ask a question like that, we just break down, or we try to fit the question into the way we live our lives. This is significant because we live as if time and as if space really exist, don't we? Are real, aren't they? We live as if all these things are real. Yet to these questions, and the things to which I've been referring, we have no answers.

But we don't live like that, do we? We don't live like we don't know what the center of space is. We don't live like we don't know what the center of time is. See, if there's no center of time, then perhaps time *isn't*. If there's no center to space, then perhaps space *isn't*.

So you understand that we're talking *questions* here.

Scott: *We're sure not talking answers! [laughter]*

PR: What is the center of mind? Perhaps it isn't—like time and space isn't! Do you know why it's so difficult for you and Zen people to find out who you are?

Have you ever looked into trying to find, really truly trying to find, who you are like as a center? I know some of you have, you've done some ontological work and have diligently looked into trying to find who you are—like where is the damn thing?

See, I know what I'm saying doesn't make much sense and is

not acceptable. But you see, whoever said that the truth was dependent upon what you can accept or not?

Questioning

PR: If somebody asks a question looking for information, they should know that's what they're doing and should ask for information. Then I can give information quickly and handle it. But you should know that's all you're doing, because you will just get information—like, "Where's the bathroom?" "It's that way." That's a completely conceptual realm; information is totally conceptual. But there is another kind of question, like the kind we ask in the ontological work. Sometimes stupid questions or little questions are really parts of a bigger question in which you are not trying to get a resolution or a closure on the question, you are trying to feed the question, further it, or open it up.

Feed any response or answer or information into your question. Not necessarily as the truth. Just feed it—like fueling the question. You add fuel to it, or clarity to it, or power to it, or depth to it. The one you ask might seem like the stupidest question. What we call stupid questions are often questions that question something assumed, and so it looks like a stupid question. Do I exist? Well, it looks like a stupid question, but you don't know that, really. It's an assumption. You don't know. So it looks like a stupid question but it's not—if there's a question there, a real question. A stupid question might be a part of a real questioning.

The Cheng Hsin endeavor is like a big experiment. What's not the experiment? The teachings of Cheng Hsin aren't an experiment, that's not the experiment. The power of Cheng Hsin is not an experiment. What is the experiment? It's seeing if we can have it on the planet. That's the experiment. Maybe it's impossible, I don't know. The experiment is whether it can show up in human beings, that's the experiment. Cheng Hsin isn't the experiment. It's whether it can show up or not that is the experiment. So this is a big experiment . . . or project.

The Principles vs. Winning

PR: As you must realize by now, none of the courses that I do are sufficient in the practice area. They are not designed to be sufficient. They are what we call insufficient in the practice area. They are not designed to be a development in and of themselves; they are designed to be a communication.

When we've got nothing and we get something, we have 100 percent more than we had before, right? Yet when we have a new possibility, insight, understanding, or an increased consciousness regarding any matter, now we can get many more things from the one thing—we have a new base from which to create, gather, or build upon. When we have nothing and we get a basket, we have 100 percent more than we had before. But when we have a basket we can pick many things and put them in the basket . . . if they'll fit. [chuckles] . . . Just more analogies.

And so each time we reach a new level or we start to truly grasp a principle a new world opens up. . . . When we hear about the principles, great, we've heard about them once and so we have something. When we understand the principles we have 100 times more. And when we interact from the principles then we have a completely new domain in which to live and in which to have millions of new experiences and insights that we could never have had prior to grasping and practicing the principles. It is in this that we actually begin to grasp the communication.

In any course of study that I do there's not enough time to cover everything we need to cover about the subject. So I address what I feel are the most important things to address—the basic principles and dynamics of effective interaction, an effortlessly effective body-being, or the nature of mind, experience, or Being. But you should understand that my basic communication or instruction is not basic. Do you know what I mean? I call this the basic principles and dynamics of effective interaction and there's more function in this course, there's more profound communication in the area of effective interaction in this course than you'll find in twenty years studying anywhere else. That's the way it is, I can't help it.

Our cultural programming has it that you must regard most of what you hear here as "information." There is information, but consider: all that information, all the stuff that you hold as information—which is a lot, right? A lot of information—all that you hold as simply information is actually real communication, an experiential opportunity for breakthroughs into the presence of ability, skill, the principles of interaction—not just "information."

You know how from time to time, at least in some small way, you have had an experience of what's going on? And that experience often seems to cover much less time than the amount of information that has come down the pike. You have had an "Aha!", and you really grasped something, or a "Wow! This stuff really works," or "Oh, this is what he means!"—one of those. Imagine that all of the information in this course could be like that. Deeper and more profound than what we usually experience. Do you see what that does with the communication? Makes it kind of huge, doesn't it? I'm telling you it is that way. I'm telling you that if you got this communication, as an experience rather than as an idea or as information, you could be very masterful.

Now what keeps us from being masterful is that we get things as information, not as an experience. Because mastery shows up in the experiential realm, which is effortlessly effective interaction. It doesn't show up in the information realm of ideas, concepts, fantasies. In seeing that, there is an opportunity for us in this. It gives us something worthy of study—the end product of which is what we call mastery, and mastery is a transformation of being. And the transformation of being is about the only thing really worth doing while hanging out on this planet. So it gives you something worth devoting yourself to entirely. Why waste your time on anything less than that?

In our study of this, however, it doesn't seem that we should expect to win a lot. We should expect to do or be the principles of an effortlessly effective body-being, and the principles of effective interaction, and not expect to win a lot. Just expect to relax, blend, feel, outreach—just study that. But I don't think we spend enough time with that. I think we spend more time trying to win than we spend studying the principles. Isn't that true?

All of the time spent trying to win is like building a house on toothpicks. Merely trying to win is precariously perched. There's no transformation in that kind of winning, that's just learning how you can get yourself, as is, to win. It's a makeshift job, like when you stick the rag in the hole, the penny in the fuse box. We just want the thing to work. If it works, who cares if it will burn the house down? We don't see the ultimate danger of our approach. Because inevitably the house will burn down, someday.

It's so funny because when we study winning we are not studying Cheng Hsin. Cheng Hsin is not a study of winning. Yet we all want to win. But Cheng Hsin is not a study of winning. When you study Cheng Hsin, if winning occurs it just occurs.

Winning is in a different domain, or like in a different house. When you are studying Cheng Hsin, winning comes about during the times when you are just working on your principles—you are concentrating on blending, using intrinsic strength, or whatever, and all of a sudden you step in the right place and bingo! Or you happen to get into the rhythm of things and it works to your advantage. I don't want to say that you are not responsible, but you may well get the feeling that you weren't trying to win. So if you aren't *trying* to win, how can you ever bring about winning? When you are trying to win or you are struggling and you win, you might think, "Yeah, I got 'em!" ... but it's a completely different experience from simply doing the principles. It's in a different realm—like in a different house, a different domain—it is totally different.

In the domain where we are not trying to win, winning is like a side effect. Not like it isn't a goal, not like you are not participating, not like you are trying to lose—I know some of you just go ahead and lose [laughs]—it's not that. You must fully participate, but without concentrating on winning. In Cheng Hsin, as you try to study the principles you will fail to do them, you will move in and out of them, and you will learn. Trying to win is different.

Instead of trying to win, participate in such a way that if all things come together in a workable manner, a result is produced. But, you see, that's trying to get all things to come together in a workable manner, not trying to get some result. The result is then produced intrinsically. All things coming together naturally turns out a certain way, because a result is only a part of a process. It's like dominoes, where you set up all of the dominoes and push the first one, all the activity that has been set up to happen happens. But if one domino misses then the whole thing misses. That's just the way it is. You have to get used to that. Because more often than not one domino is going to miss somewhere. More often than not something is going to be just a little off or out of whack—the timing is just a little off or something—so it won't work, or it won't work well.

When you are studying the principles, and you have an "Aha! that doesn't work," you should also have an "Ah, I get a sense that the timing was off, and when the timing is off in this situation it doesn't work, I see." Or "My distance was off; if the distance is off, it doesn't work." It shouldn't be like "OH MY GOD it didn't work! I'll try harder next time." No, no. Just adjust the timing. Adjust the distance, the angle, the intrinsic quality, the degree of relaxation, the feeling, your attitude, your blend, whatever—adjust. And then it should work.

If it still doesn't work, there's something else out. Just keep working with it and making adjustments. Like if you're trying to find a station on the radio and it's not quite there [makes garbled sounds] and you turn the volume up [screams], [laughter], it's not the right knob, you know, it's the other one.... Trying harder is like turning the knob that we have, but it might not be the knob that works. We have to find another knob.

A Commitment to Mastery

PR: What I'm trying to do—it seems overwhelming—is to penetrate the nature of humankind enough so that we can break through our incapacity to learn things in such a way that it becomes natural to learn things. As human beings we have a right to learn things much, much faster than we do. This is simple. It is easy. The hard stuff isn't the stuff we make hard. The hard stuff is paradox. We make stuff hard that has no business being hard. We have to break through that. We have to make it easy.

One way we can do that is to hear what is being communicated and throw ourselves into it. We throw ourselves into it in a way that is really here, present, open, a way that lends itself to the encounter and touches our being. Throw yourself into it so that it touches your whole being, not just your skin, not just your brain. It's all right if it touches your skin and your brain, but that's not where we should stop. That's why we are so slow, because we don't encounter with our being, we encounter with our "stuff."

It's an immense affair to encounter things with our being, but what else are we going to do? Think about it for a moment, what are we up to as beings? Learning T'ai Chi? I mean, is this what we were born for? Making sandwiches at the deli? Programming a computer? Or doing whatever our work is? Is that what we were born for? Getting a new car? Living in a shack? Living in a big house?

You would tell me in a resounding voice—on a good day, when you are in touch with your self—you would tell me: "NO! I was not born to flip pancakes. NO! I was not born to program computers. NO! I was not born to drive a car." You don't EXIST and BE and ARE for that stuff! That's not what you were born for. YOU would tell me that, I am certain, if you knew what I was talking about. And I would tell you that.

But at the same time we spend our time with that. And when we get together for the purpose of encountering the nature of being—which you would probably sense is more in the area of your aliveness, what you were born for—we don't come up with a vision that matches how we live our lives. You say that you were not born to commit yourself to all of the petty and superficial concerns to which you have become so bound. You would stand up on a hill and yell it at the world. You would, without qualms, if you felt free, tell everybody how magnificent you are. You want your being to shine. I know that about you. But you don't lend your being to touch things—things as simple as relaxing, and using intrinsic strength, investing in loss, having a receptive attitude, listening, and staying conscious. You don't lend your being to it. You give your mind a little bit. You kind of put yourselves into it sometimes, but you don't open up completely, you don't fully encounter what's here ... genuinely, authentically, at risk, with abandon, and with genius.

One thing we need to do is to de-confuse—to make a distinction in—what it is that we do from what is actually powerful or effective. From time to time things work out for us. Most of us don't hold ourselves as masters because we spend a lot of time with things that don't work. And every now and then something works out. How we relate to things follows the same patterns of interaction over and over again. The way you relate to something is the way YOU relate to it. There is no power or expansion in the sense of learning, growing, or mastery there ... by definition. You can see it as a truth or a belief, but it's also so by definition—there is no expansion or growth or mastery in relating to something the same way that you relate to something. You're bringing your fixed conclusions and assumptions to the relationship, and that's the same activity again and again and again. So it's not expansion. It's not growing. It's not mastering anything. It's just repeating.

You need to get into mastery. If you want to get into the workability of something, you have to know what it is that you do that is NOT that. You have to know, admit, see, experience, be with, encounter what it is that you do that isn't effective.

The information you get will not do that. Just like the information that you've gotten throughout your study doesn't change a thing. It doesn't change the way you relate. If you relate differently than you did before, even if you had the same information that you have now, and there's a difference in the way you interact, that difference is some experiential learning. Notice that the difference is probably not huge. Probably for the most part you relate very similarly to the way you would have related a while ago. And maybe in some ways there have been real experiential changes, and that is the real learning; the rest is just information. What did you take into your being that shows up no matter what you think, know, feel, or remember? That's real learning. The rest is simply gathering information. So if you get something out of what I am saying today, the next year can be an even more transforming experience than this year has been.

Often we confuse real workability with "getting by"—what I've come to call "survival." In the getting by sense, it will always work out, until you die. You will get by, until you die. And then you'll probably get by that way. Sometimes we think we make things work out when we make things not work. Often we don't allow things to actually work out. When we get by with something, we "get by" it, and so to us the appearance is often similar to letting things work out, but actually the two are totally different.

Whatever you do is powerful. I'm not saying that it is necessarily very workable, but it's very powerful. You don't have any choice. You could use that power in many ways. You could use that power to lock yourself up in a closet and become a drunk. That might not be the most workable thing for being alive. We all have power simply because we are alive. But we abuse our power. When we engage someone or something, ninety-nine percent of the time we act out what we have powerfully created to survive—historical patterns.

Notice the power of being you. Pretty powerful. You started from scratch, pretty much. See what you did with it. Pretty powerful! I mean from nothing, that! Look what you did from nothing. It's pretty powerful. Dumb, but powerful. You put a lot of power into creating from nothing, THAT! THAT! THAT! THAT!

Pretty powerful, right? You didn't have to do that, like that, with that much power. But you did. And you're pretty good at it, aren't you? I mean hey, talk about tenacious strength! Take that and try to rip it apart! Damn near impossible, right? Pretty powerful, isn't it? Not necessarily that intelligent, but it's pretty powerful. Not necessarily that workable, but it's pretty powerful. And it will survive!

We survive our mind-set and point of view. What we are not awake to is the way we hold the world. You work hard at holding it . . . your own way. And you contend or you give up contending, which can be the same as contending. Perhaps effective interaction lies in not acting out old patterns. We do things generally the way we have always done them. You have to differentiate what is the result of beliefs and old patterns and what is genuine experience. How can you tell if you are fooling yourself? When you try to learn something, when you sweat it out and only move a little bit, this is a result of doing the same thing the same way every time.

Look into your experience as one who knows nothing. When you sweat it out, when you do it over and over and over again, and in the end it's basically the same as it was in the beginning, where is the transformation? When you're still doing the same thing, and what you say is that you were opening up, encountering it with your whole being, encountering it in a way to actually move, or transform, then probably you're wrong. When you actually encounter something as a being, you wake up to a different experience.

On the Nature of Communication

The following dialogues were taken from the beginning of a Communication Workshop in 1985 that was part of an intense series of seven consecutive weekend workshops on the nature of "Being."

The Question of Communication

PR: So, if we are talking about communication, what are we talking about? What is the subject that we are talking about?

If we want to contemplate grounding, we would first have to get what we're going to contemplate. What is grounding? If we started contemplating ice water and it had very little to do with grounding, it might take a long time to experience grounding.

So what are we talking about when we are talking about communication?

The "components" of communication? Ah, now we got it [laughs]. One: present time. Two: your being. Three: another being.... What? What is present time? What is your being? What is another being? What is a question?

There are a few questions here. Actually, I'm supposed to go over these more carefully and completely. So, consider it carefully, deliberately.... okay? However, the components of communication are not an experience of what communication is. Although they do seem useful at some level.

David: *I just want to say that it seems to me that you've gone over these carefully and deliberately, and the fact that we're going to do a whole weekend on communication, tells me that I don't know what communication is. Here I was thinking, "Boy, we spent all kinds of hours on communication, so now I know what it is and now I'm in communication!" I don't think that you would just arbitrarily put the Communication Workshop on this weekend. It seems to me that that says we need more work on it, and that I don't know what it is.*

PR: All right, thank you. I'm certain that by and large if you people wanted to do a workshop on communication you could do it without me. I am not certain you'd stay on purpose. I'm not certain you would continue to generate the intention for as many hours as we will when I'm here. But I am certain that you are totally capable of looking into the question and designing your own workshop. You have already gotten the ball rolling just fine.

So, we have components, but it doesn't tell us what communication IS. If I go into a method of consideration for these components and try to create the presence of them like an experience, that would be powerful, but what IS communication? We still don't know what communication IS.

Unless we do. Maybe we're in communication ALL the time. Maybe we're never in communication. Maybe we're in communication sometimes and not in communication sometimes. But if we don't know what communication is, we don't know if we're in it or not, do we?

In either case, what we're looking to do is set out to experience what communication IS, to have a direct experience of communication. For this group a direct experience has become such a burden and work that I can't use the word anymore. Tell somebody in this crowd to have a direct experience, and uh oh . . . [laughter], ughhh . . . [more laughter] . . . So we're not going to do that. We're here to experience what communication is, to be in the presence of communication.

Communication vs. Being at Effect

So let me ask you a question. Remember all the work we did about being "at the effect" of everything, when we talked about the domain of condition-effect? Does anybody not remember? [chuckles]

Do you remember that we confronted the probability that our entire experience may be nothing but effects? Remember those confrontations? Everybody can get that they are at the effect of something, now and again. Right? Like reacting to something someone says. At least that, right? If somebody sticks out their tongue at you, and you have a reaction, you would say "Okay, now I'm at effect." If somebody calls you a name, you notice you are at the effect of that when you feel badly. If you're going to ask your boss for a raise and you are standing outside the door, breathing heavily with sweaty palms, you get "yeah, I'm at effect." Those are clearly being at the effect. Right? [chuckles]

All: [in unison] Yes.

PR: Then we start to notice that effects don't have to be big emotional turmoil; it could be a little emotional turmoil, or it could be just a concept. It could be something that seems very mediocre and ordinary. We notice those are effects also. Then we might start noticing from moment to moment there's a lot of that going down. There is all that's called the "condition"—circumstances, events, this moment of cognition—and then there is our relationship to the condition. Something appears to be the case, and then a particular feeling arises. Something else appears, and there's another feeling, or a thought, a concept. Whatever arises in our cognition we are at the effect of it, we have a reaction to it, we are affected by it. So let me ask you a question: is communication possible in condition-effect?

Matt: *No.*

PR: How come?

Matt: *Because if it's all condition-effect and everything they get is just an effect, then they don't get your communication; they get an effect. They are always only getting their effect. If the same experience is going to be cognized by both people, then there has to be some place where you can get another's experience and not just effects. Then you can get the same communication.*

Long Dialogue I

PR: Anybody else?

James: *When Matt was talking I just had a thought. If you are at the effect of my effects, you are at least getting the effects. There's something happening here. It's not like I make it all up—well, I don't know, maybe I make it up—but it seems to me there's communication happening, but it's not purposeful. I have this concept of communication where we're communicating but we're always at effect ... and then there's communication where I am vulnerable and I communicate to you what is truly going on for me, and that's another kind of communication. But it seems to me that there is communication going on in condition-effect, because you're always getting something.*

PR: What am I in fact getting?

James: *If I make it all up ... [laughs] ... this is weird [laughter].... I'm confused—if I'm at the effect of what you're doing, is it something that I totally do myself? If it is, then communication doesn't matter. Or is it something which we do, in communication? Do I do something to you, you receive it, and give something back, or is it just me spinning stuff around? ... I don't know.*

PR: So, if you're doing the whole thing, or even if I'm doing it with you, do we call that communication?

James: *That was the thing I had in mind. I didn't know what communication was. Are there two different types of communication?*

PR: We have a computer up there. You put disks in it and something comes up on the screen and if you push the right buttons— the computer being hooked up to a typewriter—the typewriter starts printing ... like this [chattering sound]. It's really neat.

Now, is the computer in communication with the typewriter?

James: *It seems to me.*

PR: Okay. So what's going on that the computer is communicating with the typewriter? Why do you call that communication?

James: *It's getting information.*

PR: What's getting information?

James: *The typewriter is receiving information from the computer.*

PR: Is it?

James: *There's information in the computer and it's sending a signal to the typewriter.*

PR: What's actually going on? Do you mean that the typewriter is saying, "What was that? Okay, got it." [laughter] … "Am I doin' okay?" [more laughter]

James: *No.*

PR: No, that's not happening. So what is going on?

James: *The computer is sending stuff to the typewriter.*

PR: Does the computer decide to send commands to the typewriter?

James: *No, you did that by typing in the command.*

PR: Yes, so does the computer know the typewriter exists?

James: *Um, well, no.*

PR: Do you think that it cares?

James: *No.*

PR: Do you think that the typewriter knows that the computer exists? Do you think it cares?

James: *No.*

PR: Hmm, when the typewriter has activity happening. . . .

James: *Is this an analogy or is this for real?*

PR: For real. Let's say I have a device, you push the right buttons, and your experience is gotten across to the typewriter. Does the typewriter have any sense whatsoever of the distinction between your experience getting across to it and the computer's experience getting across to it? Do you think?

James: *No.*

PR: Or anybody else's experience, or anything else for that matter?

James: *No.*

PR: We wouldn't say that the typewriter had any experience at all, would we? There's not really any experience going on; all that is there is a condition and an effect, no experience. Like a charge in something which sets off something else, etcetera. It's just a whole system of trip hammers. Do we call that communication?

Do we call this communication? [bangs on chair] My hand hitting the, um, what's this called? Ah, chair [chuckles]. Am I communicating anything to the chair?

James: *No. I don't know what communication is, but there's something happening.*

PR: Something happening. Okay.... If something is happening, is that communication? Is that a definition of communication that would work? Something's happening [chuckles]? If suddenly a fan dismounted from the ceiling and crashed to the floor, would we say, "Hey, communication!"? We'd say something is happening, though.

James: *Yeah, something's happening. The chair is not getting anything. It's getting hit, but it's the chair's experience of getting hit.*

PR: For the chair there's not even a hand!

James: *Something is happening to the chair, but the chair isn't aware of it at all.*

PR: If my hand is hitting this [smacking sound], we'd say my experience is this sensation [same sound], right? The chair's experience is "that"—whatever is occurring upon getting hit. Where is *my* experience getting to the chair? I don't experience "that" and it doesn't experience this sensation . . . right?

James: *Yeah. . . .*

PR: If you're standing over there, and I'm standing over here looking out at a great sunset, and I have an effect called WOW . . . or something like that, since I'm receiving this great experience—would you say that we're in communication? You and I?

James: *You mean a shared experience?*

PR: No, no, no. You could have your head in the sand.

[laughter]

PR: I'm looking at the sunset, and something is coming to me; would you say that we're in communication?

James: *No.*

PR: So if all of a sudden I look up and you're displacing the sunset for me, and I have a "Oh wow," are we in communication? Are we in communication just because you happen to be what's in the way?

James: *No, I guess not.*

PR: So when are we in communication?

James: *Well, your experience is not communication unless it's something shared. It's something like, if I was a chair I would get the experience of you coming down, your fist and . . . your feeling of the fist. But I've never—maybe never—had a shared experience where I really know what's going on for someone else and they know what's going on for me—normally. I don't know what to say about what communication IS. It's not hitting the chair and it goes ouch, and it's not the fist or its motion.*

PR: Well ... is it all right with you that we say the chair doesn't get anything, that we're not going to communicate with the chair anyway.... Does that seem reasonable to you? That I don't communicate with the chair? There's no communication, it's just a vibration in the chair, or whatever it is, not communication. If the fan falls from the ceiling it's not communicating with the floor. It's hitting the floor. If it falls onto my head it's still not communicating to me. It's hitting my head. So isn't it the same thing for the computer and the typewriter? I mean, isn't the computer and the typewriter a more sophisticated form of the same event?

James: *How about when you and I are talking?*

PR: Yes, how about that? Is this a sophisticated event like the computer and the typewriter?

James: *I don't know what you're feeling.*

PR: Yes, that's what I'm saying. What do you think about that?

James: *All I know of is what happens for me.*

PR: So you say there's no communication.

James: *That's kind of hard to swallow because ... well, I get a little hit of something and then it disappears. Are we just an elaborate system of trip hammers? That makes sense, since I don't get what you are feeling. Then I try to back out ... but it's fuzzy.*

PR: You say it's kind of hard to swallow. Maybe it is hard to swallow. Maybe it's not true. Maybe it is true and it's just hard to swallow. Perhaps the truth is not dependent upon its swallowability. [laughter]

So, what are we talking about here? Maybe some real considerations are starting to arise about what we are talking about.

James: *My sense right now is that communication is when I get into the presence of your experience, or I'm having the experience of you experiencing me.*

PR: That's communication?

James: *Yeah, because it's the presence of you, not you in the sense of simply my effect ... more like you in the sense of presence.*

PR: That's good. Now, what if I told you that I'm a robot. I'm an exact replica of Peter Ralston, but I'm just a robot.

James: *It doesn't spoil it. ... In one sense it doesn't seem to matter.*

[laughter].

PR: Can you be in communication with the cup?

James: *Yes, in another way. I'm being available to the presence of it.*

PR: Why do you call that communication? What is the cup communicating to you?

James: *The cup is communicating cup.*

PR: And what do you communicate to the cup?

James: *Well, my being conscious of the presence of the cup is ... is bringing it into a reality, into my reality.*

PR: Why do you call that communication?

James: *It strikes me as "being with" it.*

PR: So if you are being with something it's communication?

James: *Yeah.*

PR: Sometimes you are "being with" a sensation in your body— is that communication?

James: *Yes.*

PR: So, what's communicating to what? Who is communicating to whom?

James: *Well, my cognition is within the realm of condition-effect. I know myself as a self, and that interferes with the power of my senses, since the effects dominate my experience, and when I'm not sensing outside of effect, I'm not in communication.*

PR: Let me step it down once. Do you hold that the computer is in communication with the typewriter?

James: *No, I don't.*

PR: Why?

James: *I hold that there's no experience of the presence of me in the typewriter. I have no experience of it having an experience of me, of itself, or of the computer.*

PR: Am I in communication with the chair?

James: *Well, what I would say about that is that you as a human have the capacity to be in the presence of the chair in a way that is different from the computer.*

PR: So could you be in communication with the computer?

James: *I could be in the presence of the computer as it is of itself.*

PR: Now, being in the presence of the computer as it is of itself— why do you call that being in communication?

James: *I don't know.*

PR: Isn't what you're getting cognized conditions that you're at the effect of, and that have meaning? There are words on the screen that have meaning—even that they are words, and then the object or computer itself has meaning and you hold it all a certain way, and feel a certain way about it, right? And you're saying this is the presence of the computer?

James: *Right.*

PR: If there is all of that meaning being applied, wouldn't that be a problem in getting the computer for itself?

James: *You could get all sorts of meaning, but I'm not calling that communication.*

PR: So, I want to make sure I'm following you. . . . As you're getting all of this meaning going on, what would you call that?

James: *I would call that going through a conceptual evaluation.*

PR: Can you get a sense of things in the domain of pre-conceptual evaluation? Is it like when you sit down and you see a computer—some glass and all those keys and things—is that what you're calling conceptual evaluation?

James: *No, I'm talking about simple perception and what comes out of it.*

PR: What comes out of it?

James: *The distinction I'm making is that there is something for me to experience. Let's say that I'm sitting in front of a terminal and it's just it—it's being a terminal. It doesn't mean anything as far as what it is doing; it's "doing" terminal.*

PR: I just want to make sure I'm clear. When you sit in front of a terminal, it's different than sitting in front of chalk, right?

James: *It is in terms of making a distinction that this object's not that object, but in terms of objects, it's not.*

PR: So you're not at the effect of the terminal?

James: *I wouldn't say that. I'd say that in that reality chalk and terminal both present themselves as objects . . . and that's all.*

PR: Okay. Now, where's the communication? Do you understand what I'm trying to clarify?

James: *In the fact that I'm experiencing something.*

PR: If you're sitting with a terminal, and what's happening is you have effects about it—there are some thoughts and feelings relating to the way you hold it—is that communication? Do you know what I'm saying?

James: *Yeah, yeah.*

PR: ... You like it, you don't like it?

James: ... *A sense of security, does it look good? If it does look good then "wow, it's shiny...."*

PR: ... And all that is effect, right? All that stuff is bouncing off over here as a result of the condition.

James: *Right.*

PR: Are you all following this Okay? ... Okay, so all that activity is going on, right? Now, would you say that that activity going on is being in communication with the terminal?

James: *No.*

PR: It's not the terminal, it's the effects.

James: *Right.*

PR: Okay, fine. So partly I wanted to get clear for you and partly I wanted to get clear for them, that that's not what we're talking about. Now, what we're talking about is the possibility that you can get the terminal, without effect, is that right?

James: *Yes.*

PR: So there's just the presence of the terminal and there's nothing over here related to that.

James: *Well, it's more like I would have the capacity to have that be what it is.*

PR: Do you? ... have the capacity for that to be only what it is? I mean, is that something that is here, are we talking about a probability or a possibility?

James: *I'm not certain it's here. I have not gotten to the point where I can disappear perception. In other words, I still see a terminal and I still have color and so on.*

PR: Okay, let's work with that for a moment. So what we're talking about looks like it's outside of the normal way we hold condition-effect, doesn't it?

James: *Yes.*

PR: So, outside of the normal way we hold condition-effect—we could say outside of condition-effect, but I want to leave open the possibility that it's not. If we say outside condition-effect, then we're talking about communication as being outside of condition-effect. Remember, that is the original question that I asked. Just to make sure we're following all of this, the original question I asked was: "Is it possible to have communication in condition-effect?" So far we've gotten a lot of "no's," that it is not possible, and a lot of I-don't-knows.

All right, so here we are with a terminal, or a cup, or whatever, and let's say we could get to pure perception, what I call real perception. Okay? That is, we get to experience it—not at the effect of it, but at the experience of it—so that the only thing that is there is the thing-itself.

Let me ask you: Why do you call that communication?

James: *It just brings me back to the sense of being capable of joining with the presence of something.*

PR: Okay. [Peter picks up an object and stages a puppet show] . . . [laughter] . . . [more laughter and applause].

See, now dig it. This is a lot of fun and I love this one because you always buy it. You go right into it and think you are really communicating with this thing. Isn't it cute? [laughter] . . . It's cute, let me tell you . . . [more laughter]. . . .

James: *. . . And what I'm saying is that?*

PR: Possibly.

James: *That what you're doing. . . .*

PR: What I'm doing is a dramatization. See, I suspect that in large part we are doing something like that. Obviously this object isn't walking and talking, but you give it that. You say you're in union. Now let me ask you this: What's here that you don't give it?—question one. Two: What is *its* experience?

James: . . . ?

PR: I'll ask it another way. What is it experiencing?

James: *That's a very powerful way for me to hold that question—what is it experiencing? I have a sense of that question. So I would say: itself, it is experiencing itself, but to me that implies that it has self-consciousness and is able to be in the presence of itself.*

PR: Does it?

James: *I have self-consciousness as a being. I think it resides somewhere more in human beings. . . .*

PR: Okay. So first of all you hold that this doesn't have a self-consciousness. If it doesn't have self-consciousness, then its experience is actually nothing. Isn't it?

James: *Its experience of itself?*

PR: Right.

James: *Yeah.*

PR: So do you experience nothing in relationship to this?

James: *Well, actually if we go to the first question, yes—the first question being, what is there that I don't give to this.*

PR: . . . Is in fact nothing. So you don't experience anything that this actually *is.*

James: *I would have to say yes.*

PR: So how come you say you're in communication when you aren't experiencing anything?

James: *Well, now holding it that way, it's like I'm in communication with my own experience and not that.*

PR: If this did have self-consciousness, you wouldn't know about it, right? So, why would you say you're in communication with this, then? Isn't it clear that either way it's hard to say you're in communication with it?

James: *Yes.*

PR: That either you're getting its experience, not what you give to it, or it has an experience and you don't know what that is?

James: *Right.*

PR: So far it looks to me like we are on pretty shaky grounds to say we're in communication with this thing.

James: *Yes.*

PR: But let's continue. . . . Say you experience its experience. Let's just say that there is no experience, and you get its no-experience. Why would you call that communication?

James: *That's where I have that sense. . . . Well, I don't know why I would call that communication.*

PR: Let me ask you another question. If I locked you away in a dungeon with a terminal, and you spent your time relating to this terminal, do you think over time that you would get the sense that you are really deeply in communication with this terminal?

James: *No.*

PR: What's missing?

James: *Well, I do not consider it to be a living thing. It also doesn't have the capacity to experience me.*

PR: It is similar to this discussion, right?

James: *Yes. So even an experience of the thing as itself would not be communication, since there is no mutual experience of one another.*

PR: We could call that getting its experience, or getting the presence of it-itself.

James: *Yes, yes!*

PR: But not necessarily communication. Do you notice how far down the line we've come from where we were in the beginning of this dialogue?

James: *Yes.*

PR: Great, what else?

James: *Nothing, that's all I have.*

PR: Thank you.

So, the two questions floating around the floor are: "What is communication, what are we talking about?" We've kind of kicked that one around and have gotten into the ballpark, we've narrowed it down. Actually, if you've all been paying attention we've narrowed it down quite a bit, like we've really gotten on top of it. The other question was: "Can communication exist when we are being at the effect of whatever is occurring? Is there communication in condition-effect?" And we've played with that for a while.

Short Dialogues

PR: Okay, so did you all get that?

Maggie: *With the kids that I work with who are deaf and have a hard time speaking, I really have to want to get what they are saying. I don't have any attachment to it, mostly; I just want to serve them or help them get what they want in terms of basic needs—food or going to the bathroom or something like that—and I was trying to think, "Was that just condition-effect manipulation?" I was thinking no, in some cases when I was relating to a child who was trying to sign something to me I really wanted to get what they were telling me and that was it. And I really felt when we were in communication it was like, "Yeah, lets go eat dinner" or let's go do whatever. And I didn't feel anything, except I was really glad that they gave their experience to me and that I could get it.*

PR: Good, thank you.

David: *Well, whatever it is, I haven't been doing it, and I get along. I'm not doing real well, but I'm certainly surviving....*

PR: Hi, David. [laughter] You're just that kind of guy, I guess. Yes, go ahead, I didn't mean to interrupt you.

David: *Also, your being alive doesn't seem to have anything to do with what I've got going on at all. Because you're being alive doesn't matter, to me. I mean, there's not a whole lot of difference to me.*

PR: Great, thank you. Is that it?

David: *Yeah.*

PR: Okay, Something over here?

John: *David's communication reminded me of an experience I had with David. We were doing a diad together and it was very clear to me that I experienced him and his capacity to experience me, and that he experienced that also and we were absolutely in communication. I don't know what that is, and I don't remember if it was a process in which we were even saying anything. I have no memory of that at all. All I have is getting him, the presence of him, and him very clearly getting the presence of me, and my getting the presence of him getting the presence of me. It was very clear and there was no need to do anything and no need to stop doing that. And when the exercise was over we stayed in communication. It was a very powerful and real experience of each other. I'd say that's communication.*

PR: Okay. Thank you.

Long Dialogue II

Alisia: *It seems to me that hitting the chair can be a form of communication.*

PR: So are you saying there are two kinds of communication—this is one kind of communication and that is another?

Alisia: *Yes, and I do that kind of communication—hitting a chair—with other people and call it communication.*

PR: And that may be exactly what is going on, and you call that communication. But I want you to watch something. I'm going to use two hands.... I'll put this hand here on the chair [hits his hand with his other fist and shakes the chair]. What's going on in my experience that actually gets to the chair?

Alisia: *The force?*

PR: As far as me and my experience is concerned, what gets to the chair? I don't experience the force; I experience this [thumping sound]. So as far as my experience goes, what gets to the chair?

Alisia: *... I don't understand what you are saying.*

PR: Okay. Let me do the sunset again. If I'm looking at a sunset and you're looking at me ... or whatever, it doesn't make any difference, you're reading a book. I'm looking at the sunset and I have something going on in relation to the sunset. Are we in communication?

Alisia: *We're not in communication, but you are communicating?*

PR: With what? The sunset?

Alisia: *... Nothing.*

PR: I'm communicating with nothing? Why would you call that communication? Do people looking at a sunset call that communication?

Alisia: *When they go and talk about it, yeah.*

PR: Then they are talking about it and they call THAT communication, but not looking at it itself, they don't call that communication, do they? They call that having an experience or something. We call it being at the effect, right? We have some effect pop up from this condition out here. So if what's coming to me is an effect, how is that any different than if you and I are just passing what we call information back and forth, and what I do is get an effect and you get an effect?

Alisia: *It's not.*

PR: I'm going to suggest something. I want to suggest [hits chair—thumping sound] that there's nothing over there [thumping sound] that's the same as what's over here [thumping sound]. I mean, right about here, let's say [where his hand touches the chair] [thumping sound] the experiences are completely different. See? It's like there's something here [points at his hand] and then there's something else there [points at chair], and this isn't this, see?

Alisia: *That's what I hold all communication to be.*

PR: Right! This is true, I suspect. What I'm suggesting is that— that's what you hold all communication to be. Obviously I'm suggesting that is not communication. If what's here isn't over there, why call that communication? What's being communicated?

Alisia: *Well, the communication's just that contact.*

PR: So when this fan falls down on the floor and makes contact, it's in communication with the floor?

Alisia: *Yeah, but I was thinking of this as two people.*

PR: Whatever, I don't care if they are two rocks.

Alisia: *NO! You can't have two rocks in communication. I don't feel that two rocks are in communication just because they are bumping into each other.*

PR: You just told me that it's communication if the fan fell on the floor ...

Alisia: *No, it was an analogy of communication.*

PR: Okay, what's the difference then between the fan falling on the floor and two people doing the same thing? One person falling on another person?

Alisia: *The difference is that the people are alive.*

PR: And?

Alisia: *Perceive.*

PR: And?

Alisia: *That's all.*

PR: So because they are alive and perceive, that is communication, and if they are not alive and they don't perceive, it's not communication?

Alisia: *Um hmmm, yes.*

PR: Ah! So if what goes on over here is the effect of what goes on over there, and there is nothing shared, you call it communication because there's something happening.

Alisia: *Mm hmmm.*

PR: So this is communication simply because there is something happening. So when there is something happening with what we call living beings, that's communication?

Alisia: *Yes.*

PR: What is a living being? Is an effect living?

Alisia: *No.*

PR: It's not? ... I agree with you, it's not. See, if it's not living then how can we hold this to be true? If effect is not living and all that is here is condition and effect, this is still non-living activity even if you say there are living beings partaking of it. And if there are living beings that happen to be perceiving it, and what's going on is condition-effect, why do you say that just because they perceive, they are in communication? What does communication have to do with my looking at a sunset? I'm not in communication when I'm looking at a sunset, but there's an effect, there's condition-effect going on.

Alisia: *I'm not saying that all effects are communication.*

PR: Simply because it's with a person—see this is the argument that you have to hear—that simply because you say it's a person, you say you're in communication. And I'm saying that what's going on is you're in condition-effect. You agree. You are perceiving the effect of some condition, you've agreed. You say that effects aren't living and that only perception indicates life, so this whole thing is based on the fact that you simply say it is a living person, therefore everything that you're at the effect of must mean something is communicated. And I'm suggesting that that might not be true.

I'm suggesting that there's a great similarity to looking at a sunset, getting pissed on by a dog, or getting hit by a fan. That it's where you're at in reaction to it that determines your experience. That what you perceive is your own effect, and has nothing to do with what experience is over there or whether or not it is a living being out there. It makes no difference ... like the kid said over here, when he suggested it makes no difference if there are living beings out here. It really doesn't, and the only reason that they are called living beings is because you say they are living beings. It works and it's fine, but it makes no difference. I mean, I'm at the effect of this when I'm not in communication and I'm at the effect of this when I say I'm in communication. What difference does it make? It's my effect, that's what's going on here.

Okay. So I want you to take a look at whether there are two kinds of communication or there's something we "call" communication that's not, and then there's communication.

The Truth vs. Manipulation

PR: Now I want you to consider that we're actually very habitually into all kinds of manipulations in our experience, as well as our communication and the form of our communication, and most people aren't up to hearing that yet. That we can actually "lie" by having thoughts and feelings. That we lie through manip-

ulating our own experience. For example, consider what you
ignore or what you avoid, what you allow yourself to think, how
and why you produce feelings, how you distract yourself with
emotions. Consider that this is possible. As matter of fact, that
it's done habitually, it's done a lot. You do that a lot. You don't
just alter your communication, you feel something *as* a manipulation and then of course act in relation to that feeling, and say
it's the truth—since it's really there. If you manipulate the experience you can say it is really what is so for you, what you are
experiencing.

David: *I would have to have had some experience of telling the truth,
or have had something in the area of experiencing the truth, in order
to know that it's possible. If what you're now saying is true. . . . I suppose I had a suspicion that such a thing was going on, but without the
experience of it. Certainly it's a lot easier to ignore the possibility, or
deny that it is possible at all to have had the experience of the truth.
How am I going to know?*

PR: Well probably . . . you were lying about it. Probably you have
some experience of what the truth is—like you say, you suspect
it already, you had a sense of it already—and you just lied about
it. We do that. And your lie seems straight up. You've got a good
rationale for it; it's very logical. So something that is very logical
and rational must be the truth, right? We have the reasons and
explanations all laid out, so it's got to be the truth. It makes sense.
And there's nothing that exists that can't be the truth, right?
Nobody said . . . well, probably a lot of people said . . . but somebody didn't say . . . that the truth had to be rational or make sense
or be logical or linear. The truth just has to be the truth. See, rational and linear and logical may perform a different function. The
truth is the truth, and those are functions for something else. So
the truth may or may not fit in there.

So when you tell me the truth, it has got to be *as is*, the experience has got to be as it *is*, doesn't it? You've got to get it across
as it is. So what comes across over here can't be different than

what is over there, otherwise you wouldn't call it the truth. You couldn't withhold something or manipulate something.... So intention also seems to be an issue; you have to have the intention that you're going to communicate the truth.

So let me talk to you about a couple of ways we're very clever, diagrammatically—not diagrammatically clever—I'm going to talk to you diagrammatically—about being very clever about lying. One, you give someone symbols from which you know they will produce the wrong experience. You know where they're at, you get a sense of where they're at, or whatever—I'll just use the word "know"—and that they are going to produce the wrong experience if given those symbols. It's all factual, it's all the right symbols; you can say honestly, "Well, those symbols agree with my experience." But you know that they are going to reproduce another experience. They are not getting your experience. You don't intend for them to; you're not really communicating with them. You just give them the symbols so that they produce a different experience. You can even give them all the "right" symbols. All of the pieces are there. But they produce another experience with it, and you know they are going to do that. That's very clever. You ever watch yourself do that?

All: [nervous laughter]

PR: I know you've all done it. I don't know that you are all conscious of it, though.

Integrity and Communication

PR: Telling the truth comes from and makes real the experience of being whole and complete. Integrity. I'll say that again.

Telling the truth comes from the experience of being whole and complete. Telling the truth makes real the experience of being whole and complete. Telling the truth comes from and makes real the experience of being whole and complete, the experience of integrity.

Liz: *If I tell the truth, it threatens my sense of survival. The reason I tell the truth at all is because I think that if I can survive it and get past the pain of telling the truth then I'll feel better.*

PR: It might be true that if you keep telling the truth and keep surviving telling the truth, that you might also start feeling better. The effect might occur that you start feeling better. But if you try to tell the truth again, and again, and again, and again, usually what you do is just back down. "Oh, forget it. Haven't I told the truth enough? Is there no end to this?"

[laughter]

PR: Perhaps sometimes we tell the truth so we can feel better. But predominantly we are at odds with telling the truth, it's an ordeal that we have to go through, it's a threat to our egoic survival. If it is something that will make us more effective or feel better then we may want to do it, but just once in a while. It's as if we would like to tell the truth about ourselves and then just lock it away in a box or a safe and be done with it. In this way we aren't continuously threatened by it, and we can still manipulate our communication to serve various ends.

The Communication Is Not the Form

PR: Communication is other than the form. Communication implies more than the form.... Experience also implies other than the form ... and not another form than the form. So do you get that implication?

Matt: *Ooooo! [smacking sound]*

[laughter]

PR: Anybody else get that implication?

[more laughter]

PR: So, does anybody not get that?

Bob: *Well, I got it but I wonder if I got it superficially. I just thought that experience isn't what the condition looks like; it's what you experience. I mean, you said that the experience isn't the form the experience takes, and so my first thought is what it looks like, like when you are swimming.*

PR: Okay, so we have it that the experience of swimming is other than the form of swimming, other than the posture and the movement—that's an interesting distinction. So the experience of swimming isn't the form of swimming. How we usually hold that is that the experience of swimming is the perception of swimming, or the sensation of swimming. If we hold perception or sensation as form, perceptive form, then what else is there? . . . What is the experience of the perception sensation . . . what is the experience of swimming that isn't itself the sensation or the perception of swimming? That is different than the form of swimming, and the form of the perception of swimming?

Bob: *Right now I can't answer that. I'm just feeling more and more abstract forms. . . . Like exactly the way you describe it—the muscular experience of being the swimmer, the emotional experience of being a swimmer, all of the senses, not just visual forms. . . .*

PR: Right, so the emotional experience, the sensations—all perceived experiences, in other words—and your reactions to them, let's call all of that "form." So then what is the experience of that? We commonly say experience is the sensation, or the emotions, or the physical sensation. What's the experience of what we call experience, when we call all of that the form?

Bob: *Emotional reaction?*

PR: But that's at the effect of what we're calling the occurring event, it's later than . . . like in relationship to . . . I have an emotional reaction to it, but I'm talking about the experience itself.

Bob: . . . *I guess I'm always interpreting it, so I can't get a handle on it.*

PR: Okay, I can imagine you can't get a handle on it. What's the way we get a handle on things, how do we handle them?

Bob: *You observe them and look for a handle.*

PR: Yes, you look for a handle [laughter], right? So in looking for a handle we have to find something. We have to find some "thing" as distinguished from other things that we can "grab." And generally we find some thing that we can take with us, so to speak. So we call that a handle. I have a handle on it. See? So you don't want something that will slip out of your hands, because then you wouldn't call it a handle. Right? You've found something and then—whoosh—you lose it; you wouldn't call that a handle. You'd call it something else, slipperiness—those are all analogies.

I suggest the way we do that is conceptually and rationally. That's how we get a handle on things. I'm suggesting that what I'm asking you about now concerning experience—and I'll get back to communication in a minute, but I think this is a good probe into experience—doesn't lend itself to "handleability." It doesn't lend itself to anything that carries on, since it doesn't. It "is" only in the present moment. It doesn't carry on. Experience just "is."

So we look for a handle on experience. It's almost like looking for a handle on what you call the experience, all the forms— the movement, the posture, the emotion, the thought—what is it that's having that experience? When we ask that question we're not even clear on what experience is, right? What you do is put your attention on the forms of your experience. When we're saying what is it that is having your experience, usually what we're asking is, what is it that is aware—of the forms that we're cognizing? What is it that is cognizing or formulating our experience?

We would say that your experience of swimming is different than my observation of your postures, or your movement. Superficially that is pretty easy to get. Then if we ask, what is implied that is completely other than the form, what shows up? Well, you might say, "An experiencer is implied, one who is experiencing, or someplace the experiencing is being or taking place." Yet that gets tricky because what is implied other than the form? What's implied other than something? What is implied other than all that is perceived as there, all that is distinguished as there? All of that is showing itself as something. It has to show itself as something, doesn't it? It must show itself as something in particular. And that's contrasted to something other than particular. Even if it's an infinite in-particular.

So . . . experience actually looks a lot like nothing. When you look for something, that's down the line. At cognition experience looks like or is recognized more like nothing. Now there's a distinction I want to make. I already did that. See? It looks like nothing . . . it looks like nothing! It smells like nothing, tastes like nothing, feels like nothing.

All of that is not the communication! Communication implies more than the form. Communication implies other than the form. It's a great way to get to experience.

Bob: *I'm having a hard time distinguishing . . . well, that's not true. I want to say that I get that communication isn't an object. . . . I don't get that communication isn't a form. And I did. You're making a distinction between not being an object and not being a form.*

PR: Yes, communication doesn't appear to be an object. Where is the object communication? Show me the object, show me the thing that is communication. Bite on that for a moment object fans. Where is the "thing" that is communicating? See? You can't find it. [laughter] Communication isn't an object, obviously. Now this brings up that I might be saying that it's also not something that isn't an object. It's not even that! In other words, it's not even the intangible somethings that aren't objects. Okay?

Bob: *I just don't get that. I could be making that distinction but I don't believe you. Communication "has" to be a form.*

PR: Why?

Bob: *I hold that if I'm communicating, or receiving a communication, I have to know what it is, and I don't know what no-form is, therefore ... [laughs]....*

PR: Okay, but what is it you are saying you're communicating—knowing what is? Is communication something communicated?

Bob: *No.*

PR: So what do you know? Do you know communication or do you know something communicated?

Bob: *I suppose something communicated.*

PR: Yes, like an experience, which is also not an object.

Bob: *Right.*

PR: An object is perceived, not communicated. Get it? The rock got it too, right? [laughter]

So an object is perceived, not communicated. Perhaps it's received by you but that's not communication. If we say I'm communicating something by throwing an orange at you; is it the orange that is the communication? No. So the orange thrown at you, being the thing gotten, say, implies something other than orange, doesn't it?

Bob: *Yes.*

PR: If it doesn't imply something other than orange, all it implies is orange! You go to an orange tree, you walk over and there's an orange flying by [laughter]. An orange hit me in the head, and that's all. Right? You just had an orange hit you in the head over there. So if you say that's communication, or symbolic of the communication, then that implies something else, something other than the orange.

First of all, you have a hard time with that, right away. "What do you mean, something that's not an object? Well, of course my thoughts and my feelings aren't objects, but kind of ... they "exist" somewhere and they're about so big and stuff like that...." But notice that they aren't that way—they appear that way. That's how they appear to you. They appear as somewhere, right? But where? You notice that when you look into it, you are not clear on where they appear somewhere. So you say they appear "in my head" or something like that. Because you can't find them. So you say they are not an object, but they appear as some form or other, but not as an object. I want you to challenge that. They are not an object, not even subtly. So, in communicating an experience something is recognized as a result of the experience that takes place with another.

Bob: *I just realized that I hadn't been making the distinction of not perceived or pre-perception experience. I had been holding that somehow it was something there like an experience that I feel, or see.*

PR: Yes, cognition, or perception . . . experience being communicated, kind of like an orange, but not. You getting my experience is like you getting the orange. Is communication the experience?

Bob: *I don't think so.*

PR: Is communication any more the experience than the orange is?

Bob: *No.*

PR: Did I say that right? Is the experience any more communication than the orange is?

Bob: *Not that either.*

PR: Not that either, Okay. So then you are saying communication implies other than the form. See, communication might not even be a process.
    What did you say?

Bob: *I said I couldn't distinguish a non-objective form from no form at all. I could only hold communication as a non-objective form.*

PR: Clear now?

Bob: *Well, I'm clear that ... wow, it's really not what I think. That I don't distinguish experience OR communication. Not really, not experientially.*

PR: Do you get that it implies other than the form? You say you perceive the blackboard. Now, other than perception—unless you are one of the people walking down Telegraph Avenue mumbling to themselves—other than perception you say you are not communicating with this [blackboard]. Unless you say perception is communication, but let's not do that. You would say you're not communicating with this, wouldn't you?

Bob: *Right.*

PR: How come?

Bob: *I don't get its experience.*

PR: Right, you don't get its experience. What "this" implies to you is itself, period. You call it inanimate. You call it inanimate because it doesn't imply anything other than the object. What you call animate implies something other than the object. Otherwise you'd call it inanimate.

"Who" implies something other than the form. Communication implies other than the form. If all of a sudden this thing started communicating to you, or you started getting experience coming from this, you would go aaagh!! Besides that that's weird, it's other than the form, right? It implies a distinction of other than the object. I mean, all the way down the line! It implies the creator of experience, or the communicator of the experience, which is where the experience is coming from, ergo, creator of the experience, which you can't find! You can't find it in form! ... Try! [soft laughter]

Bob: *"Who" is a distinction between inanimate and...?*

PR: ... Animate, yes. That's wild isn't it? Now about animate ... don't make the mistake that we do, and say ah! that's the "thing" that's animate. There's some "thing" hanging out in there! What thing is hanging out in there? All the things you'll find hanging out in there are the same, just other forms. Even the intangible forms are other forms. They are things expressed ... they are things seen, perceived, "known." They themselves imply other than they themselves. All of it. They themselves imply other than they themselves. Hmm? Thoughts, feelings, emotions, don't they imply other than they themselves? So I'm suggesting that communication implies other than the form.

It's very simple, you just look at this [bangs the wall]. It doesn't imply other than the form.... Does anybody not get this? It's very simple, it's ultra-simple. It's so obvious that it's miss-able. If you think about it, you've lost it already.

Being and Communication

PR: Now I want to ask a new question. What is it that is communicating? And what is it that's receiving your experience? Do you get that? Great. Now, knowing that I'm speaking in that mode, what is it that's having an experience? What is it that is communicating to what? What is it that you're communicating to?

Liz: *Oh god!*

[laughter]

PR: What is it, first of all? What's communicating to what? Okay? Now I'm going to say it in a strange way. What is it that's communicating to whatever it is that it's communicating to?

Simply considering the matter of communication brings up such powerful stuff. How is communication possible? If you don't take it for granted, but look deeply into it, how is it possible for communication to take place? For the experience of one to be received by, experienced by, another? What does this say about the nature of being?

Does this stuff excite you as much as it does me? I suspect if it doesn't excite you as much as it does me, you may not be actually in the experience of it. It's pretty exciting stuff. [laughter]

What Is Enlightenment?

This communication was taken from a talk given by Peter Ralston to Level One Apprentices in 1981.

A Direct Experience Isn't an "Experience"

Somebody asked, "What is enlightenment?" So I thought I would come by and talk about it a little bit. There is a lot of confusion around the issue of enlightenment, so I will share with you some of the things I've encountered. I thought it might be useful.

Usually we think of enlightenment as something like a state, something to get to, and when we get to it everything will be great. So I want to acknowledge that notion, not challenge it or destroy it, but put it aside. That's not what I want to talk about tonight. I want to talk about the possibility of directly experiencing something—an enlightenment experience. I don't want to talk about anything else.

What is a direct experience? I would like you to listen to this experientially. Begin by getting a sense of you. Get a sense of you "inside there." Now I would like you to get a sense of the "in"ness of you. You know, that inner quality of you, the one you call *"you."*

Where are you?

You usually say you're "in there" somewhere. You're "in" something, somewhere. Well, I want you to start to open up a little bit and get the sense that you don't know where you are, where you're "in." There's the sense you are somewhere, but you don't know where it is, you don't know where that is.

You figure you're not in here [points to briefcase] because you don't know what's in there. You figure you're not in here [points to his own body] and you're not in there [points to his cup]. You're kind of "in-there" somewhere [waves his hand at them]. The closest place you have to refer to is your body. It's like you're in there. I want you to get a sense of "that" in there. Not to worry too much about if that is really where the "in-there" is, just that it seems to be in somewhere. You seem to be somewhere inside your body. I want you to look at that sense. The one you call "I."

Take a look and see if it's not true that that sense, that in-there sense, goes back as far as you can remember. There has always been an in-there sense as far back as you can remember, and so you suspect that it was there before you can remember, or assume it must have been. It seems to go way back—this sense of you. It has as one of its main qualities the sense of being exclusive. By exclusive I mean it's not in here [banging on briefcase]. In other words, it doesn't include being in here, does it? Make sure you know where it's not. It's not in the briefcase; it seems to be exclusive. But I mean really exclusive, like it's over there, not in here [points to his own body]. It's not in here, it's over there, and it has always been that way. It has always been that way as far back as you can remember. Isn't that true?

So, imagine this—this is very simple—that the possibility of a direct experience is the possibility that that in-there sense could actually and directly be in the same place as something else. In the presence of something else, or in the presence of itself.

So far this doesn't have a lot of power to it—what I just said. So now we have to look at it in a way to which you can relate, a way that has some power to it. Imagine, if you will, the possibility of that in-there sense actually feeling . . . well, how about the sense of being crowded, like there's company. Imagine the inward sense having company. But not company like right next to the inward sense, but *in* there, in the same place! That's company. That sounds a little strange. It is. It should sound strange. But we have to start somewhere.

Just imagine that. Imagine that, really. What would it be like for that inwardness, that "you"ness to have company? Imagine that just a bit, right now. Just sit there and imagine that very "you"ness having company. Not like you are in one half of your body and the company is in the other half of your body, and you are squished. Not like that. But like the inward sense is partaking of the same space with another sense which isn't different from the inward sense. When I start talking like that, I start to lose you, right? So, imagine you have company. Just do that for a second.

Imagine, if you will, that you want to directly experience something in here [banging the briefcase]. Perhaps you want to directly experience my watch, or maybe this [holds up a used teabag] . . . well, probably not [laughter]. How would you do that? How would you directly experience something? Ah, my cup. How would you directly experience my cup? Well, as long as it's "out here," you don't know what's "in" here. It ain't in-there, it ain't wherever you are. So direct experience refers to there not being a different place where the experience is from the experiencer. The cup is experienced. So, think about it in the sense that we would then have to have the cup in-there, or the you-in-there out here. But, if you were out here then you would be in-here. If the in-there was out here, it would still be in-there, so to speak. Remember, we don't really know where in-there "is." We don't know what it's "in" anyway, but whatever that in-there is, or wherever it is, it would have to be the same as the cup. The experience of the cup. Not in-there's experience of the cup out here. But the cup's experience of the cup being the same as in-there.

So we could call that a direct experience; there is no this and that. See? Let's have the cup represent the "in-there." [Holds the cup next to a watch.] Now, the cup's in-there is experiencing the watch. It is "this" looking at the watch, the cup looks at the watch. You see? It's like a reference point. Oh, but now if it was a "direct" experience it would have to be more like they would occupy the same place [moves as if to put the watch in the cup]—this is an analogy; don't take it seriously. If you did take it seriously you might fall in the water. This talk could get my watch wet. I'll only go so far with analogies. [laughter]

Now, we could put our attention on having a direct experience of the cup here and see if we could do it. Another thing we could put our attention on is having a direct experience of you, like the in-there. But you don't know where you are, you don't know where the in-there is. You don't have a direct experience of the in-there; you have a "sense" of in-there. And that's kind of indirect in a funny way, isn't it? So there is the possibility of having a direct experience of the in-there. Of "I." There is the possibility of having a direct experience of another, of an object, life, or what anything is. Am I making any sense?

Q: *Excuse me, I had a question. This morning you were talking about outreaching. I was wondering if you were talking about outreaching as experiencing another person? I don't see that as the same, but is it a similar sense of experiencing another? In other words, a direct experience?*

PR: No.

Q: *So they're different.*

PR: Right. You are talking about "perceiving" another. That's not what I was talking about. You are talking about perceiving another, very simply, very directly, perception-wise, but they are still held as outside of you, right? Both your own inner-sense and the other are held as outside of you. You see? "You" are held as outside of you. Do you know what I mean? You don't like to say that because what's the use of saying such a thing? You don't go around saying, "I don't know where I am." You say, "I am here." You see? Direct experience has nothing to do with perception. It has nothing to do with experience. It has nothing to do with cognition. It has nothing to do with the senses or making sense. See?

The Context of "I"

Q: You just said it doesn't have anything to do with experience, and yet you are talking about direct experience.

PR: It has nothing to do with language. We are using metaphors that can only be cognized in perception. In other words, everything we are doing is indirect. Anything we are talking about now is not being talked about *as* it. It is analogous.

So, what would happen if I experienced I? If I on the one hand experienced I on the other hand? This isn't experiencing I. This is I holding itself as outside of I, experiencing what is held as outside but called I. Looking back at itself, like that. I experiencing itself is I experiencing itself. So there is no I experiencing I. If "I" experiences I, that's indirect. That's what we do already. We get these vague notions and feelings and qualities, and identify sensations and thoughts, etcetera.

There isn't a "me" in direct experience. For example, when I experience the cup it is indirect in that there is I and then there is the cup—do you understand? But, if there is a direct experience, then there's no distinction between "I" and "the cup," right? So then you would say I isn't different than the cup. You would say that there is no I. When "I" directly experiences the cup, it doesn't show up like a perception of the cup. It's a perception of the cup when it's experienced indirectly.

I want you to understand that we are talking about something that is not possible [laughter]. It's not impossible, either. You see, we think our whole world is I. Our whole world is held in the context of an objectified I. You are somebody, you are doing something, you are thinking, you are feeling, you are living, you are frightened, you are happy, you are getting something, you are losing something, you are surviving, you are eating, you are perceiving the rug, you are walking down the street, you are looking at the cup, you are listening to somebody talk. It's all always that way. It's held in the context of I. And it's even worse than that.

We hold that this *is* I. Like, for example, for you, I am your thoughts and feelings and perceptions—yet all that stuff is you. So you see, I *am* you, aren't I? Don't you think about me sometimes? Notice you have a certain relationship to me, you look at me. You have thoughts, you have perceptions. Where is that going on? You say it's over here, that's what *you* say. You see? I am suggesting that our life "is" I. Mostly, that's how we live it. All that goes on is assessed in terms of I and done in relation to I. More than just your thinking and your feeling and the "I am this and I am that," or playing a role, etcetera. Open it up a little bit. It's not just this petty stuff that goes on in-there; I'm saying it's also the stuff out here. This is what you say it is.

If our entire world is dependent on I, our entire world is seen as I. I is the context for all that is. Then a direct experience is certainly a ridiculous thing, and a direct experience is certainly impossible, right? There is no I in a direct experience. You see, there is no thing experiencing itself, there is no thing separating itself and observing something—it's direct. I am not talking about a direct feeling, or a direct sensation, or an emotional encounter—I am talking about a direct experience.

The word "experience" doesn't really apply. No inward sense, no outward sense. A direct experience of you is you, but not "you." It's whatever's there. Now it gets tricky because we don't know where "there" is. So, when I say there, I am speaking loosely. And when I say whatever, I am speaking loosely. And when I say you, I am speaking loosely. I am just speaking loosely. But do you see what I am saying?

I can imagine what you're thinking: "Let's see, I can kind of rationalize that, I understand what he's saying" or, "I don't understand what he's saying." Trying to find a place to put it doesn't put it anywhere. Behind all of that mental activity there might be a kind of resistance to it—even just the notion of it. Not resistance to the fantasy—the fantasy is nice, right? For most of us the possibility of enlightenment is really kind of nifty keen! "You mean I could not suffer anymore! Whoa!" That's one of the things that goes along with the rap . . . you too could not suffer. "Have you been suffering? Do you exist as a human, having a hard time with life? Well, enlightenment is for you!"

Q: *Ever sell used cars? [laughter]*

PR: In your fantasy of enlightenment, there is no more suffering. It is only bliss and joy, true freedom. Freedom from life and death. Ever read that one?

The Context of Time

Q: *Is it impossible, from the nature of enlightenment, to sustain enlightenment?*

PR: It's impossible to have it. See, this is where it gets tricky. I think I can say yes. I think I can say yes, it is impossible to sustain it, but there is no sustaining necessary, because it doesn't exist. It is not some thing that exists in time. There is no time in which something is and is and is. It is not a thing. What "is" in time? Some thing. The only thing that is in time is something that you can say it was and it is. Right? And how do you say it was and it is? It can't be in time unless you can say something like, it has been here. You have to identify it. It has been here a long time, it has been here a short time. It's this. It wasn't here before, it's here now. Do you see what I'm saying? If it was something to get as a thing in time, we would have to say it wasn't here before, and now it is. If it wasn't here before, and now it is, then it would have to be something. Wouldn't it? It would have to be something that wasn't here before and now it is, and is sustained, and could go away. You would then have to get it back. That's something, isn't it? Because it has the possibility of going away, coming back, not being here, or being here and carrying on—that's all the rules for something in time.

Q: *But isn't it like that? Someone has a direct experience, say, in a workshop—they have a direct experience in a diad. They are experiencing another person directly and then it goes away and they never experience it again. Isn't that something that existed in time, existed for a certain amount of time, that wasn't there before? I mean, it was there, and then it wasn't there again.*

PR: We think things in reference to time. So then the only way we ever think about something is that it came and went and that it's "in" time. Outside of time is a funny way of speaking, because outside of time isn't outside or inside of time. It's not like it's over here and can be referenced to time. It's not referenced to time at all. And if all we can do is reference to time then there is no place to put it, and we've got to put things, so we'll put it in time.

Let's say that you experience your true nature, directly. Experience "you" directly. You would not say, ah, this was never the way it was, suddenly it is this way. You might not say anything. You might say this is the way it has always been, it has never been any different, and I've always known this.

It has always been that way, and yet you have been living like it hasn't been that way. For all intents and purposes—in your speaking, in your feelings, and in the way you lived—it wouldn't have been that way. And when you recognize it, you say it has always been that way, and you've been doing something else.

Q: *Like just noticing the truth.*

PR: Yes, like noticing the truth. Yet we still think the truth is in time. You see? Like a long time ago it was true and it's still true and it's going to be true for a long time. When we think or speak it will conventionally always fall within the context of time, and so everything we are cognizant of will automatically refer to time. Remember, we are not talking about some "thing" that is a direct experience; we're talking about directly experiencing the very nature of something, becoming directly conscious of its nature, or being "one" with it. These are all ways of speaking. The truth of the matter is whatever it is.

The "Tabloid"

PR: So let me tell you some stories. Now, I'll bet the subject will be more palatable to you, but less true. A long ago and in a galaxy far far away [tongue in cheek], I did some very intense work. I'm a very lucky guy, because each time I had a direct experience, I had little or no confusion with anything. One time I had a direct experience and it was accompanied by lots and lots of phenomena, and still I was clear that the phenomena wasn't it. I had a direct experience before this, and it wasn't confused with anything, there was NOTHING there. There was nothing there but the direct experience. The second time it was with lots of phenomena, brilliant phenomena.

Q: *Like what? What was there?*

PR: You want the fantasy stuff, right? Okay. Light, brilliant colors, stuff like that. An unconventional perceptive framework, positioning, observation. I couldn't say where these things were, but they were. That was going on, and the enlightenment occurred when I dissociated myself from all the phenomena that was occurring. In this case I was setting out to experience another. Do you really want to hear about this stuff?

All: Yes!

PR: Okay. There is really no way to talk about it. So I want you to know that, and I'll talk about it. Also, you should know that this will MAKE NO DIFFERENCE! It's a lot like looking at a sleazy tabloid; it has nothing to do with the truth! But just for entertainment purposes I'll tell you a tale.

As I set out to experience this person, phenomenologically, all bodies disappeared. It didn't have to happen, you know, it's just what did happen. It's not in the blueprint—"Oh, I've got to get the bodies to disappear"—it has nothing to do with it, I mean nothing to do with it! I spent thousands and thousands of hours in contemplation, and lots of stuff like that would happen and it wasn't enlightenment. Do you understand? It has nothing to do with it; stuff like that is just another mediocre experience in the world. Do you understand? A direct experience has nothing to do with anything subtle or gross, up or down, in or out—nothing, nothing! I don't want you think that this story has anything to do with enlightenment. Clear? Okay. Then I will go on.

So, bodies disappeared, and there were blue lights, weird stuff. I forgot all about that ... blue lights, and then there were red stars, and I was committed to experiencing this other. No, it was the other way around—red first then the blue. All this phenomena was going on and I'm going right through it. Kind of like the guy in "2001," going through all that stuff. Thinking where is it, where is it? I'll tell you, the red lights, they didn't do it, but the blue lights, the blue lights almost got me, they were so beautiful. All right, so I wasn't on purpose [laughs].

So anyway, I was holding all that as a distraction. As a matter of fact, I was holding it like the "other" was throwing it up as an array to distract my attention. Like they were afraid of me experiencing them; as if they could get the presence of another was closing in, and the phenomena was being thrown out like, "Look over there, take that, take anything!"

And then all of a sudden, I just had an experience where there was no time, no space, no location; all of a sudden that became present for me, that the thereness and the hereness … it's the same thing. The thereness and the hereness [slapping briefcase]. All of a sudden it became apparent for what it was. I don't know what else I can say about that. Sounds like an anticlimax, doesn't it? You say, "Let's go back to the lights."

It was like this. The other was not different from me. There was no place and no location. They were the same self that I was. There was no difference, there was no distinction between I and you. There was no you there, me here, it was the same experience. Don't try to think it.

Q: *Was there an us?*

PR: No. No us. There was Being, only. There was no time, there was no space, there was no location, there was no distinction, there was no us, there was no I, there was no you.

Q: *Was your experience in your body?*

PR: I could say in this case, no. But it wasn't an exclusive event either. There's just not a distinction, so no bodies. It wasn't exclusive like I can't have a body. It wasn't somewhere else where there are no bodies. See there is no way to speak of it.

Q: *Isn't it. . . . Isn't it. . . .*

PR: No. [Laughter]

Q: *So there isn't an external element?*

PR: Who?

Q: *At that point, there is no external?*

PR: There is no internal.

Q: *If there is no external, of course there's no internal.*

PR: Now that's impossible, isn't it? See, that's definitely impossible. And how would you do that? "You" can't.

Q: *But you did it.*

PR: We could say "I" didn't do it.

Q: *Isn't it more like something you get into?*

PR: You don't experience yourself as completely meaningless—yet. Probably what you guys are hearing is a lot of meaning. In other words, meaningless like meaning "less." You see, but that's meaning—that's less value. Valueless, less value. I mean NO value. No value, no meaning. I mean no meaning, nothing, zero, zilch, zip. No value. No you. Not as a negative. Do you see the easiest way to hold that is that it wouldn't be very nice? Right? Meaningless, what me? Holding ME as meaningless, valueless, ME? That wouldn't be nice. But that has a lot of meaning in it, doesn't it?

So anyway, really what I wanted to do with you was to try and support you in taking the mystery out of what enlightenment is. I don't know if I've done that. I've tried to support you in being more responsible for it. Direct experience means there is no separation between you and what you are directly experiencing.

Q: *How do you know it then?*

PR: You'll know it when you get it.

Q: *If there is no meaning, why go for it?*

PR: There is no reason to go for it, none. There is no reason. But if there is no you, there is no suffering. Sounds like a bad trade-off [laughs].

Q: *What do you do with the recollection?*

PR: Recollection is the memory of the phenomenon that went on around the event—the ideas and thoughts and concepts that arose, and new thoughts and new concepts created at the time, plus a sense of the openness that was there, and whatever else your attention happened to fall on immediately afterwards. And that's what you recollect.

I've done a lot of work with others and have seen people have a direct experience, and yet the phenomena were so strong that they would completely go into the phenomena, completely go into the sound and color, and they would get lost in that—it's more interesting. It's not, but it seems that way at the time. It's the only thing to look at. So any direct experience that they had is lost or confused with "experience" rather than the direct consciousness. Not that they didn't have a direct experience, it's just as if it's "overlooked," because the only thing that's related to is the phenomena, the experience, the sensation, the concept, the "whatever" that comes into cognition at the time.

Direct experience is not anywhere. It's not this big thing that you get into and the light descends upon you. Unless it does, but that's a light descending upon you. You know what I mean? That's what that is. So if you wonder if you're enlightened when a big light comes and sits on your body, I'll tell you: "What's happening is a big light is coming and sitting on your body." Enjoy! If it's enjoyable, enjoy it. See if you can do something with it. But that's all that is. It is NOT enlightenment.

Q: *So if you have a direct experience, as you were just saying, what you would call "it" is the concepts and the new perceptions or whatever that you experience immediately afterwards. So can you open yourself up like that without having the enlightenment experience? Can you open yourself to that space where you get new concepts, without having a direct experience, and then go backwards to the direct experience?*

PR: It's not going backwards. There is no backwards to it. There is no method or process that you can do that forces a direct experience. No matter how clever you are! [laughs] You see, even after having a direct experience, first of all we try to package it, and then we try to relive the package or the notion of it. It's NOT the package. An experience of nothing is still an experience of nothing. It's not an experience of "something" that is "nothing." It's not an "experience." It is pure Consciousness, not "Ah, I experience nothing."

Q: *But don't you have to go out of here to get there?*

PR: No, there is no out of here. This is it. That's enlightenment.

Q: *But you have to take the external out of it. You know the divisiveness.*

PR: You don't have to take it out. There is nothing you have to exclude. As a matter of fact, it is usually dangerous to exclude. There is nothing you have to exclude or take out. You have to recognize what's true. That's all. And it's true now. This! Not somewhere else. It's not true up there. Or over there. It's just true. It's recognizing what's true. So you may develop an ability to listen to what's true, and you realize it's in a completely different context than what you are living in—it's no context at all.

Q: *Is it the way you hold it that's the secret?*

PR: [Laughter] There is no secret. Just freedom. Freedom.

Q: *Is that counting when you just experience an experience?*

PR: I understand your questions, and I understand the desire to know. Where it falls apart is that you're speaking of it as if it were something. What I recommend is that you have lots of direct experiences. I recommend you have them frequently, and I also

recommend that you train yourself. I recommend that you practice. I recommend that you practice changing the context, the
way you "hold" things. I recommend that. You see, most of us
don't know that we hold things. We think things are the way that
they are. And I am suggesting that we hold them that way, and
that's why they are the way that they are. We can hold them very
differently.

So there is nothing exclusive. See? It's not like over here is suffering, and over here is freedom, and over here is the teabag, and
you have to get from suffering to freedom. Of where I am speaking, you can be in the middle of great misery and be in great joy.
And I am not saying that this joy is only in pretend misery, in
pretend pain. In real pain there is joy.

Recently, I have been saying that joy is the presence of freedom. That when freedom is here, presently, really, actually freedom—that's what we call "joy." It's freedom. Joy is what we call
the presence of freedom—when we encounter real Being. I don't
mean joy as in happiness, or giggling, or pleasure, or something
nice. I'm talking about Joy.

All right, I thought that might be of service. Thank you for
your attention. It was fun.

The "Lollipop" Talk

These dialogues were taken from an Ontological Study Group meeting in 1993. A dialogue within a series of dialogues is underway. In this section Bob is experiencing pain in relation to losing an intimate relationship.

The Function of Pain

PR: As I've said many times before, "It's a problem of identification." When we say "I," we've said a mouthful, but we take it all for granted. In our experience, "I" is a function of "being," isn't it? When we say "I" it is so for us that I is occurring, and that I is here objectively. And that you are in the place of yourself, ergo "I am here" is a reference—you're referring to some thing being there, and pretty much taking for granted that that's so. And so wherever being is, I is there. I is here.

So the phenomenon of "being" lies in this experience that appears to be—and is called I. And it appears as an exclusive event because it's held that way in the distinction we make called self. Right? And so when you say, "I am at cause,"—like when you say, "I'm causing my own suffering"—really what you're saying is that when you engage in a particular activity, you "relate" to what occurs out of that activity—what comes to pass, what seems to be a result or an effect of the activity—with another activity called pain.

Why? Well, take a look. Something's up, huh? You're trying to accomplish something. So we can assume for the moment that the relationship of pain to that activity is part of what you're try-ing to accomplish. It seems to serve some function.

What function? Well, it presents the circumstance as unwanted; giving it a particular orientation. What is that orientation? I think we need to know more about pain.

If we entertain the possibility, just the possibility, mind you, that there is no such thing as pain—to say it another way, that pain doesn't really exist—well, that's a pretty weird thing to enter-tain, isn't it? Clearly pain exists and it hurts and it's one of the biggies. Without pain, so much isn't possible, right?—fear, hurt, anger, and many more—we've talked about that. That's why pain is one of the key points to our work.

So entertain as an opening, which right now lacks grounding, that pain isn't really there like pain. We've done enough work so that it may have a little grounding, a little possibility, but still it's pretty far out. Which is to say that pain isn't really there like something as itself. It's not really occurring. What it is is a con-cept. As if it's an activity of—I don't really mean it this way—but as if we "make believe" pain is there. And that's what hurts. That's the kindest, simplest, most childish way to say it—and that's not it. It's an activity of creating a phenomenon called pain or hurt. And that doesn't quite say it, either.

Another way that's not saying it is having the "illusion" of pain. I'm just trying to create a position to talk around. An activ-ity that presents something that we call pain, that is serious, important, and heavily motivating. I mean really critical as a moti-vation. But I want you, just for the moment, to entertain the pos-sibility that there's nothing really there. I know that you can intellectually zing that one by, but see if you can get semi-seri-ous with it—that there is really nothing there, any more than there's anything there as fear without an unwillingness to expe-rience something unwanted—painful—arising in the future. And remember, the future is totally conceptual.

There's no future if there's no concept. No concept, no future, eh? Future is conceptual. Why? Well, because we say the future isn't. And anything that isn't has to be conceptual—if you say it "is." It is what? It is a concept. See, it's an idea, it's a thought, it's an image, it's a possibility. It's not "is" like an occurring event, except in the conceptual domain. No future, no unwillingness, no unwanted conceptual possibility of experience—no fear. No fear. There is no fear. So fear lives in that domain. So in one sense, you see, we could say it's like an illusion. A very serious, pragmatic, incredibly grounded one, but an illusion.

That's what's taking place such that we think fear is like a solid. It really isn't solid at all. It's not solid. See, there's nothing there like a solid. There's nothing there even like a circumstance that's presenting itself. There's only something there like a conceptual activity that appears like a solid. I'm saying the same thing with pain. But pain doesn't have that same kind of future construct to it. So you can't take it apart the same way. But it's the same thing. Pain.

In order to consider the matter you must look past the taken-for-granted relationship to that experience. Sort of like getting past the notion that food comes from the refrigerator, you know? If you thought food originated in the refrigerator, and I asked you where does food come from, you'd say refrigerator. And if I pressed on, you would have to simply insist that food comes from the refrigerator and that's the end of the story. You would probably get irritated at me for pursuing such an inane questioning. Since you and I really know food comes from the store—okay, the farm—so we see that it's silly for someone to think that food comes from a refrigerator. But we don't know where food comes from past "farm." At some point we stop. Like thinking fear is fear, anger is anger, and that's the end of the story, without really knowing what makes up fear or anger. Or, in this case, experiencing the nature of pain.

You're just entertaining this, I'm not asking you to believe it. You can believe it, you can not believe it, I don't care. Just entertain it.

I'm not saying fear doesn't occur like an occurring event, but it's a conceptually occurring event. And what we call fear like a solid is illusory. I'm not saying that when you're afraid, you're not afraid. Clearly you are. In your experience, you are afraid. In your experience, it is real that you are afraid. It's just that in your experience, it's also real that fear is there like a solid thing. I'm saying that's an illusion. It's not solid. I'm saying that's also true of pain. That in our experience, pain is very much there like a solid thing or a circumstance, and like it is circumstantially created. It is not a solid, unavoidable occurrence.

I'm suggesting that this is true in the objectively physical sensation domain of pain also. But it's easier for you to think it if we just eliminate the objectively occurring sensation domain, such as getting your leg cut off. I don't care about that. That's not important right now. But if we direct our attention toward emotional pain, the pain of loss and that kind of hurt feelings, it becomes possible to entertain this notion, right? "Okay, if you just leave out my leg being cut off, I can accept it better." I don't care about your leg. In the way that I am saying it now—there's nothing there that pain is. To say it in another way, the pain isn't really there like an objective solid entity. It's not there like an entity, it's not there like an object. It's not like something there that has to be. None of that.

Then pain is an activity. Some kind of conceptual activity, albeit reflexive, albeit almost genetic or instinctive, I don't care, primal for sure, but still a conceptual activity. If there's what we call pain in our experience, then we could say that pain is causing pain. That means something different, now. That pain is causing pain. Then we could say that the activity of pain is causing the activity of pain. Having the activity of pain is causing the activity of pain, see? Indulging in that activity, reflexively creating the illusion of pain, is creating the illusion of pain—however you want to say it. The "pain" causes pain.

Pain causes pain. Nothing else causes pain. Pain causes pain. If you and I engage in a conceptual event, the result of which is pain, or the activity of which is pain, then we might say that I caused the pain. But we're still abstracted from it because that's like an assertion and not a source. See? "I cause pain."

If you take a hammer and whack your foot, having a sense of volition in it, and say, "I whacked my toe and boy it hurts, therefore I caused pain," that's different, isn't it? You're not saying then that you caused pain. You caused whacking your foot, which caused pain. Because of your sense of volition in the matter, when you say I caused the pain, you're really saying, "I caused whacking my foot, I did it." "See, I can not whack my foot, I can whack my foot, I can not whack my foot, I can whack his foot." So it looks like you're causing it because you whacked your foot. This is because you have a sense of volition in there. But you still didn't get a sense of actually, directly, causing the beingness of the pain. You caused whacking your foot that seems to result in pain, or the sensation to which you attribute pain.

If you notice an activity taking place—like an image and expectation of the future—and circumstances destroy the possibility of that image coming true, so you feel loss, and thus say, "I caused that, I did this conceptual activity and out of that, that resulted in pain"—a loss, ergo pain—then you've really not said anything closer than I whacked my foot, right? You're saying, "What I have a sense of volitionally being responsible for causing, caused the pain."

But you're still not in touch with the source of the pain. And if pain is itself an activity, then obviously, you'd have to be in touch with pain as an activity to be at the source of that, right? You'd have to actually be in touch with the "grabbing" of the pain, the "holding" of the pain, the "squeezing" of the pain— metaphorically speaking. You'd have to be in the place where you are actually "squeezing" out the pain—and if you're actually creating the pain, you could not create the pain.

So there is a legitimate place now in your experience to say that the activity you're attributing to causing pain doesn't cause the pain. Do you see what I'm saying? If you want to say I swung the hammer, okay, you swung the hammer. What did it cause? It caused nothing but swinging the hammer. Understand?

Bob: *Okay, I get all that, but I'd like you to say again, in the example I gave, what is my activity?*

PR: Well, the activity that I identified for you is the image of the future event, and the thwarting of the expectation, and so the loss of something that you didn't have. Which is the loss of the possibility. That was the activity, right?

Bob: *Yeah.*

PR: And you say that causes pain, right? Really what that causes is itself. I mean, if you take a look, what you got is that conceptual activity and loss. Here's the scenario: I had expectation, I expected it, whatever that means, I expected it, wanted it, and now it's not going to happen. Uh ohh. Okay, now loss. There's no pain there. What's there is I expected something to happen, I expected some scenario to happen, and now it's not going to happen. So obviously there's got to be something else, it's got to "mean something" that it's not going to happen. And, out of the meaning that it's not going to happen, pain occurs. You relate to that with pain. Loss of the expectation has to mean something.

It also has to be set up a certain way, doesn't it? It has to be set up such that it's unacceptable and intolerable for you not to have that scenario. Obviously it's tolerable, you'll get through it, but it's got to be resisted. How come you weren't happy about it? How come it didn't tickle you, you didn't jump up and down and laugh?

Bob: *Well, I was looking forward to being with this person, and I was expecting to have a good time. And I received a phone call, and now I've lost that potential good time. But then again, it could be, "Well, so what?" But I still don't get the function for the disappointment and pain. It's like, why did I do something like that? That makes it worse. That adds pain on to a potentially neutral situation.*

PR: Not having the good time, now you're having a bad time.

Bob: *Yeah, that the expected future will now not occur. I mean, I could have left it at that, but I don't. What I do about it doesn't help me at all. You know, it's just pain. And it feels so arbitrary that I do that.*

The "Lollipop Talk"

PR: If you had a lollipop and it tasted good—what is tasting good? It's sensations in your body about which you're saying pleasure, right? "Oh, feels good, Oh, feels good." And if I took it away from you and you cried, you'd say, "I don't get more feeling-goods", right? "I'm losing my feeling-goods. You're taking my feeling-goods away from me. I don't get my feeling-goods, so I have to feel bad about that." Why? Why do you think? Take a look.

You want it, you covet it, you thirst after it, desire it, but what is that about?

Bob: *Well, it seems to be all about me and not about the lollipop.*

PR: Okay, all right, let's go back to the first question that I asked. Why pain, simply because I took away future good times, future good feelings?

So you're having good feeling and I take it away. If you were having good feeling, good feeling, good feeling and then there was the absence of good feeling, that doesn't necessarily mean, ontologically—for you and I it means it, but ontologically—it doesn't necessitate the onset of bad feeling, right? There's just good feeling, good feeling, and then no more good feeling.

If you have good feeling, good feeling, good feeling, you eat the lollipop all up and there's no more lollipop, that's different than me taking it away, isn't it? And then you might say, "Oh, darn," you might be disappointed there's no more lollipop. Or you might say, "Well, that was good, I'm glad." You have the memory of the good feelings: "Oh, that was good, oh boy, I had a lollipop," and you're happy that you had a lollipop. What's the difference between being happy that you had a lollipop and going, "Oh darn, it's all gone, I don't have any more lollipop?" Ontologically, what's the difference?

Bob: *In the second one there's an orientation towards the future. I was expecting that I would keep on having this lollipop as long as there was lollipop. That it would continue , but then you grabbed it.*

PR: No, I'm not on to that one yet. Certainly that's true, yes, but I wanted to make an even subtler distinction before I go back to the gross distinction, which will help us. In this distinction, there are two different endings when you finish the lollipop. In case one, you finish the lollipop and you're, "I had a lollipop, that was great, I'm so glad I had a lollipop. That was so much fun. Oh good, oh good." Okay? Second scenario: "I had a lollipop. It's all gone. I'm so disappointed. Awww, my lollipop's gone." What's the difference?

Bob: *I ate it all?*

PR: Yes, you ate it all up, right. Same circumstance, but different ending. What's the difference between those two? And on occasion, you've had those two, right?

Bob: *Yes.*

PR: Maybe even with a lollipop. But go ahead, what's the difference? Some possibilities.

Bob: *I'm a neurotic little kid?*

PR: Okay, but ontological possibilities rather than psychological possibilities.

Bob: *Well, okay. In the first one, there's just one activity, eating the lollipop. And it became a memory. In the other, there are two activities: eating the lollipop and then the action of having myself feel bad because there's no lollipop.*

PR: You feel bad because there is no lollipop, right? So obviously there's a "future" relating to the "past." There's a present which is rolling into the future, relating to the past. You could say a present relating to the past—that's good enough, right? But that's also true in the first one. What's the difference?

Bob: *There's pain in the second one.*

PR: Well, that's true. If we use this like a tiny itsy bitsy metaphor or example of an ideal, or analogous to an ideal, in the second one, you've got another way things should be, or could be, that you're contrasting with the way things are, right? I have a lollipop, I'm into pleasure, pleasure, pleasure. Now here's the absence of lollipop, I could have a lollipop now, I could have the pleasure now, and I don't have it. I'm upset.

In the first one, I have the lollipop, and now I don't. What's so in the first one is the past is still the same past. But now there's no "supposed to be any other way." I just don't have a lollipop. But I had a lollipop. I had a lollipop, that was fun, and now is now. Now I have the memory of having the lollipop and that it was fun. That was fun, right? And now what I've got is, "I had a lollipop, and I'm having a pleasant memory of the lollipop." The other one is, "I don't have a lollipop"—and that's in relationship to the memory also. However, the first one is, "I *had* a lollipop," and the second one is, "I don't *have* a lollipop." And that's in contrast to the possibility of having a lollipop and so the desire or the preference for having a lollipop. I want to have a lollipop but I ate it all up.

Well, let's go back to the original scenario. Now I take the thing away from you. You have a lollipop, good sensation, good sensation, and whommp! Now what's so? You're upset. Why?

Bob: *What's so is there's also the situation that things aren't the way I think they should be.*

PR: What way is that?

Bob: *Well, we've got three examples now and the second one was I wish I had a lollipop, I ate up all my lollipop, and I would like there to be a lollipop now but there's not. Okay. And if you snatch it away, well, what I think should be happening, that I should be allowed to continue with this lollipop, is not happening. Something wrong is happening and it's wrong of you to take the lollipop.*

PR: Oh, certainly.

Bob: *And somehow I get something out of being upset at you for being the bad man who takes my lollipop.*

PR: Now that's important—you need to grasp that.

Bob: *It's like I don't have the lollipop anymore and it was really important to have the lollipop, and now I'm upset at you and that's just as important. If I can't have the lollipop, I'll be upset at you. There's some equivalence here that is important.*

PR: Yes, yes, there is. Now what do you think? If you have a lollipop and you've had a few good licks and I take it away, do you suspect you'd be more upset than if you finished the lollipop and it's not there?

Bob: *Yes.*

PR: Yes, probably significantly more upset. If you finish the lollipop and it's all gone, well, you're disappointed. Now, what are some of the significant differences between being disappointed because your lollipop is all gone and when I take your lollipop away? I dropped some hint there.

Bob: *Okay, if I simply eat up all of the lollipop, there's no blame assigned. I mean that's the nature of food. You can't eat it and have it, too. That's just the way of reality.*

PR: And we could resist that too, but....

Bob: *Yeah, if you're six years old, you probably will. Whereas if you snatch away the lollipop, it's unfair, it's not the way it has to be, it could be otherwise.*

PR: It's seen in your own experience that it could be otherwise, very pragmatically. We've got a lot of evidence here, right? What evidence do you have?

Bob: *Well, it's in your hand.*

PR: Yes, I have the lollipop, I have your lollipop, right? The evidence is the lollipop. It's a real objective circumstance that you can see. Look, over here is the lollipop and I'm licking it. Whereas in the other scenario, there is no lollipop. Nobody else is licking it, nobody's licking it, it's all gone, right?

Bob: *Right.*

PR: So you have a couple of things. One, you have an objective reality that you attribute to your pleasure, a lollipop, like an object that's occurring. And relative to the objective occurrence you have an assessment that you must have at least another hundred good licks on that thing, right? So there's a future assessment in relationship to this object that you have another hundred good licks on it and I just ripped off your hundred licks. It's like the phone call you received from your girlfriend—the future part, the hundred licks. You already had twenty licks or whatever, but she ripped off a hundred good sensations there. And it's still objectively occurring.

There's another thing too. It's your lollipop. And so now there's an object that's your lollipop and it still exists as "your" lollipop, right?

Bob: *For me, sure. You're holding it, but it's my lollipop.*

PR: That's right. And I took away *your* lollipop and so *you* should get those hundred licks. Clearly, just like in the first scenario, the possibility in pleasure is the same. You lick it, it's pleasure; you lick it, it's pleasure; you lick it, it's pleasure. I take it away. You had some pleasure, you had twenty licks on the lollipop, right? No difference. "Oh good, pleasure, pleasure, pleasure, gone." No difference, except "your" lollipop is still occurring, and the concept of what could have been.

You can accept, especially as you grow older, that the damn thing disappears when you eat it all up. That's it, and you go on. But in this scenario, you didn't eat it all up. You have the image of eating it all up. You have the image of a process in which you're going to have all these licks until the thing's gone. It's your lollipop—possessive—and now I took away your pleasure, which you have a right to. Those things have to be there, right? Yours, and the object lollipop. Now I'm interrupting it. I'm interrupting your relationship to your pleasure. I'm taking away your pleasure.

So, the pain isn't in the pleasure that you had—obviously—the pain is in the pleasure that you didn't have, that you say you should have. And so you feel a pain because you don't get the pleasure—interesting. You feel a pain because you don't get the pleasure that you were supposed to have. Because clearly, if you weren't supposed to have it, no pain. If it was my lollipop and I gave you twenty good licks, you'd say, "Thank you, that was nice, I got twenty licks." Because you weren't supposed to have it. So you got something that you weren't even supposed to get. You got licks on my lollipop. "Oh good, I got extra bonus licks," or whatever. You had your lollipop plus licks on my lollipop, "Wow, bonus points, I'm in lollipop heaven." But no pain.

If you had the same amount of licks and it's your lollipop, if I take it away, you're in pain. How come? Same thing, same amount of pleasure, same twenty licks, but now you're in pain. You're crying, bawling, throwing a tantrum, why? Obviously, it's related to "I should have had that pleasure, that was my pleasure and I didn't get to have it." Which is clearly conceptual with a nice objective reference, the lollipop. I didn't get that pleasure. Now, why the upset?

Bob: *Why, indeed?*

PR: But that's critical. A crucial point. Because definitely there is upset.

Bob: *I just keep going round and round with this. I'm upset because I'm not getting what I want, I'm not getting what I deserve. Yes, I'm upset. Yeah, it's conceptual, it's a loss of imagined future pleasure, so what?*

PR: Why didn't you get up and take the lollipop back? You might get up to take the lollipop back, but you'd be pissed while you did it, huh? See, you're already upset. You can see it's different than pleasure, pleasure, pleasure, I take the lollipop, you come and take it back, and more pleasure, pleasure, pleasure. No upset.

From time to time we see little babies look like they do something like that sometimes, right? One baby's playing with something, another baby takes it and they go take it back, with what looks like very minimal amount of upset about it. They took it, and I took it back. Then of course, there's the other more frequent scenario. One takes it and the other bawls. Or one takes it and the other gets angry takes it back and hits them with it, or whatever—that whole business.

So there's obviously something taking place there. Interesting phenomenon, this pain. Pain at the loss of something you didn't have, didn't get. Let's see, loss, loss, loss. Doesn't loss always refer to the future? You lose your wife, what did you lose? Well, she was alive up until when she wasn't, and she died. What did you lose? You lost the future of her. You lost the future. Oh, loss. Or the lollipop. Whatever. We don't usually look at it that way, right? If you had a car and you lost it. . . . "I lost my car." What did you lose? Well, you lost "having" the car, which is using the car in the future, which looks, right about now, like I can't use my car anymore.

Bob: *It looks like now because I don't have it now. I want it now.*

PR: Right. You don't have it now. But clearly you want it now for the future, right? Especially in the case of the car.

So there's a point here. Is everyone up with me on the point? A point where the upset is. See? The pain, the upset. Why? You say it seems to relate, somehow, to me taking your lollipop—obviously. It relates to that, but there's something else. You being upset relates to you having the lollipop and then not having the lollipop. What it means to have the lollipop, and what it means to not have the lollipop, proportionally.

Obviously, if you were chewing on a piece of grass, and you really didn't care, and I took the piece of grass from you, you'd probably not be very upset. Would you? The most upset you'd be would be at my rudeness for taking the piece of grass from you, the social boundaries that I've crossed. I'm not supposed to take a piece of grass. But if I was a very good friend and I was just teasing you—I'm your wife or your husband or something like that, and I giggle and I take the grass from you—you might be slightly irritated or amused. You'd probably just pick another piece of grass or something. So the upset seems proportional to the significance. But what, what? What does it do? What does it do? What does it do?

Well, here's a place in which to look—although I don't want to assert this as the answer at all—but one place to look. . . . Did I ever tell you about a Russian movie I saw once? The "hero's" wife died, and he dragged her conceptually around throughout the movie—mourning, mourning, mourning, pain, pain, pain. Russian pain, throughout the movie. He beat everybody else up, his new wife, people he knew, himself. Suffer, suffer, and this was somehow glorious—his suffering, you see? What I suggested to the person I was with at the time is that his pain and suffering relative to his wife kept his wife "alive." Kept the presence of his wife around. That was the form in which he kept the presence of his wife, because he wouldn't let her go. He wouldn't let go of the wife.

Obviously, if he let go of the wife, he wouldn't suffer, right? Because he wouldn't be suffering the absence of her. And so the only way he could keep her, since he couldn't keep her as a presence, was as an "absence." And the only way he could keep the absence was to continue to have pain about the absence, so he could have the absence as a presence. And the absence was there as a presence in the pain or the suffering—the loss of the wife. So he turned the absence into a presence. And given his disposition was clearly to want the wife rather than to not want the wife, then this presence appeared as an unwanted. The only way he could have her there as a presence was to have it be unwanted. Weird, huh? You following me on that?

Bob: *All except the very last one.*

PR: Well, given he wanted the wife, and she was not present, if he let her go, there would be no absence of wife, there would just be the room, the chair, his new wife, or whatever was next, right? But to have the absence of his wife remain as a presence, as a strongly felt presence, he couldn't have it as a strongly felt positive presence, given his preference for wanting the wife. See, he wanted the wife, so he couldn't have it there as a wanted presence, right? Because it's the "absence" of his wife. So he had to have it there as an unwanted presence. And his reaction to the unwanted presence looks like loss, pain, suffering, you see? It's an unwanted presence, persisting into the future. Wild, huh?

Liz: *Is another way of saying that, the pain is a placeholder for the wife?*

PR: Sure. We started that way, the pain acting as a placeholder, which is to say, to hold the place of the thing that's gone, right? And so if it holds the place, then somehow, in some weird way, the thing isn't gone. But since there seems to be something undeniable about its goneness, we can't hold it as thereness, right? So we have to hold it as an absence by having something hold its place—so it can remain in some fashion. And since there's a preference for its thereness rather than its goneness, then whatever's holding the place has to look like a non-preference or something unwanted. So, we want the unwanted. We want the thing to be there as an unwanted, and present as a presence. And in his case, a strong presence of something unwanted so that he could keep his wife. . . . But over the years, she started to stink!

So how did that relate to the lollipop?

Bob: *It looks like the same operation; if you take away my lollipop then I'll carry around the loss of the lollipop as a presence.*

PR: Right. So then you still have the lollipop as the presence of its loss, which is unwanted. And since it's unwanted, you call it pain. Because it's the presence of an unwanted experience—that you want. Clearly if you didn't have the unwanted experience, then you would have no lollipop, right? It would just be gone, and what would be next would be breathing, playing in the sand, whatever. But the lollipop would be gone and you don't want that to be the case.

Bob: *It looks like I'm hanging onto the lollipop whether I've got it or not. If I've got it, I've got it. If I don't have it, I'll switch to being at the effect of the loss of the lollipop. I'll carry around the lost lollipop. But why would I do that? Why would I opt for that, rather than just letting it go?*

PR: Why indeed? Well, if you didn't do that, what would you get?

Bob: *I wouldn't get anything. I would just be back at point zero.*

PR: Okay. However, obviously in our looking at it, in the scenarios we've run down, being back at point zero actually seems like the more pleasant position to the whole matter, right?

Bob: *Right. Well, at least it's the absence of pain. It looks like a no plus or no pain situation.*

PR: Which is to say that whatever's next is whatever's next. But that's not the one we go for, so what's missing?

Bob: *What's missing? I'm thinking of what's there. What seems to lead me down this path of loss and pain is value. I value this lollipop. I mean, when you take it away, I still maintain the value of the lollipop, and if I didn't hold the value of the lollipop, I probably wouldn't go into pain. That's one thing.*

PR: So why would you keep the lollipop as an unwanted presence, which is to say, the absence of the lollipop as an unwanted presence?

Bob: *To me that's the same question as what's the function of pain?*

PR: Okay, what's the function of pain? Just off the top of your head, what do you think the function of pain might be?

Bob: *Well, it keeps life interesting..*

PR: Nahh.

Bob: *I mean, because if I didn't live with pain then I couldn't experience pleasure.*

PR: True, but we don't know that.

Bob: *What does that mean?*

PR: We clearly don't grasp that pain and pleasure are the same phenomenon, right? We always try to go for the pleasure and avoid the pain. Which, if pleasure and pain are the same thing, is not possible.

Okay, so maybe pain keeps life interesting, what else, what function does it seem to serve in your life?

Bob: *Well, when I'm in pain, it's not just that I don't want to feel this pain, the pain hurts. It's that it isn't right that I'm in pain and if it isn't right that I'm in pain, then I'm a good person. Then if bad things are happening, and I have pain, then somehow, I'm right or I'm superior to something.*

PR: Let's back up for a moment, let's hold on the "right" and "superior" thing for a moment. I want to go down that avenue, but let's back up for a moment. All of your emotions, all of your feelings, what do they seem to do for you, what's their primary function?

Bob: *Well, they feel real familiar, they give me a sense of me.*

PR: Okay, what's their function? So, maybe it's possible to have a sense of you without emotions, right? It would just be an emotionless sense of you. So how do they keep you around? What do they do? What do you do when you're hungry?

Bob: *I go out for food.*

PR: Yes. What do you do when you're afraid?

Bob: *Try to make it disappear.*

PR: What do you do when you feel loss?

Bob: *Try to get laid.*

PR: What do you do when you're in pain?

Bob: *Try to get rid of the pain.*

PR: Etcetera, right?

Bob: *Yeah.*

PR: And so, the feeling and emotions obviously serve some kind of orientation and they also serve as motivation for you, don't they? Primarily, grossly, simply? Motivators tell you what to do. Do this, avoid that, get this, move away from that, right? And so if you yourself are creating pain in yourself to act as a motivator, you could make it stop. Since basically, you create it to get rid of it. So, in relationship to the lollipop, you're having pain you're supposed to get rid of, but you're having it be there yourself. You're putting it there to get rid of it. So now, what function could it serve to have something there that you are motivated to get rid of? That you're putting there yourself? What might you do? Well, one thing, obviously—you're upset, you're hurt and you're supposed to get rid of the pain. If I have your lollipop, what's the simplest thing you could do to get rid of your pain?

Bob: *I could take back the lollipop.*

PR: You could take back the lollipop, right!

Okay, but say you don't take back the lollipop, or perhaps I eat it up real quick or something and you still keep the pain. How come?

Bob: *Well, so I can still feel the pain, and so keep something around indirectly.*

PR: Why? If the pain's a motivator to get rid of itself, but you're keeping it there, how come? Now you can continue to relate to the lollipop as an unwanted presence—the absence of the lollipop as an unwanted presence—what could you be accomplishing in that manipulation? In this way you provide something for yourself beyond clinging to the lost presence, don't you? You provide a function designed to motivate you into some kind of resolution to the resisted circumstances. And there's more, but the more is difficult to speak about without an experiential understanding of what I'm pointing us towards.

Well, we've gotten pretty deep into this issue in a short period of time. So this "no cause" business that we tackled last time has revealed a relationship to something that probably wouldn't have been revealed without the "cause/no cause" work.

And now there is a proposal about pain. A proposal about keeping the presence of something wanted but lost, in the unwanted presence of its absence. Some kind of dynamic which appears inversely proportional in the amount of future you had planned, and the amount of value and attachment to it, related to the amount of pain—the extent of the pain, the suffering, the absence felt.

But we're still at a loss to get what's going on with this. We need to see—ontologically, not psychologically—that we conceptually create the presence of the lollipop through its unwanted absence. We create an unwanted absence that appears as pain which motivates us to resolve it—like going to get the lollipop and sticking it back in your mouth—and so now it's a wanted presence. Without which you wouldn't go get the lollipop to put it in your mouth, would you? See what I'm saying? If the lollipop simply disappeared, there's no getting the lollipop back. If the lollipop wasn't there for you as a motivating unwanted absence, there wouldn't be a motivation to get the lollipop back, and so you suffer the unwanted absence to drive you to recreate the presence of the lollipop. ... It's a possibility.

However, we can see a maintenance of, even sometimes an increase in, the unwanted presence when there is no apparent possibility of getting the lollipop back. Is that just a mistake or what? Or does it serve some other purpose? Well, let's do some homework.

Coming from the position of the possibility we create the pain, I want you to discover for yourself as an experience, psychologically and ontologically, what function does pain serve? So if there's any domain in which you say, "I'm not responsible for the pain, I'm not creating the pain at all," okay, then pass on it for now, because then it looks to you like it's circumstantially derived. It looks like it's caused by something other than you, so pass on it. But wherever you can get some responsibility for being hurt, such as loss, or being upset or in pain, then what is the function or purpose? If you can get it as the unwanted presence of the absence of something, then ask why? Since that's all conceptually derived. Why are you doing it? What's going on? It's a critical point. What's going on there?

Dave: *I'm already thinking of past situations. So do you want this to be present, this week's situations?*

PR: Any way that will serve the investigation. So if you want to consider the past and try to work something out, that's fine. But definitely take the opportunity when something arises fresh to work with it. The data you get when something's occurring or fresh is often different than the data you have when it's a memory. It usually has more charge, more reality to it.

Thank you and good night.

Thank you.

Thinking Beyond Objectification—
On the Formation of "Mind"

From an Ontological Study Group meeting in 1992. Another series of dialogues is underway. In these we are working through some rather difficult considerations related to the nature and design of mind. It will take some serious reflection on the founding structures and assumptions of your experience to fully grasp what is being worked out in these dialogues. This chapter should be used mostly as an exercise or an example of ontological work following a certain investigation. Much more work would need to be done to clarify and ground what is being considered.

Thought and Emotion Are Distinctions within the Same Event

PR: I'm talking about a lack of separation in the distinction between thought and emotion. In order to pursue this further, I want us to look into the conviction that we have of an objectified reality. It's pretty easy to see that we have objectified our thinking and emotion. In other words, we hold that thoughts are some "things" that are. They come and go perhaps, but it's held as if there is something there. We really think there's something there. You have a thought. You can look at it. You can share it, you can kick it around, it can be wrong, it can be right. It has all the attributes of a thing, and we assume it also has the attributes of location, space, substance, and qualities like that.

And emotion . . . emotion is definitely something there. Right? Something that is "in your body" and it has a "location" and maybe even a color and volume, and the like—you can be right and wrong and all that, and you can "trust" in it or not! [laughs] Trust it . . . see? I mean it's all in the domain of being right and wrong if you have to "trust" your feelings, you know?

So that's how come I went into this whole business of objectified reality—as a conviction. Because if we're going to speak about emotion and thinking as not separate—as a distinction within the same event—we don't want to make some new "thing" out of it. I don't want you to jump on to a new notion and say, "Okay, there's emotion and thought, really they're not different, they're the same thing, but it's a new thing. It's the "megoo" thing." Still holding it in an objective form, but as if thought and emotion are now the same thing. I don't want you to do that.

I'm suggesting that thoughts and emotions are already the same thing, that they're already made through distinction and reflection alone. So if I'm going to draw our attention to the activity of reflection that I'm talking about, we have to completely get past this notion that everything has to be an object. That everything has to be objectified. That everything has to "be there." That everything has to fall into an "is there" for it to "be." You can see by ending that sentence the way that I did, how you're left with nothing, and you're sort of waiting, "Well, go on . . . what are you talking about, you didn't say anything just now." That shows us what I'm saying. So, in order to take away this distinction. . . .

Kim: *What distinction?*

PR: Thinking and feeling—and objectified reality. I'm not suggesting you take away the distinction, really, but take away the separation. Take away that a distinction is necessarily there like an object or like something that is. So I was thinking that eventually if I started to work on thinking and feeling, we would come face to face with the impossibility of thinking this matter, because we would come up against our inability to think beyond object. So it wouldn't occur.

Kim: *We can't think beyond object?*

PR: My assertion is not that we cannot think beyond object, but that we do not think beyond object. Not just object like a pillow, but the domain of objectification. There is an activity taking place—if you think, you think *that*. You think something, don't you? You think some "thing." And you think some thing in particular, right? You feel something, or you think something, right? So when you have a thought, do you see how objectified that is? You "have" a thought. Say you have a picture, an image, of some thing—an object. Every image is of an objective event, isn't it?

So that's one of the reasons I tackled this. Now what I'm going to work on is the other side here, so that we can see why I was tackling this objective distinction.

How Does Objective Perception Determine Concept?

PR: Every image you have is a whole lot like looking at a pillow, isn't it? You have perception, and you say that the perception of sight is your eyes seeing things. Your eyes see "things." Your eyes never see nothing; your eyes see things, right? We say conventionally that light has to bounce off of an object to see it. Otherwise we don't see it. You don't say you see the air. You can "feel" the air, so you say, "Ah, it's there, I know," but you don't see it. You could see it moving things, so we have it that air is there mostly because we feel it and because we see something moving, right? If we never saw anything moving and we didn't feel air, I bet you we wouldn't make that distinction. There wouldn't be any experience called air, would there? So we would not have the thought of air or any feelings for air.

Leslie: *What you're talking about are "objectifying" characteristics. For example, you're talking about identifying characteristics. Without characteristics, things wouldn't be there for us.*

PR: These are all a matter of objectification.

Leslie: *Objectified, like air is an object or a characteristic?*

PR: Yes. However, what I'm suggesting is not characteristics, as if we have any choice about that, but more like we hold characteristic as all there is. If there is something, there is a character to it. In other words, it has qualities. And what are the qualities? The qualities are about its "objectified existence." It has space, it has substance, it's cold, it's hot, etcetera, etcetera. All of which for us are . . . well, let's just take a look.

Like I was saying, we wouldn't have air unless we saw a thing move and said, "Aha, since nothing's touching it, it must be the wind," or feeling a certain sensation on our skin. Say we didn't have any of that. There would be nothing there for us. But then through a rigorous method and a very specialized event called science—it's a very specialized, rigorous, and also limited event, or way of looking at things—let's say we discover air. We would say there is air, that we live in air. But we still wouldn't live, or experience, that air was there.

Watch, I'll show you. It is so that we have now a belief, a distinction, that molecules exist. Right? Everything is full of molecules. But we don't live for a moment that anything is full of molecules. See? Because we don't know. Science says everything is molecules, and when we apply that model to things, we can get certain results . . . plastics, for example. But we don't live it because there is nothing for us in our experience called molecules, right? Except the thought, and the thought appears as a "model" without any experience that matches the model in our perceptions of the world. So, now take a look and see how much of your thinking is like that.

Now, begin to consider that every image you have, everything you can imagine—like a picture—how much of that is identical to a visual field, an imprint on your visual faculty? You could say all of it. Anybody find anything that isn't?

Leslie: *Well, I call the conceptualization of other senses images too.*

PR: ... I'm just talking about pictures for now. Like we have in our memory a picture of our high school, as if we can "see" it. That's certainly from seeing it, right? But then we can have all sorts of images—you could have an image of being in a vast expansive nothingness with a sort of....

Leslie: *Light?*

PR: Okay, light. And the image of it is as if we "see." Do you understand what I'm thinking? The image of it is what comes to our attention. What I'm pushing here, what I'm about to assert, is that all of our imaging—visual memory, pictures, imagination, etcetera—is a replication of what we call visual perception. It is consistent with our visual perception—like we're wired that way. Our "feeling" is from our sensations, and sound from our hearing, like that. In other words, our senses. So when we think about something or imagine something, how much of it is coming from what we call our experience, like our sensorial experience?

Linda: *Wow. I was just thinking sometimes, not so often but occasionally, it seems to me I think with words and there are no images, but that's just another of the senses. It's my hearing rather than my vision that I'm relying on!*

Leslie: *And also there are some very kinesthetic conceptualizations. A real feeling, a sense of something by its feeling—how I "fit in," so to speak, or how a movement feels—and it's not a visual thing at all. So when you broaden your platform for leading us to your assertion about thinking through the senses, it makes more sense to me. Since not everyone does it the same way; people think very differently.*

PR: I'm not stopping there, I'm just starting. So the question here is—how much of your thinking is reflected in that field?

Leslie: *Of the senses?*

PR: Yes. Is there anything that goes on outside of that? Let's take a look—let's create a model and see.

Perception without Association

PR: Let's begin with an activity—you perceive. Let's say you perceive and are even cognizant of what you perceive. You feel, you see, you hear—it's cognized as that—and that's all there is. You see a pillow. If the pillow's out of sight, there is no such thing as pillow. It's not there. You feel your body. No sensation, no body. You hear the sound—without the sound, there is no sound, there is nothing to be heard or not heard, nor could be heard. Okay? Now consider that.

For us to do that, or even move into a state where we could imagine that, I bet would be a big deal for us. We might say it is like what we call "being present." I think when most people say they are being present, they are saying something like that, right? What they're being present to is their immediate sensory perceptions. What they call the experience of being present is attending to their immediate perception of objectified reality. Because you don't say you're being present if you're attending to some conceptual domain. We don't associate that as being present, right? We'd say no, no, I'm not present because to be present means for me to see the room. To hear the cars. To know I'm here sensing what is really happening right now.

Linda: *Which excludes thinking about other things that aren't present—all that kind of abstract thinking. That definitely is what happens....*

PR: So, in what I'm suggesting now, we'd have to exclude thinking about present things also. We couldn't stand it, could we? It's like "waiting with an object." Do you know the practice waiting with an object? Look at an object—like a marble or a pencil or a pillow or something—and stay with what's there as merely the perception, the unchanged cognition of that object for as long as you stare at it. Without trying to make it any different than you get it at first glance. The whole waiting-with-an-object practice is that when you see a pillow, you see a pillow. Not trying to get past cognition, or investigate it, question it, allow it to get weird, hallucinate, go to any other perception, think about it, or feel anything about it. To do nothing that isn't there when you first recognize it. See a pillow—and then do nothing but see a pillow, and see a pillow, and see a pillow, and see a pillow, and see a pillow. Go ahead and try that.

You see, a pressure builds up, doesn't it? Immediately we get crazy. More than likely what happens is you start bouncing around. Like you investigate the pillow. Or you start throwing things in, like thinking about the pillow. But when you saw the pillow the first moment, the first millisecond, you weren't investigating; it was just pillow, a recognition of pillow. But then to stay there seems for us impossible. More than likely you don't even want to keep investigating the pillow. You want to think about it, "what am I doing, am I doing this right?" It gets really involved. If nothing else, as you are looking it starts to change, you start to see weird things about it. But that's not the pillow, that's visual phenomena.

So we seem to be dissociated from the fact of the matter of our own cognition. It seems as if it's important for us that our cognition is piled on top of itself. Piled and piled and piled and piled, with many levels and a lot of activities occurring relative to it.

So let's go back to the model that I was creating for the purpose of looking into the formation of our concepts. In this model we just have perception, and we can't mess with it. We can't think what's for lunch, we can't remember what happened a moment ago. Five hours standing there is the same as one. It doesn't make any difference. It doesn't have a watch, you know. [chuckles] So, imagine that we had no capacity to mess with it whatsoever. That there is only perception—basic cognition, this is that, but that's it. You don't get to mess with it. So a pillow's a pillow and you can't do anything about it because a pillow is only a pillow, do you know what I mean?

Now, say that perception—sensory perception and cognition— is only occurring if it's occurring, which is to say, it's only occurring now. Whatever's occurring now is it. End of story. Nothing else can exist. There is no distinction of anything existing, except for what's occurring now. No memory, no thought of the future, none of that. Only what is occurring immediately. Only whatever you are currently cognizant of in this very instance is all that is. Completely all that is. It's not contrasted with the possibility that there is something else not presently being perceived, right? "This is all there is and I'm not thinking about anything else." There is no "not thinking about anything else." There is nothing else. Nothing else. There's not an outside, there's not an inside. There's not a coming and a going, there's not a home, there's not an other place, there's not a future, there's not a going to be—none of that exists at all, period.

Linda: *Given this, is it possible to understand the language then? Without memory?*

Leslie: *That's what I was just thinking, too.*

PR: Why do we need to understand language?

Linda: *How could we understand you talking if everything was just now?*

PR: Maybe you couldn't understand, it doesn't matter. Do we need to figure out if you could understand language?

Linda: *No.*

PR: Okay. So there may not exist what we call language, in this. There doesn't exist much, there's no future, no past, no memory, there's no coming or going, there's no inside, there's no outside. Now that's radical. See, we have it that there is an outside. There would be no outside.

Linda: *There would be no outside?*

PR: Right, there would be no outside.

Leslie: *Why? I don't get that the distinction of distance—in other words, the implication of in and out—would disappear at that point.*

PR: If we're not seeing outside right now, then there is no outside.

Leslie: *But if you're having cognition, to me that doesn't eliminate objective distinctions, or trying to make sense of it.*

PR: You would have to think about something that's not being perceived, wouldn't you? Wouldn't you have to have the thought of something not here, something not perceived, something not cognized? Don't you have to extrapolate? "Ah, yes, there is the other side of the wall." If I just see the wall, I don't see how I could do that without having a thought about what isn't perceived.

Linda: *So there would just be seeing, like now I can see outside.*

PR: Yes.

Linda: *But there would be no call to call it outside. I would just be seeing.*

PR: No call to call it outside. Obviously, when we start to move in this direction, a lot of what we hold simply to be so would be damaged. I said that you could have cognition. Right? We're allowing in the model at this point that you can have cognition. You recognize whatever is there as that. So if you see outside, you can cognize it as the outside. However, outside may take on a completely different relationship than what outside usually is for us. Outside and inside would only be an immediately seen relation, and nothing else. There would be no "around the corner" now, would there?

Leslie: *It's funny, I just can't get it. I can consider going into perception about it, but once you add cognition, to me, I can't exclude the distinction of depth and scope. It seems inherent in cognition. It's like cognition is relative.*

PR: Depth and scope?

Leslie: *Distance and time, sort of?*

PR: Well, time's gotta go. We're not saying that this cognition would be the same event that we are used to—like a bug's cognition is probably nothing like what we call cognition.

Leslie: *Can you define that for me then?*

PR: What?

Leslie: *Cognition? Distinct from perception at this point?*

PR: Sure. Interpreting something to be something. Like it is something. That is a fly. This is a rug. Not necessarily naming it, but getting it, making a distinction, that is not that. What I was allowing in this case was interpretation like it's a rug, or it's a pillow. Yet, obviously our framework of interpretation is extremely sophisticated—and by that what I'm saying is that it seems absolutely dependent on association, time, extrapolation, thinking, and feeling, so that it is absolutely infused with all that. That perhaps is most of what cognition is. So if we take those away we're totally crippled in our ability to say what something is. Like this fly sitting here on the rug, for the fly that may be interpreted as something, but it ain't a rug and it's probably not even something you sit on. It's so radically different in interpretation. It may not even be something he has seen before even though he has lighted on it six times in the last minute, see? But the fly does, I would assume, get it as something. So that he puts on his brakes before he crashes into it.

Leslie: *And he doesn't eat it.*

PR: And he doesn't eat it, right.

Linda: *So in that sense of cognition, even an amoeba would be cognizant in the sense of distinguishing things.*

PR: This is possible, and the distinctions that amoebas make are undoubtedly extremely simple. First of all, we say that the amoeba can't hear or see or smell—that wipes out a whole bunch. I would guess that an amoeba has no "other-than-itself," really. I doubt the amoeba thinks, "Gosh, I stop here, I wonder what's past that?" "What's out there in the petri dish?" I bet you amoebas don't suffer. Even if you burn them up with a match. It's probably a completely non-reflective event that's kind of more or less itself, you know?

Linda: *Doesn't even make a face.*

PR: Right, doesn't even make a face.... Well, it's curling up, except it's not "what a trip," it's just "what is."

Leslie: *I'm not sure if it's where you're taking us, but at one point during Pleiades, when we had looked for a while at perception and interpretation, there was someone who was part way in front of me so that my field of vision of what I was trying to put my attention on wasn't completely visible to me. So I was looking out and there was a blank in something on the board, so I couldn't see everything. Within my conventional thinking I was holding that the person was in the way of something on the other side and I needed to see beyond them or around them. It was a little irritating.*

So I put my attention on the irritation and realized that there wasn't anything in my way—for a moment anyway there wasn't anything in my way. What "was" was simply what was there. There was nothing in the way and there was nothing on the other side of that. I mean, that sounds pretty silly because I could move and would get the field of vision that I wanted. But there wasn't anything else—that was that. And I got that's what was there. There wasn't another side of that. That was just perception. That was all there was and I would get a different perception if I was coming from a different location. Is the thing that you're drawing our attention to now getting cognition without contingency?

PR: Maybe. It seems to me that probably the best that we can do tonight, or the best we will do tonight, is imagine the model. But imagine it like a present occurrence. To actually get it, I think, would be unusual.

Perceiving Our Projections

PR: For example, in relation to dogs.... Personally, I'm certain that dogs have some form of language. They definitely make distinctions. They have association, memories, all sorts of interpretation. However, it's absolutely not like ours. And what we can't get is that it's not like ours. So it's best just to say we're making it all up—what we attribute to dogs. And I imagine most of the time we'd be right.

You think that a dog puts on some kind of a face for you. Do you think it knows what it looks like? As if it stood in front of a mirror and thought, "Oh god, that's cute, I bet I could really just bend them out of shape if I look like that."

Linda: *It stands in front of the mirror of a human.*

PR: It gets an effect. But I suspect it has no idea what it looks like. No idea. There is no idea. I imagine also that a dog does not recognize itself in a mirror. Even if it did stand in front of a mirror, it doesn't recognize that as "self." That whole domain is a completely different event than what we imagine, because *we* are entrenched in self-consciousness. We're entrenched in interpretation, meaning, emotion, thinking. Dogs are not into thinking, they're not into emotion. That's a human invention.

... I love it ... she's a dog lover, I can tell.

Linda: *They seem to suffer.*

PR: [tongue in cheek] They do seem to suffer so. And they're so cute sometimes. "What are you trying to tell me, Spot?"

Jef: *They know when they're bad.*

PR: Oh, they know when they're bad.

Bob: *They really love you, too.*

PR: What I think has a lot of power is to recognize that that's "our" conversation. That he loves me, they know when they're bad, they're suffering, aren't they cute. That's totally *our* conversation, not theirs! They're not going, "Golly, I'm cute. God, I'm suffering, or this hurts." They're not carrying on a conversation like that. Their "conversation" is radically different. I mean, try to get what the cup thinks. We have it that the cup doesn't think, so it's a little easier to imagine a radically different experience occurring over there.

If we attribute to animals an experience that is more in the domain of whatever is "is" only in the moment, and without a "conversation" about it of any kind, then I suspect we'll be closer to the mark. It's probably a little easier for us if we move down to a lizard or a worm or a fly.

Linda: *Because I don't think they love.*

PR: Right, because you never see a fly getting cute.

Linda: *Like its little face crossing its eyes for you.*

PR: Crossing its eyes, loving you, knowing that it's bad, things like that. . . . In any case, we could imagine or attribute to them a domain of just what is is only as it is, just immediacy in perception, cognition, and nothing else. There is that, that's it, end of story. Sensation, end of story. Doesn't mean anything, it's not going anywhere, didn't come from anywhere, it's not an emotion. Moving in that direction. So now let me tease out the model.

Creating "Mind"

PR: Now we have a basis for the model, in which there is merely perception and the simplest form of cognition. We will have to go in the other direction in a moment and put all this stuff together, but for now, imagine that we have just immediate cognition. That's all there is. Now imagine that a new dimension is entered here. A sudden possibility. Heretofore, if you gaze on the cup, the cup is "that," end of story. Now a sudden possibility enters in which we can reproduce these perceptive experiences at will. We can conjure them up and make them disappear. They can come and go. That's all. In other words, we can represent them. We can reproduce or "mimic" them, I should say. We can symbolize, mimic, reproduce, them at will. Or as if at will. Okay? That's all. Just add that one possibility, and see what happens. Just that one possibility.

We can now have a sensation that's not occurring. You can have an image that isn't there, one you're not seeing, so that now you can mimic an image. What image do you mimic? Well, you mimic some image that you saw. If you add to the image "I saw it," we call it memory. Right? "That's my high school," is a recognition of an image in some relative position, like you place the image somewhere. See, if you could only reproduce a picture of your high school, it would probably be pretty weird, right? "Hey, high school, wait a minute, what's going on here?" You would simply have an image occurring out of the blue. So, you put it in a place. "Ah, I know, that's my high school, it's not here, let's call it a memory." When we have this possibility, a whole new demand takes place. In order to make certain distinctions, interpretations, and organizations, time must enter. Then everything has places, has sequence, and all of that is done in an objectified manner.

It's okay, it's somewhere else in time. "I'll just build "time blocks," and I'll throw it back into time," in an objectified manner. Do you see what I'm saying? It "was." It's not now, it was. It's not here. Is it in my wallet? Well, no. If I want it to happen— then I must create a future. It's not here, that's something I'm imagining "wanting."

So we start to see, by producing a possibility, what occurs from that possibility—the moment that possibility occurs. Say we could create perceptual mimicking at will. Just conjure it up. Have a feeling. Have an image. Have another feeling. Have another image. Remember a sound. See? Immediately—see what I just did? I said remember a sound. Have a sound. We've got it that in order to have a sound, we have to remember a sound. We have to have heard a sound, and then remember it. Make up a new sound.

Katie: [Shrill sound]

PR: Well, that was a squeaky sound [laughs]. I don't know if it was new, but it was creative. It was loud, too.

If we just started cranking out perceptive mimics ... that would be strange, right? You'd just, for no reason, start whacking out perceptual phenomena at will. Which is to say creating it, for no reason, out of the blue, not preceded by anything, and without motivation. From the position that we operate from now, if we suddenly started doing that, we would be mad. Absolutely insane, right? If we continued to interpret in any way, shape, or form, we'd have to say we were insane—or at least everybody else would say we were insane; we may be having a field day. But they would put us away. It wouldn't make much difference, though, because we're just making it up anyway.

Leslie: *It would be hard to go into reaction about it. I wouldn't place listening to the stream of perceptions one way or another. If I just let that keep going, that would eventually show up to others as madness.*

PR: At least one event that we call madness. There's probably a huge array of possibilities. So I'd imagine that others of us have opted for a possibility in which the mimicking occurs in other ways. Here are a couple of possibilities: No mimicking whatsoever, no interpretation, that's one possibility. They'd be catatonic. Not interpreting. Or, perhaps interpretation, but no reaction, no response whatsoever, no effect, nothing, not in a dance with it at all. No correlated activity going on with it. Merely the perception and interpretation of the activity that is. That's another possibility. We'd call that something. We call it catatonia, because there doesn't seem to be anything going on; we can't figure out what's occurring. In madness there seems to be interpretive activity and reactions taking place, yet it doesn't seem to be fitting with our interpretations and so it's called madness. There is correlated activity occurring in relation to something, but we can't figure out what it's in relation to. They could be mimicking perceptive experiences that we would say are not occurring or never occurred.

So we can see that for us, in order to maintain this order to our experience, we need a distinction between what is presently occurring as perception and interpretation, and what isn't. We need a distinction we call memory, fantasy, imagining the future, and what we call occurring reality. Then there are many other distinctions we make. Such as that's a fantasy, and that's a memory. And in order to do that we have to say this one's here and that one's there, and this one's real and that one's not, and this one has happened and that one hasn't, etcetera. And we do that with objectification. I don't think we have to, but we do. That's our way of doing it.

Linda: *What don't we have to do?*

PR: Objectify it. I don't think we have to objectify it but that's what we do. We make everything like an object. For example, have you heard about the three hearts of the Japanese? No? Well, that's an example of an objectification that we don't do that somebody else does. They have the heart that they show people, most people—heart to them is a lot like "self." They have the heart that's secreted, that they show themselves and only share with very, very close friends or family. And finally there is their true heart. So, there's a heart they show people, a heart that's secreted that they only share in intimacy, and then the heart that nobody knows—their true heart that even they don't know. Kind of like that. And so the way I hear it it's almost like separate boxes, one within the other. And perhaps the distinction I just made is too much influenced by my culture hearing theirs. Do you see what I'm saying? Then it's not like the way it is for them. Anyway, that's just what came to mind. . . .

The Mind as Creatively Reproduced Mimicry of Sensory Perception

PR: Now you see, we started to look into this matrix of reality and it's a real mess already, isn't it? In order for us to think through the distinctions that we've drawn out so far in this model, I've spent a bunch of time just on cognition, immediate cognition, and then added one possibility, and that one possibility suddenly blossomed into a million distinctions. And we have a hard time simply looking into the distinctions that result from this one possibility of "mimicking experience." I'll just call it experience, okay, just to make it easier—or sensory perception.

What experience do we have that isn't sensory perception? We might say we have lots of experiences that are not sensory perception. But now, take a look. Could you take that experience—one that you say is not sensory perception—and add a dash of perception, a bunch of feeling, some visual imagery, some memory association, a sprinkle of fantasy, blend it all up, and end up with that experience? Now I challenge you to find anything that you couldn't do that with.

We have another distinction arising out of the possibility of reproducing past perceptions, but I think it's in the same domain. Once the mimicking, the ability to mimic perception occurred, I think this other possibility occurred. I think it's a correlate of that, like an offshoot of that. Not the same one necessarily, but an offshoot of it.

Kim: *What is this second possibility?*

PR: Mimicking something not perceived. As if to extrapolate from perception. Like you've never seen a plane of blue light as far as the eye can see, but you can imagine one, right? You've never seen it, but you've seen blue, you've seen flat surfaces, you can see as far as the eye can see. So you fill in a brilliant blue light like a flat plane as far as the eye can see. You never felt vastness as far as the eye can see, but you could drop in a feeling that you would equate with or relate to "as far as the eye can see." You've never seen anything bigger than the biggest thing you've seen, but you could imagine something bigger. Now I want to go for something really abstract, so you have to do it yourself—imagine two nonexistent, really loose dimensional worlds in which there's a cleavage down the middle and the two dimensions are coming together, and you have no body, you don't exist, but you are observing these dimensions. Now whatever you just made up you undoubtedly have never actually seen before, but still you could construct something, yet it remains objective and can be related to as a mixture of historical sense perceptions.

So, I'm talking about another possibility, not just the one that we call mimicking perception as a memory. We can obviously mimic perception. So that's why I'm calling it a correlate, not a new event. It's mimicking a perception that we've never had. Mimicking perceptions that we've had is its own distinction. How do we know we had them? We have to make a distinction. How do I know I had it? Because I remember it. See how that's a double bind? You're saying you remember it because you say you had it. You say you had it because you are remembering it. Well, which is it?

The new distinction is one of putting together possibilities, given in the ability to represent sensory perceptions, in a new way. Like creating new forms of perceptual mimicry.

Linda: *So this correlate has to do with the degree of abstraction? It seems more than just putting together different memories. It seems like it's recombining patterns and designs.*

PR: It's even more involved than that. But let me ask another question. Does the possibility of association occur before the possibility of mimicking? It's hard to say because our association always goes along with the mimic. Like when a ball is flying at my head, I get—or have some experience of—impact before it hits me, right? So I flinch. I flinch because I get impact before it hits me. The fly doesn't flinch. It moves out of the way. I suspect it doesn't get impact. In other words, it doesn't extrapolate or mimic an experience. What it gets is an associative one. The distinction I just created with this association thing, is no mimic of an experience but an association of past experience to present without having the past experience mimicked, you see? We do both. We have past experiences reproduced as if they are coming from present experiences occurring, so we associate them with what's happening and interpret from that position. So what I was just asking about is the possibility of associative perception. Associating perception without any mimic. Without mimicking experience. Associating the experience without mimicking the experience.

Kim: *It seems possible. In limited amounts.*

PR: I'm just talking about its possibility of being. Certainly if it's a possibility of being then it seems perhaps that it's possible for us. There's an immense amount that's possible for us that's still inaccessible, right? Like cognition without association seems impossible for us. It's possible—it's a possibility of being—but it doesn't appear readily accessible for human beings.

The whole model that I started with is inaccessible to us. It's possible, therefore, obviously possibly accessible, but it's not conventionally accessible to us. We'd have to make a dramatic shift out of the domain of being human or merely being human or conventionally being human, in order to have that possibility realized, appear, be—like an "is." However, we could say that the possibility is existing right now, but it's so fundamental it's unrecognized. For us, it can't exist by itself.

This mimicking of perceptive experiences—how do we do it, how do we mimic? We don't just mimic. We also correlate, extrapolate, we associate, we make many, many, many distinctions. All of this conceptual activity is taking place, and none of that do we call thinking. We call it reality, as a matter of fact. It's just like a so. That's a memory, this is a fantasy, and this is a pineapple. Did you all just think of pineapples? As a matter of fact, you probably tasted them, right? Had some kind of taste, smell, vision, touch—of pineapples. Also, immediate associations arose, such as liking it, not liking it, acidic qualities, Hawaii, whatever—the whole thing, instantly, the moment I mention pineapple. Like it occurs when a pineapple shows up—whether it's a mimicked perception or what we call an actual perception.

Mind, Self, and Survival

PR: We make a lot of distinctions. We have to make sense out of them, and it all has to serve a purpose. And the purpose it has to serve is our self-survival. In this experience that's taking place, there's something that occurs called the self, right? We make the assumption there is a self. Like a perceiver. Now you tell me. How does it come to pass that self needs to be?

Self "needing to be" gives us meaning. It gives us good, bad, right, wrong—survival. All of that just floods out from there. Pretty simple, right? Okay, once all that occurs—needing to be, survival, right, wrong, good, bad, etcetera, etcetera—is established in some sort of structure, then emotion and thinking occur relative to that structure and purpose.

Since we can mimic perceptive experience, we could imagine what emotion might be. Can you see how easy it would be to create emotion in the immense field that we have here? Throw in survival, right, wrong, motivation to get it all handled—and emotion is an activity that has a lot of possibility. It is a mimicking of experience that's full of sound and fury. And in the field of emotion, we make all sorts of distinctions. This emotion, that emotion, the other emotion, and they all mean something and carry a lot of information at a stroke. It's all survival, and it's all a manipulation. It's an activity that is in relation to, but for us really in reaction to, what we interpret to be—for the purpose of survival. So is thinking. We make a distinction and we separate the two. But I want to suggest that they're actually the same activity, and we separate them into thinking and emotion. But now I've gone too fast, so let's back up.

What is, or how did it come to be, that "self needs to be"? How does that come to be? Do some work here. I don't know how you would know. But you do need to be, right? You're the most important thing in all this. Okay, so it's already here. How come that? How did that come to be?

John: *It doesn't feel like I could know that. Like it's not allowable. I* mean, it's like a magic trick. If you know the magic trick, it's not the same anymore.

PR: Risk it.

John: *When you know how the whole magic thing happens, nobody's going to applaud at the trick.*

PR: How does it come to pass that self needs to be? We would say that self "is." Somehow self-consciousness arises. There is a distinction—self. Having made the distinction self, how come that distinction needs to be? How come it occurs that there is a need to be in there? How is it that that comes about through the distinction self?

John: *It's almost like the science-fiction stories where the computer takes over—suddenly it's just self-conscious. It's not going to turn itself off, right? It's kind of like, as soon as it comes to be, as soon as that happens, there's no question—it simply needs to be. So your question is how does it come to need to be?*

PR: Uh-huh, that's the question.

John: *But the need to be seems to be so obvious. That's inherent in self. But how does it come to pass? That's weird. "Needs to be" just seems to be so.*

Kim: *When we start mimicking, we start making distinctions, and when we start making distinctions . . . I just lost it. . . . Before that there is no self because there is just what there is. So if we throw in the mimicking we start getting the distinctions and when we . . . I just had it, I keep losing it.*

PR: Okay, so you're working from a base that there is no self without the mimicking of experience.

Kim: *Right, and that's when self happens because. . . .*

PR: . . . In order to get a reflection occurring? Like you can't have self-consciousness unless there's a reflection—you "reflect" a self?

And out of the reflection make a distinction this and other—the distinction of self.

Kim: *... And once you make that distinction, then that needs to be. I'm not sure if that's exactly it. ...*

Leslie: *I'm also seeing the possibility that the need to be arises first, and it is this very "need to be" that is the self.*

PR: Okay. Now here on the floor we have two very interesting points, and very different. We have that perception and even cognition is not enough for a self, that there has to be the mimicking of experience or a reflective quality in order for a self to be distinguished out.

And then over here we've got "need to be" *is* self. So you're saying the need to be, that the coming to pass of the need to be, is the distinction of self?

If it came to pass that this cup needed to be, would we call that a self? We might even call it our self. If I made the distinction that this [points to body] is not this [points to cup], yet that [cup] needs to be—like it just comes to pass that it is the primary distinction that needs to be—it then becomes self. It's possible. It's a possibility. It doesn't become this [body] since this isn't self. We say it doesn't become this body, but it becomes my self, since it's what needs to be.

Leslie: *Also, it seems that the quality of reflection is not different from "need to be." I mean, it's because need to be "is" to be "distinct" and to be unique ... but I can't get a good look at the rest of it.*

PR: I think the distinction seems to be that there's something about creating "self,"—simply self—and there's something else about creating "my self"—like identifying with self. However, I can see the possibility of the creation of self without any identification with it.

Leslie: *Don't we need the quality of reflection in order to distinguish and so experience what is self and what is other?*

PR: With or without reflecting—I would just have to not reflect on this as myself. I could reflect on this as myself. I could also reflect on this as self, not my self, in which case there's no ownership, and there's no relationship except for I am "other," or the base in which this exists, or some such possibility.

Leslie: *Reflecting on that "self" is, but not identifying any quality as my self?*

PR: Probably. And in this way, we could see how opinions and beliefs then become self, by needing to be. See, we think that our opinions need to be, our beliefs need to be, our concerns need to be, our relationships need to be—all those things that live in apparent abstraction that we identify with, we say need to be.

Leslie: *If you get that the whole emotional realm, or the need to be "that way," doesn't have to be self, your self anyway—generally, where I live is that all of my thoughts, opinions, and feelings are also my self—if I got self without "mine," then that need to be, that self—my thoughts and feelings and opinions—wouldn't have to be identified as me. That's powerful for me—just imagining it.*

PR: Well, what if this needs to be? [Picks up cup] And these need to be? [Picks up paper and pencil] I've got my hands full. What seems so for me in this, is that if this needs to be and this needs to be, it is still self. If this needs to be [cup], this needs to be [pencil], and this needs to be [paper], it's all self. So then self is found in all that is held as what needs to be. It seems then that every opinion, belief, conviction, assumption, cosmology, moral code, behavior, emotion, or attitude that is identified with, that is held as self, needs to be. Also, if it needs to be perhaps it is self.

Somehow the survival of self becomes the operating principle for being a self. In this the "need to be" appears synonymous with the experience of being a self. Is there such a thing as being a self without any need to be, without survival? If so, then perhaps this would be an experience of "being"—or the nature of being. In this perhaps we can begin to get the possibility that self is not an object. If this is so then an experience of the "nature" of being can only be had outside of "objective" thinking or experiencing.

Such confrontations as trying to experience the possibility that thinking and emotion are not really different push us in a direction that forces us beyond conventional and objectified cognition. By so doing we come closer to a confrontation with the source of our own experience and self.

Tonight we have challenged many assumptions and opened up a lot of avenues for further investigation. We must continue to be very rigorous in our questioning, however, and not allow it to fall into mere abstractions or philosophy, but ground it with the demand to realize the truth of the matter within our own experience.

Thank you and good night.

Thank you.